MW00633409

Praise for *Nothing But Net*

"People always ask me what investment books can help them understand how to value technology stocks. I gave up suggesting them a long time ago; nobody knew enough or had enough history with the most important sector in the market. And then along comes Mark Mahaney with *Nothing But Net*. The problem's solved; I have the answer. Read this book. It's the most comprehensive, self-deprecating, and insightful book I have come across that explains how tech stocks really work: which ones go up, which ones go down, from the only person who has opined for the entire era. I thought I knew these stocks cold; I learned a ton. You will too."

—JIM CRAMER, host of *Mad Money* and cofounder of TheStreet.com

"Timeless insights into stocks, management, and what makes a company worth investing in. Required reading for the next generation of investors."

—SCOTT GALLOWAY, Professor of Marketing at NYU Stern School of Business, cohost of the *Pivot* podcast, and author of *The Four*

"Mark's book will help all investors—from novice individual investors to seasoned institutional investors—gather the confidence to invest in the future today. *Nothing But Net* offers important investment lessons that I have not forgotten and, thanks to his analysis, will never forget."

—CATHIE WOOD, founder, CEO, and CIO of Ark Invest

"Mark has been one of the sharpest, smartest, and most reliable analysts on my show for the last 10 years. He takes it to the next level in *Nothing But Net*, a remarkably personal, witty, engaging, yet informative read. You'll laugh and learn, not just about picking tech stocks, but also about the meteoric rise of the world's most dynamic and valuable companies, and where they're going next."

—EMILY CHANG, host and Executive Producer of Bloomberg Technology, author of *Brotopia*

"This fun, informative book is Peter Lynch meets Michael Lewis. I've long known that Mark Mahaney is a top player, thinker, analyst, investor, and human being, and now I've learned, he's also an amazing writer. His 10 Timeless Stock Picking Lessons are really insightful and useful. Read this book."

—ED HYMAN, Chairman of Evercore ISI and the #1 Ranked Analyst for Economics for 40 years by Institutional Investor

"Wall Street analyst Mark Mahaney has been watching Internet stocks rise, fall, and confound investors since the start of the web era. In this personable, compelling book, Mahaney reflects on both the hits and misses from his storied career while dishing out critical tips on how to appraise tech companies, when to invest, and how to stay sane through it all."

—BRAD STONE, author of *The Everything Store* and *Amazon Unbound*

NOTHING BUT NET

10 TIMELESS STOCK-PICKING LESSONS FROM ONE OF WALL STREET'S TOP TECH ANALYSTS

MARK S.F. MAHANEY

New York Chicago San Francisco Athens London
Madrid Mexico City Milan New Delhi
Singapore Sydney Toronto

1 2 3 4 5 6 7 8 9 LCR 26 25 24 23 22 21

ISBN 978-1-264-27496-3
MHID 1-264-27496-3

e-ISBN 978-1-264-27497-0
e-MHID 1-264-27497-1

To My Sons—Noah, Carter, Aidan, and Malcolm
All My Love . . . ALWAYS

In Memory of Robert and Olga Mahaney
ETERNALLY Grateful

To Brother Brendan and Sister Alex
FOREVER Thankful

To The Abbey Boys
Pax in Sapientia

CONTENTS

The Oldest and Longest-Lasting Internet Analyst on the Street

I am the oldest and longest-lasting Internet analyst on Wall Street. And I have been lucky. Very lucky. For almost 25 years, my job has been to cover Internet stocks—to write about, model, analyze, discuss, and explain arguably the most dynamic and interesting investment sector on Wall Street. I have had the opportunity to track some of the most innovative companies of the last quarter century—Alibaba, Amazon, AOL, eBay, Expedia, Facebook, Google, LinkedIn, Netflix, Pandora, Priceline, Snap, Spotify, Twitter, Uber, Yahoo!, Zillow, and others. I have had the chance to meet and get to know (sometimes barely, sometimes well) some of the leading entrepreneurs and CEOs of the last 25 years—Jeff Bezos, Reed Hastings, Meg Whitman, Steve Case, Mark Cuban, Eric Schmidt, Jack Dorsey, Jeff Boyd, Dara Khosrowshahi, Tim Westergren, Evan Spiegel, and Doug Lebda, to name a few. And my stock calls have had their share of failures, but also many dramatic money-making wins.

I've had a Buy on Google for most of the past 10 years as that stock has climbed 465% from $310 in early 2010 to $1,750 at the end of 2020. I upgraded Facebook to a Buy after its 50% post-IPO correction and have reiterated that recommendation ever since, as the shares have jumped 1,265% from $20 to $273 at the end of 2020. I've had a Buy on Netflix for the last 10 years, as that stock has soared over 2,000% from $25 in early 2011 to $541 at the end of 2020. And I've had a Buy on Amazon.com for 15 straight years as that stock has exploded 7,300% from $44 in early 2005 to $3,250 at the end of 2020, making Amazon one of the most valuable companies on the planet. Those four stocks helped create one of the most lucrative investment portfolios (FANG as in Facebook, Amazon, Netflix, and Google) of the past several years. And I've been with them every step of the way. Lots of skill. And lots of luck.

I have also been unlucky. I was laid off by Morgan Stanley in 2003 in the wake of the dot-com bust, after working there for five years as the top associate to legendary analyst Mary Meeker. I was also fired by infamous hedge fund manager Raj Rajaratnam at Galleon for "not getting enough edge" after grinding it out in that trading snake pit for a year. (That firing turned out to be a blessing, in hindsight. Still, firings are never fun.) And I was "terminated" by Citibank for a violation of that company's media disclosure policies—a highly painful experience on both a professional and personal level—after working extremely hard there for seven years building the leading Internet research franchise on Wall Street.

As I look back on my career, I was hired into the dot-com boom (highlight—the eBay IPO in 1998), fired out of the dot-com bust (lowlight—the 90% correction in Yahoo! shares in 2000–2001), rehired into the dot-com revival (highlight—the Google IPO in 2004), fired out of the dot-com controversy (highlight—the Facebook IPO in 2012), and hired back in for the dot-com takeover (highlight—three of the largest market cap names in the world are now GOOGL, AMZN, and FB).

Throughout these years, I have been "All Net, All The Time," "Nothing But Net," and "Always Online"—my email signature taglines over the past 25 years. Like most people "growing up" over the last 20 years (I am now modestly over 50), the Internet has been deeply interwoven in my life. When my first son, Noah, was born with Down syndrome, I begged for access to a computer in the NYC hospital so I could order every book on Down syndrome that

Amazon had and join every Down syndrome user group hosted by Yahoo! And every year on the anniversary of my dad's and mom's passings, I repost on Facebook the eulogies I gave at their funerals. (Yes, this is gonna be a personal book.) I also was consistently among the earlier adopters of services and products like Gmail, Netflix streaming, Facebook, Twitter, the Kindle, Alexa devices, Google Glass, Snapchat Spectacles, the Amazon Fire Phone, Stitch Fix, Oculus Virtual Reality headsets, and Uber, partly out of a fun fascination with new services and products and partly out of a need to stay on top of my sector. Later, my four sons came to generate (not always consciously) some of my best insights into the newest social networks, like Instagram, Snapchat, and TikTok.

Analysts do a lot of odd things. Like looking for correlations in unusual places. Here's one. My oldest son, Noah, was born on March 12, 2000, just two days after the NASDAQ peak of 5,048. Almost from the beginning, I nicknamed Noah "The Bear," not at all realizing that his birth date marked the beginning of a multiyear bear market for tech stocks. Then came Carter, born November 20, 2001. I nicknamed him "The Kangaroo." And what do you see if you start the NASDAQ chart on Carter's birth date? Lots of ups and downs. Then there was Aidan, born on August 5, 2003. His nickname? "The Bunny." And lo and behold, you'll notice a lot of big hops if you start the NASDAQ time machine on that date. Finally, there was Malcolm, "The Monkey," born April 4, 2007. And yes, the NASDAQ charts show mostly an upward climb if you start on that date. Anyway, I told you analysts do a lot of odd things.

Because of all my work on the Internet, and because of the growing importance of tech and Internet stocks, I have become something of a trading floor name. Over the last 10 years, the number of TV interviews I have done on CNBC, Bloomberg TV, Fox TV, and other outlets has totaled well over 500. Over that time, I have also done over a thousand print interviews with the *Wall Street Journal,* the *New York Times,* the *San Jose Mercury News, USA Today,* the *San*

Francisco Chronicle, and a series of other publications, including one with an obscure French business magazine (*Le Capital*, I think) that helped lead to my firing by Citibank. Two years ago, *Business Insider* published an article on "36 Hours in the Life of a Tech Analyst" and featured me. If you Google "sexy Internet analyst," you will quickly find a link to a *New York Times* article about me and two other analysts. The article had nothing to do with our sex appeal, which was surely pretty limited unless Excel spreadsheets are your thing. But it had a lot to do with how influential we had become regarding publicly traded stocks. And if you work through the Twittersphere, you will see a graphic reference to me as a horse's ass for having a Sell rating on Twitter. So, yup, lots of publicity . . . most good, but some bad.

I've now covered the Internet sector for almost a quarter century. Longer than some of my clients and colleagues have been alive . . . that makes me feel old. But it has been an extraordinary opportunity. To watch, track, and analyze the birth and growth of an entire new industry. Kind of like being an autos analyst in the 1920s, when cars became popular and common. Kind of like being an airlines analyst in the 1950s, during the golden age of air travel. And kind of like being a cable analyst in the 1970s, when cable TV expanded into major cities and metro areas.

GOOD CALLS, BAD CALLS, PETER LYNCH CALLS

Over the last quarter century, my job has been to make calls on Internet stocks—to Buy, to Hold, to Sell. My job has been to answer questions about Internet stocks—Which ones to buy? When? What price levels? What are the catalysts? Which management teams appear great? Which appear suspect? What are the biggest competitive risks? How big or how small are the market opportunities? And perhaps most importantly (as I've learned over time), where is the product/service innovation the best? The worst?

I have experienced some truly memorable moments covering Internet stocks. (1) Gazing in awe, along with Mark Cuban, as Broadcast.com's stock soared 249% on its IPO trading day—at that time the biggest one-day pop for an IPO ever. Was Cuban upset about all that money being left on the table for investors? Nope, he viewed it all as a great marketing event for his company. (2) Watching Jeff Bezos leg-wrestle Joy Covey, Amazon's then CFO, at a dinner following a 1999 Investor Day in Seattle. I actually don't remember who won. But it sure was entertaining. (3) Watching eBay CEO Meg Whitman celebrate (very briefly) when eBay's market cap surpassed Yahoo!'s for the first time during a Morgan Stanley Tech Investment conference in Scottsdale, Arizona, in 2000. You bet CEOs keep score. (4) Having Marc Andreessen, founder of Netscape and now arguably one of the most influential venture investors in the world, warn me at a 2005 industry conference that Microsoft would never allow Google to succeed.

And (5) . . . A series of phone calls with famed investor Peter Lynch.

Lynch actually called me several times in 2015 when he was doing research on Groupon, the online coupon/shopping deals company. Groupon was arguably a classic Lynch stock. At the time, it was widely hated and dismissed by tech investors and had materially underperformed its peers and the market. But the company had a rock-solid balance sheet and was in the process of a potential turnaround. Lynch's questions to me were detailed and insightful. He totally challenged me. And then I challenged him to avoid Groupon and instead to dig into Google and Amazon. I don't know how or whether Lynch decided to invest in the net sector. But I recall our conversations vividly, with nothing but respect.

I have made plenty of stock calls. Plenty of great calls, plenty of so-so calls, and plenty of terrible calls. Among the great calls:

1. Placing and defending a Buy recommendation on NFLX from 2013 to today. Per CNBC, NFLX was the single best

performing S&P 500 stock, by a long shot, for the 2010–2019 decade, rising almost 4,200%.

2. Maintaining a Buy recommendation on AMZN from 2005 to today, from $44.29 on December 31, 2004, to $3,257 at the end of 2020—a rise of 7,254%. I am not even going to bother fact-checking the following statement—AMZN has been the single best performing S&P 500 stock, by a very, very long shot, over the past 15 years. (It helps that NFLX wasn't added to the S&P 500 until 2010.)
3. Pitching PCLN (Priceline.com, now Booking.com) as a Buy recommendation from 2008 to 2018, when it soared 1,524% from $107 to $1,738.

Among the terrible calls:

1. Initiating coverage of Blue Apron, the online meal kit delivery company, in July 2017 shortly after its IPO with a Buy call and a $10 price target with the stock at $6.55. Now you might pull up the APRN ticker and see the stock trading at around $6.50 in December 2020 and think: "Mark, that's not exactly terrible." But a quick Google search will also show that Blue Apron did a 1-for-15 reverse split in mid-2019. Which really means I slapped a Buy on APRN at $98.25. Which means an investor buying APRN on my recommendation has lost 93% of his or her stake. *That is terrible.*
2. Placing a Sell recommendation on Twitter in September 2016 with the stock at $18.49 on the thesis that it was overvalued and its fundamentals were deteriorating. Then upgrading it to Hold a year and a half later in February 2018 with the stock at $31.22, after a 69% climb. Shoot. That was also a terrible call.
3. My worst call of all time: slapping a sell on Google prior to its first earnings report in October 2004. Google shares had soared 50% from its IPO. I thought that rise was excessive.

> I wrongly believed Yahoo! to be a better fundamental asset. I made the mistake of trying to play a quarter, and I underappreciated the amazing innovation and market opportunity of Google. Despite my call, Google posted very strong quarterly results; its stock rose 15% the next day and continued to rise aggressively for another year as search advertising took the advertising market by storm and Google gobbled up market share.

How many calls have I made? One way to think about it is that every quarter I've had a chance to reevaluate a stock call. To affirm a call. To upgrade. Or to downgrade. So for fun math, over 20 years that's 80 quarters, and with roughly 30 stocks under coverage, that's . . . 2,400 calls! But that's not the right way to think about it. Because with stocks always moving and news flow constant, there's an opportunity to reevaluate stock calls daily. This is something some of the twitch-trigger hedge fund analysts do . . . and some of them do it very well. So from this angle, that works out to 20 years, roughly 200 trading days a year, roughly 30 stocks, so that's . . . 120,000 calls! My mind is spinning just thinking about that. Thankfully, that was never my mindset, though knowing why any one of my stocks was up or down materially on any given day was my job.

The simple point here is that I've made lots of stock calls. In arguably the most dynamic, best performing stock sector on Wall Street over the past two decades. And I've learned a thing or two along the way. Actually, *10 key lessons*. And I'm going to share them with you in this book.

SOME ROADS LEAD TO WALL STREET

In his book *Outliers*, Malcolm Gladwell makes the keen insight that much of success is simply luck. Being in the right place at the right time. Similar to the statement that 90 percent of success is simply showing up. But if you want to really be successful, you have to show up at the right place at the right time. And showing up to analyze the Internet sector in 1998 was exactly the right place at the right time. Like I said, I have been very, very lucky.

My luck occurred because in 1998, a Wharton Business School classmate and friend of mine, Chris Boova, was kind enough to give me some of the research reports published by one Mary Meeker, who for over a decade was the Internet analyst at Morgan Stanley. She was also the lead author of *The Internet Report*, a 150-page primer on the Internet sector published by Harper Business in 1997. I vividly remember that report because a *Wall Street Journal* article on it sent me scurrying down to the Barnes & Noble in downtown Philadelphia looking to buy it. Irony. It was my reading of that report—from cover to cover—that truly ignited my interest in a Wall Street career covering the Internet sector.

Anyway, back to my luck and Chris Boova. Yes, he was kind enough to meet me in the lobby of Morgan Stanley, where he worked, to hand me some of Mary Meeker's research reports. But he was also kind enough to inform me that one of Meeker's two associates was soon to be leaving and Meeker was on the lookout for a new hire. Was I interested? Was I! So if there's one person I am most in debt to for launching my Internet Wall Street career, it's Chris Boova. Thank you, Chris!

What then followed was a six-month interview process that ended with me joining the Morgan Stanley equity research department as an associate to Mary Meeker. That process involved me meeting several times with the associate who was leaving—a guy named Russ Grandinetti, who was leaving for what turned out to be a fantastic career with a tiny little online retail company called Amazon.com, where he helped launch the Kindle product line, among many other achievements. I remember telling a friend when I was interviewing at Morgan Stanley that my hope was to become "Russ Plus." Russ, I don't think I ever achieved that status.

That six-month interviewing process also involved me meeting with the then head of Morgan Stanley's Technology Investment Banking group, Ruth Porat, who later became the firm's CFO, and later still the CFO of Google. One of my career ironies—or lucky breaks—is that I only met Porat because Morgan Stanley became concerned that I was also interviewing with core competitor Goldman Sachs and its Internet analyst Michael Parekh. The truth was that I had met with Parekh, though I hadn't begun any formal interview process there. Somehow or other, Morgan Stanley found out that I had met with Goldman—I dunno, maybe I mentioned it in passing, don't quite recall—and that led Morgan Stanley to accelerate its interview process. Shortly thereafter, I was hired.

Anyway, that's it. All the history about me that you need to know. At least for the purposes of this book.

The Big Long

In 1989, famed Fidelity portfolio manager Peter Lynch published *One Up on Wall Street*, a *New York Times* bestseller that aimed to help individual investors succeed in the market. That book contained a lot of great company and stock stories and introduced to many the concept of ten-baggers—stocks that can rise tenfold over a reasonable period of time and dramatically outperform the market. Lynch advised individual investors to look for everyday investing opportunities all around them (e.g., Dunkin Donuts, Pep Boys, The Limited), to be patient, and to "keep a lookout for tomorrow's big baggers."

Well, the Internet sector has been chock-full of ten-baggers. By my count, the US Internet sector has produced, up through the end of 2020, at least 23 ten-baggers (stocks that went up at least 10x), including two 300-baggers (Booking.com—BKNG and LendingTree—TREE), one 400-bagger (J2 Global—JCOM), one 500-bagger (Akamai—AKAM), and two hefty super jumbo baggers—Netflix (NFLX) and Amazon (AMZN). NFLX has been a 1,500 bagger (1,500x), up from a low of $0.37 in October 2002 to a high of $557 in September 2020. And AMZN has been a 2,500-bagger (2,500x) from a low of $1.40 in May 1997 to a high of $3,531 in September 2020. Yes, there have been a lot of duds in the Internet sector—stocks that underperformed the market or simply traded in line with the market for substantial periods of time—but there have also been some dramatic ten-bagger performances.

In 2000, Lynch wrote an Introduction to the millennium edition of his book in which he touched on the hot topic of the day—Internet stocks. He described himself as "technophobic" and skeptically referred to Amazon as "one of at least five hundred 'dot.com' stocks that have performed miraculous levitations." At the time of that publication, I was working at Morgan Stanley under famed Internet analyst Mary Meeker, trying my best to figure out whether there really was value in the Internet sector. And I vividly recall Morgan Stanley's senior market strategist stopping me in the elevator, pointing his finger at me, and asserting: "You know Amazon will never be profitable!" The truth is, I didn't know.

And yet Amazon did eventually—many years later—start generating substantial amounts of GAAP EPS and free cash flow (FCF). In fact, Amazon is now on track to be one of the largest generators of annual FCF of any company in the world. And its stock became a ten-bagger many times over. Like 250 times over.

Tech stocks have delivered almost unprecedented performance over the past 2, 5, and 10 years—with the NASDAQ up 94% over the 2 years ending December 31, 2020, up 157% over the past 5 years, and up 386% over the past 10 years. For each of these periods, tech stocks (aka NASDAQ) have outperformed the overall market (aka the S&P 500) by roughly 2x. Key point—tech stocks have been where it's at.

And very near the center of this dramatic outperformance by tech stocks have been US Internet companies. Stalwart names like Facebook, Amazon, Netflix, and Google (now called Alphabet)—the FANG stocks—have dramatically outperformed the market, rising on average 52% in 2020, 99% over 2019–2020, 262% over the five years 2016–2020, and 1,219% over the decade 2011–2020. These companies have also become living room names. For good and for bad, my and your teenagers couldn't survive a day without checking in with Facebook's Instagram. For a while in late spring 2020, as the Covid-19 crisis affected our lives, the only retail outlet most Americans could reliably count on was Amazon. Netflix has become so influential that a short series it produced on a young chess wiz (*The Queen's Gambit*) caused a run on chess sets around the world. And Google . . . well, it's everywhere. It's also become part of what I call the Lucky Lexicon—company names that have become ubiquitous verbs. Like Xerox and Coke in the past. Like Google or Twitter or Uber or Airbnb today.

There's much more to the net sector than just FANG, however. Many other net stocks and companies have added to the sector's allure and investor attention—including Booking (nee Priceline), Chewy, eBay, Etsy, Expedia, Grubhub, Lyft, Pinterest, Shopify, Snap, The Trade Desk, Twitter, Uber, Wix, and Zillow. 2020 was one of the strongest IPO years on record in terms of funds raised, and several of the highest-profile, highest-popping IPOs were Internet stocks—Airbnb and DoorDash near the top of the list, with both rising close to 100% on their first day of trading. The blockbuster Airbnb IPO was particularly noteworthy because it occurred while the company was still recording—thanks to the Covid-19 crisis—30% year-over-year declines in its bookings and revenue. Growth companies are typically expected to be, well, growing when they stage their IPOs. Airbnb was declining. And it still pulled off a highly successful IPO. Wow! Reflects a *lot* of trust and hope by investors in Airbnb's secular growth opportunity post-Covid-19. A *lot*. And imagine how much interest there would be were TikTok—one of the fastest-growing Internet apps of all time—to announce its IPO intentions!

The Covid-19 crisis made some of these Internet companies indispensable. We needed Amazon to keep our pantries and closets stocked during the pandemic. We needed Netflix to keep us entertained and distracted. Pet adoption surged, and so did the customer count at Chewy—rising by at least 1 million per quarter for three straight quarters in 2020. People looking to express their individuality while staying safe flocked to Etsy to buy designer masks—in the June quarter of 2020, ETSY added 12.5 million active buyers, nearly as many as the two prior years combined. With dine-in options severely curtailed, food delivery companies like DoorDash became a lifeline to both small businesses and consumers. DASH's revenue rocketed 214% year-over-year in the June 2020 quarter and then 268% in the September 2020 quarter. The stocks of these companies and others reacted accordingly—AMZN up 72% in 2020, NFLX up 64%, CHWY up 203%, ETSY up 294%, and DASH up 17,000%! (OK, OK, that's annualizing the 85% pop DASH had on its first trading day . . .). Still, the point holds.

I remain very Bullish on stocks, especially the Internet sector and the growth opportunities it still creates for entrepreneurs, companies, and investors. And I believe that hard-earned lessons from the last 2½ decades provide several good guidelines for how to invest—not trade but invest—in Internet and tech and growth stocks going forward. Not for the next quarter or year, but for the next two decades and beyond. And given the millions of new investors who have entered the stock market during the Covid-19 crisis—thanks in part to stay-at-home restrictions and the removal of trading commissions—I think the need for a guide to growth and tech investing is as great as it has ever been. Perhaps greater.

I am mindful that in 1998 and 1999, during the dot-com bubble, the NASDAQ surged close to 100% in a two-year period, briefly topping 5,000 on March 10, 2000. Which led, of course, to the dot-com crash, declining 77% over the next 6 months and then taking 15 years to recover—15 *long* years.

I just want to make sure that today's new generation of investors doesn't have to wait 15 years to recover from the all-in tech bets made then.

FROM *THE BIG SHORT* TO THE BIG LONG

For almost a quarter century, I have been at the (Wall Street) center of "The Big Long." Michael Lewis's book *The Big Short* exquisitely told the story of the housing boom and bust that helped create the global financial crisis in 2007–2008, with a special focus on the greed and deceit that created the housing market excesses. What I'm focused on—and have been lucky enough to follow—has been the dramatic wealth creation caused by the rise of the Internet over the last 25 years. The Big Long.

The history of the Internet over the past 25 years, from my Wall Street analyst seat, has been fascinating. I've watched the rise of some of the leading companies of today—Facebook, Amazon, Netflix, Google—and the fall of the leading companies of yesterday—Yahoo!, eBay, and AOL. In such a dynamic competitive sector, it shouldn't be surprising that very few companies maintain leading, dominant positions. And figuring out which companies are going to be dominant franchises is extremely hard. But those who accomplished this generated some of the best portfolio returns in the stock market over the past generation.

When Peter Lynch wrote the Prologue to the *One Up on Wall Street* 2000 edition, he noted that the Internet—like other major innovations such as railroads, the telephone, and television—would spawn lots of new companies, but only a few of these would survive to dominate the field: "A big name or two will capture the territory, the way McDonald's did with burgers or Schlumberger did with oil services." Lynch was right. He expected the Internet to create an exclusive club of companies that earn $1 billion a year in net income. Turns out the Internet sector has already produced or nearly produced 10 such companies: Alibaba, Amazon, Booking, eBay, Facebook, Google, JD.Com, Netflix, Tencent, and Twitter (Table I.1). And five of these are generating well over *$10 billion* a year in net income: Alibaba, Amazon, Facebook, Google, and

TABLE I.1 The $Billion 'Net Net Income Crew

Company	Ticker	2019 Net Income ($MM)
Alphabet	GOOG	34,218
Alibaba	BABA	26,329
Facebook	FB	18,485
Tencent	700:HK	14,289
Amazon	AMZN	11,588
Booking	BKNG	4,866
Netflix	NFLX	1,867
JD.Com	JD	1,866
eBay	EBAY	1,516
Twitter	TWTR	1,458

Source: Company filings.

Tencent. And my guess is that another 10 will be added to the $1 billion list over the next decade.

Make no mistake about it. If there has been one Big Long over the past two decades, it has been the Internet. Famed venture capitalist John Doerr, at the height of the dot-com boom in 1999, called the Internet "the largest legal creation of wealth in the history of the planet." Two years later, during the dot-com bust, he apologized for his remarks, saying they had helped lead to a mercenary get-rich-quick attitude. The long-term truth is that the Internet turned out to be an enormous wealth-creation machine for investors who picked the right entrepreneurs, management teams, companies, and stocks and then patiently stuck with them through often wild market and sector gyrations. Or traded them like hell through all those gyrations—an approach that over time I have increasingly come to view as a fool's errand.

In 1999, the six largest US market cap companies in the world were Microsoft, General Electric, Cisco Systems, Exxon Mobil, Wal-Mart Stores, and Intel. Today, the six largest include Alphabet (aka Google), Amazon, and Facebook. The Internet is the obvious

Big Change in this list. By the way, two of the other top six market cap companies—Apple and Microsoft—are on the list primarily because of the Internet. We don't buy Apple phones to test whether you can hear me now on the Verizon network. We buy them to access the Internet. And Microsoft's success left the desktop for the cloud long ago. Yes, the Internet is the obvious Big Change.

Add up the market caps of Google, Amazon, and Facebook at the end of 2020, and you're over $3.5 trillion. Add in the market caps of some of the other major Internet companies (Netflix, Booking.com, DoorDash, Airbnb, Spotify, etc.), and you're well over $4 trillion. Add in the major Chinese Internet companies (Alibaba, Tencent, etc.), and you're well over $5 trillion. That's $5 trillion in shareholder wealth that simply didn't exist 20 years ago. There are lots of interesting debates around how much of an impact the Internet has had on the US and global economies. But when it comes to shareholder wealth creation, there is no debate: The Internet has been The Big Long of the past 25 years.

Yes, I know. There were many failures and disasters along the Internet way. Investors who bet on companies like Pets.com, eToys, and FreeMarkets could have lost almost their entire investments at some point. (Full disclosure—I was a Bull on FreeMarkets, a B2B Internet company that helped run online auctions for industrial supplies, and I got that stock completely wrong.) It wasn't just the small companies that had their share of problems. Some of the supposed "big winners" of the Internet era also ended up being massive disappointments—and occasionally, massive money-losers. Picking out the leading Internet franchises is only easy in hindsight.

It certainly felt like AOL was going to be *the* leading Internet franchise during the late 1990s. It had well over 20 million paying subscribers, a brand name practically synonymous with the Internet, seasoned executives such as Steve Case and Bob Pittman, and the momentum and chutzpah to buy one of the largest media companies in the world, Time Warner. Now AOL is a fraction of its former size, it has been gobbled up by Verizon, and its acquisition of Time Warner is considered one of the biggest blunders in corporate history. In 1999, I stood next to Bob Pittman at a small-group investor meeting in Boston as he argued that dial-up AOL didn't face a broadband challenge because it had the clout to negotiate from a position of strength with any cable company. It didn't turn out that way.

Then there was Yahoo! In the fourth quarter of 1999, its stock price practically doubled. It was a can-do-no-wrong company. Its CEO, Tim Koogle, became the epitome of "corporate cool"—he even played a mean guitar when not in the office. Or maybe in the office too. In 2000, the company hosted an Analyst Day at its headquarters in Sunnyvale, California. Everyone came to learn the secret to Yahoo!'s success. And when that "cool" CEO explained that the secret was that the company had a "no-bozos" hiring practice—it didn't hire any "bozos"—it was a moment of keen insight for the investors in the room: "Ah, so *that's* how they do it!" It was also a moment for self-reflection by the investors in the room: "I wonder if *I* would pass the no-bozos test . . ." Unfortunately for Koogle and several other executives, they were pressured into leaving the firm within the next few years as Yahoo!'s fortunes deteriorated in the dot-com bust. (Makes you wonder how airtight that no-bozos rule was.)

Finally, there was eBay, which became the bullet-proof Internet company from 2001 to 2004, surging in market value when almost every other Internet company fizzled. While NASDAQ all-in declined 14% over that period, EBAY rocketed over 600%! Meg Whitman, eBay's CEO, was considered one of the best managers in the business, dramatically outperforming chief competitor Jeff Bezos in revenue and profit growth, as well as market cap creation. eBay's job fairs were so popular they shut down parts of Route 280 near San Jose. And eBay's success under Whitman helped pave her path to an almost successful run for governor of California. Today, however, eBay's market cap is just 2% of Amazon's, and its marketplace is considered quaint and outdated by many Internet users.

Like I said, very few companies maintain leading, dominant positions on the Internet.

Still, some companies have become dominant platforms and created enormous shareholder wealth along the way. Google has become the largest generator of advertising revenue worldwide, by far. And right up until the Covid-19 pandemic hit, it had a phenomenal track record of generating 20% organic year-over-year revenue growth for 50 straight quarters (12 years, with minor exceptions in two quarters in 2014 and two in 2019). That is an almost unheard-of growth rate for a company of this size (well over $100 billion revenue run rate). And Google—now called Alphabet—is a stock I have consistently recommended for most of the last 15 years, with a brief Sell shortly after its IPO (a truly disastrous call in hindsight) and a brief Hold during the Eric Schmidt to Larry Page CEO succession. I always thought highly of Schmidt because he was personable and approachable as well as intellectually honest and open. At Google's first Analyst Day, he went out of his way to encourage me to ask publicly the investment questions I had laid out in a recent research report. I did. And he and cofounder Larry Page addressed them directly. Over the five-year period ending in 2020, Google has jumped 131%, handily beating the S&P 500's 84% performance. There's a lesson here about the wonderful stock impact of compound growth—specifically, compound fundamental growth . . . and most specifically, compound revenue growth. But I'll get into that later.

Amazon was publicly derided as Amazon.bomb and Amazon.toast in several major financial publications during the dot-com bust. *Barron's* magazine, one of the best barometers of conventional Wall Street sentiment, has carried numerous articles on Amazon over the last two decades, most of which (though not all) have been skeptical. The most famous of those articles is likely the May 31,

1999, cover story—"Amazon.Bomb"—which asserted: "The idea that Amazon CEO Jeff Bezos has pioneered a new business paradigm is silly." Well, today Amazon is the most dominant, disruptive force in global retail. Not so silly. And in an extremely impressive pivot, it also built the world's leading cloud computing business . . . and one of the world's largest advertising revenue companies . . . and potentially the world's largest grocery retailer . . . and business supplies company . . . and so on. Oh, and in 2020 it delivered its third straight year of $10 billion+ in GAAP net income.

Netflix has been a highly dramatic company. (I like puns.) Of the major US Internet companies, Netflix has been the most controversial for a variety of reasons. It was never certain how many households would subscribe to a monthly DVD-by-mail service, and then to an on-demand streaming service. And the competitive risk seemed insurmountable—how could this tiny company headquartered in Los Gatos, California, survive competition from Blockbuster, then Wal-Mart, then Amazon, then HBO, and then Disney? Yet Netflix did survive. And flourish. I recall seeing Reed Hastings pitch Netflix to a crowd of deeply skeptical investors in 1998 at the Marriott Hotel near San Francisco. If they had been able to overcome their skepticism, those investors could have enjoyed dramatic returns. As of the end of 2020, Netflix was up over 40,000% since its 2002 IPO. That's a ten-bagger 40 times over. And over the decade 2010–2019, Netflix was *the single best* performing stock in the S&P 500.

Finally, there is Facebook. It has become a juggernaut, with over 3 billion current global users, $7,186 billion in revenue and $214 billion in free cash flow in 2020, and a market cap that now exceeds $700 billion (as of early 2021). Facebook has also become a hugely influential cultural phenomenon. Some believe that Facebook helped swing the 2016 US presidential election. Again, Facebook now has over 3 billion global users. That's more than the entire population of China, the United States, and Japan combined. But Facebook didn't look like a juggernaut in the year after its IPO, when its stock corrected from over $40 to $17 on the perception that it didn't have a mobile strategy. Yet FB has been a fifteen-bagger—up 1,441% through the end of 2020.

The Big Long indeed.

WHAT THIS BOOK IS *NOT* . . . AND WHAT IT *IS*

This book is not about investing across asset classes—equities, bonds, commodities, REITs, currencies. My experience has been almost entirely focused on equities. And it's not a book about investing across all equity groups—high growth, cyclicals, slow growth, turnarounds, asset plays. I have only covered high-growth companies. Or better put, companies that compete in the high-growth sector that is the Internet. Where rarely does anything but high-growth company stocks work. Where successful turnarounds almost never happen. Where slow growth usually translates into slow death—or, better put, into market-matching but not market-beating share price performance.

This book *is* a brief review of the public market history of the Internet. The big trends that have driven Internet stocks over the last two decades. How the dot-com boom led to the dot-com bubble led to the dot-com blowup led to the dot-com blowout. Which companies succeeded the most, and which companies missed it.

But this isn't a history text. It's a series of lessons (10 to be precise) that I learned the hard way over almost 25 years of covering the most dynamic sector on Wall Street—Internet stocks. And I am hoping that these lessons can help you better invest—not trade, but invest—in the great growth opportunities that lie ahead of us. Investors who sought those great growth opportunities back in 2000 too often resorted to the expressions—"It's different this time" or "You just don't get it!" I am truly hoping that those who read this book will instead be able to decide and defend their investments in part by referencing TAMs, Crucial Combos, DHQ opportunities, and some of the other concepts I detail in this book. If they do, I will have succeeded. If they do *and* generate reasonable returns on their investments, I will have truly succeeded.

10 Lessons

Now it's time for the 10 lessons about tech investing I learned from analyzing the most explosive sector on Wall Street over the past quarter century.

There Will Be Blood . . . When You Pick Bad Stocks

"There will be blood" is a simple way of saying that you definitely, absolutely, positively will lose money in the market if you invest in and trade stocks. There will be hours, days, months, and even quarters when one or even all of your initial investments will turn negative, either because of market shocks or because even "sure thing" stocks can trade off 70%+. You have to be able to tolerate setbacks.

Stocks move. They go up. They go down. They go up big. They go down big. There's nothing you can do about that. If this bothers you, you probably shouldn't invest in the market.

By buying a stock, you are making a bet (perhaps educated, perhaps researched, perhaps considered . . . or not) on both the future fundamentals (revenue, earnings, free cash flow) of a company and the future perceptions (valuation multiples) of that company. To invest in stocks successfully, you have to be a good fundamentalist. By this I mean you have to be able to reasonably forecast what revenues and profits a particular management team in a particular market will be able to generate against a particular competitive set. That is a hard thing to do. It's like forecasting the future. No, it *is* forecasting the future. And nobody can do *that* well.

The tough thing about stock-picking is that you can be a great fundamentalist and still be a lousy stock-picker. Because to succeed you also have to be a good psychologist. You have to forecast how the fundamentals you forecasted will be valued by the market. Whether the market will ascribe a high or a low multiple to those fundamentals. A higher or a lower multiple than the stock currently trades at. And a lot of things can go wrong here.

Here's a simple example. (Investors with several years of investing experience can skip the next few paragraphs.) You have a stock that generates $1.00 in earnings and trades at a 15 P/E (price to earnings) multiple, which is close to the average forward multiple of the S&P 500 over the last 20 years. You do some work on the stock—looking at analyst reports, reading a few earnings releases, doing a few Google searches—and you believe the company can grow its earnings by 10% per year for three years to $1.33. If its multiple doesn't change, this means the stock will go from $15.00 to $19.97 in three years. It will appreciate 10% per year for three years, following the EPS growth. Bingo. Done. Easy-peasy. Next!

But what if the market changes its mind and decides that that $1.33 shouldn't trade at a market multiple? That something has changed in the business, and the future growth outlook will be materially muted? Let's say the company is a pet supplies physical store retailer. And over the next three years an online pet supplies retailer (let's call it Chewy.com, hypothetically) comes into the market and starts gobbling up market share through great customer service, savvy marketing, and broad selection. And then a pandemic comes and forces retailers to remain closed for a significant time. So the market decides it's only willing to put a 10 P/E multiple on those future earnings. Now, instead of a $19.97 stock, you have a $13.31

stock. And you have lost 11% on your investment. You got the earnings completely right—you're a great fundamentalist—but you got the multiple completely wrong—you're a bad psychologist. Which means you're a bad stock-picker.

Sounds like a stupid example. It probably is. But Chewy is, of course, a real company. And so was Pet Valu, until it announced in November 2020 that it was winding down its operations and closing its 358 stores and warehouses across the United States. Which is actually a lot worse than a 11% stock price correction. A *lot* worse.

One of the reasons you absolutely, 100 percent will lose money in the market from time to time is that a large percentage of any individual stock's movement has nothing at all to do with that stock's particular fundamentals. It has to do with the market. It's a bit of a truism on Wall Street that a third of a stock's moves can be attributed to its fundamentals, a third to its sector, and a third to the overall market. I haven't studied this. I'm sure someone has. But I have lived it, and that feels accurate to me.

Didn't we just live through a graphic reminder of this? On February 20, 2020, the S&P 500 Index was at 3,373. One month later, on March 23, it was at 2,237, off 34%. Covid-19. And just about every single growth/tech stock traded off over that month. Some dramatically—Snap off 37%, Uber 45%, and Expedia a whopping 58%, as the public interest in getting on a plane collapsed. Some growth stocks traded off more modestly—Microsoft off 26%, Akamai 16%, and Peloton only 13% as gyms closed and individuals sought to work out at home. During that time, only one notable tech stock managed to trade up. Zoom. And boy did it—up 50%. In one month! Though Chewy and Cloudflare traded up 10% and 5%, respectively. Even stocks that eventually emerged as clear pandemic winners—as great work from home (WFH) plays—including Amazon, Etsy, Netflix, and Shopify—all traded off in that one-month period, with those four stocks correcting as follows: 12%, 39%, 7%, and 30%.

The point is that investors can quite easily lose money on their stocks picks—even if they are fundamentally and valuationally sound—because of major market moves. And those moves can be driven by rare, unpredictable shock events. *Black swan* events, to use the vernacular. Nassim Nicholas Taleb crystalized this phenomenon in his book by the same name. The basic thrust of that book is that the future can't be predicted. And those who rely on confident forecasts of the future will eventually be cruelly disappointed. It's a good idea to keep in mind.

So there will be blood. Even if the market gods are smiling. Even if you pick an explosive growth sector like the Internet. How? By picking the wrong stock. I should know. I've done it many times.

BLUE APRON—NOT ENOUGH MOUTHS TO FEED

On June 29, 2017, Blue Apron IPO'd on the New York Stock Exchange at $10, raising more than $300 million and valuing the company at $1.9 billion. That day, CEO Matt Salzberg was on CNBC pitching the company's prospects. He noted that the company had grown 10x over the prior two years, that it benefited from an integrated end-to-end (farm to box-on-doorstep) supply chain, and that it had already achieved positive unit economics—specifically, that it was able to break even on customer acquisition costs in about six months and over a three-year period averaged $1,000 in revenue per customer. It was a great pitch. Unfortunately, that day marked the all-time-high for Blue Apron (APRN) shares.

Everything fell apart very quickly for Blue Apron (Figure 1.1). Within a month of its IPO, one of its three cofounders stepped down from the COO position. Within five months, another of its cofounders stepped down from the CEO position amid substantial employee layoffs. By the end of the year, the stock had declined to $4.00. Within 18 months, APRN's share price had fallen over 90%

FIGURE 1.1 APRN: Catching a Falling Apron

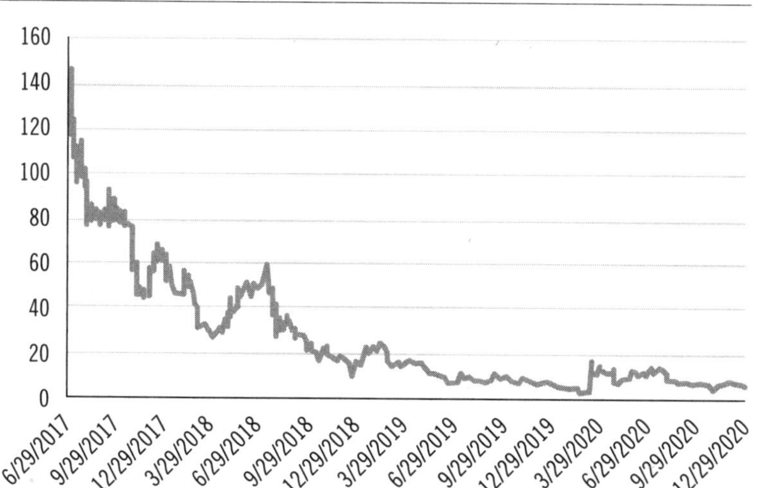

to $0.66, eventually forcing the company to execute an unusual 1-for-15 reverse stock split so it wouldn't be delisted. On a pre-split basis, the stock got as low as $0.15 in mid-March 2020, before being "discovered" as a Covid-19 play and as a beneficiary of shelter-in-place restrictions. It shot up 5x in less than a month, though half of those gains were lost a few months later.

What were the stock-picking lessons from Blue Apron? First, you have to understand the setup. For a time, Blue Apron was considered a "sure thing." In the quarter right before its IPO, it had achieved an almost $1 billion revenue run rate—$245 million in quarterly revenue—along with over 1 million customers. Those are substantial numbers. Plenty of companies have executed successful IPOs with much lower revenue and customer bases. Blue Apron management expressed its hope that it could reach 99 percent of at-home cooks in the United States. What is that number? I dunno. But it's a lot bigger than 1 million. This also looked like a massive total addressable market (TAM) play—one of the key factors to successful tech investing. According to Euromonitor, total spend in the

US retail grocery and restaurant market was $1.3 trillion at the time of the Blue Apron IPO.

The company had been operating for five years prior to its IPO and experiencing triple-digit percentage growth (100%+) for several years. There was a lot of competition in the sector—companies like Plated, Sun Basket, and Purple Carrot—with venture funds having invested over $400 million in the sector, per Pitchbook. But on the most important measures—revenue and customers—Blue Apron was the clear market leader. And Blue Apron had a subscription model, which meant high revenue visibility for the company. What could go wrong?!

When it came down to the IPO, all the major banks pitched to be part of what was expected to be the "big action." Early in 2017, my bank sent me to meet with Matt Salzberg in his Manhattan offices. And several months later, I joined my fellow deal syndicate members for a nice evening event with Blue Apron's full management team at one of the company's tasting facilities—a fabulous Brooklyn brownstone, where Blue Apron chefs prepared a gourmet meal. That meeting included a chance to meet CFO Brad Dickerson, who had joined the company the prior year, coming from a multiyear stint as the successful CFO of Under Armour, another factor that lent credibility to the Blue Apron story. The next day, we conducted a tour of one of the company's distribution centers in suburban New Jersey, donning lab coats, gloves, and hairnets to inspect the fresh food packing facility. I also became a customer of Blue Apron and enjoyed (really!) making different meals for my family.

About a month after the Blue Apron IPO, I initiated coverage of the stock with an Outperform rating and a $10 price target. The same price as the IPO? Yes, because in that short period the stock had already lost 35% of its value, trading down to $6.50. In that initiation report, I acknowledged the understandable skepticism of the market toward Blue Apron but argued that the impressive size of the company's TAM ($1.3 trillion), its leading market share position, its pending product and service improvements, and its deflated valuation all created an attractive risk-reward opportunity. Four months later, in the wake of the resignation of the CEO, I downgraded Blue Apron to Sector Perform with a $4 price target. The stock was at $2.99. A year later, the stock reached $0.66 (pre-split). And a little more than a year after that, it touched $0.15.

That's the setup. So what are the lessons?

A lot of the reporting on Blue Apron has focused on the competitive risk that dogged the company almost from the beginning. There were about a dozen competitors in the years around its IPO. ConsumerVoice.org currently lists the top 10 meal delivery kit services in the United States (and Blue Apron doesn't make the list). There was also the whale—Amazon—which announced the acquisition of Whole Foods right before Blue Apron's IPO. Investors immediately focused on this risk during the IPO road show. The Amazon threat may have been the single biggest reason why Blue Apron was priced ($10) so significantly below its initial deal range ($15–$17). But despite my respect for Amazon, I don't think this was the real undoing of Blue Apron. Do you know anybody who is currently receiving meal kits from Amazon?!

There was also a lot of reporting on what I called the Venn diagram challenge of Blue Apron. As one thoughtful industry observer "observed":

> If you like to cook but not to shop or plan your own meals, and if you weren't too hungry, and if you didn't like cooking for too many friends, then Blue Apron—the startup delivering precisely measured, prepackaged amounts of just enough salmon, green beans, butter and lemon for one meal, no leftovers—was for you.

Blue Apron's appeal was to people who liked to cook at home, but not too much. Meals were meant to be prepared in 30 to 45 minutes. Blue Apron's appeal was to couples and to four-member families. Three-member families would have extras, and five-or-more-member families would need to sign up for an additional subscription or play Dinner Table Survivor. Blue Apron's appeal was to people who didn't like to shop in the grocery store, were willing to commit to a relatively fixed delivery schedule, were willing to sign up for either $60 per week (two-person plans) or $72 per week (four-person plans) subscriptions, which were actually reasonably inexpensive on a per meal basis but still required a bit of a financial commitment. Yes, this could be described as a Venn diagram challenge. But I don't think this either was the real undoing of Blue Apron.

The company that best meets the Venn diagram challenge is . . . HelloFresh, which very few US investors know about because it is headquartered in Berlin, Germany, and trades on the Frankfurt Stock Exchange. Yet throughout the debacle of Blue Apron, HelloFresh has built up the world's largest meal-kit delivery business, generating almost $4.5 billion in revenue in 2020 (growing over 100% year-over-year, thanks in large measure to Covid-19-related lockdown restrictions), with over 5 million customers worldwide (as of the end of 2020), including over 2.5 million in the United States. HelloFresh is profitable and has seen its stock rise 400% over 2018–2020, reaching a market cap of almost $12 billion as of early 2021, approximately 6x the value of Blue Apron at its IPO. So it can be done! And many of the initiatives that HelloFresh talked about in its December 2020 investor update presentation—broadening its assortment to other product categories and new meal occasions like breakfast and lunch—are exactly what Blue Apron discussed over three years ago. So it is being done!

No, the real investment lesson from Blue Apron has to do with what is probably the single most important factor in tech investing—probably in investing as a whole: management. The market opportunity was there. The business model was challenging, but not impossible. There were no real competitive moats around Blue

Apron—competition was just a mouse click or a screen tap away, but Blue Apron was the market leader. And for a substantial period of time. For all you race fans: The track was firm, the horse was healthy, and it had the lead. But there was the slight issue of the jockey.

In all fairness, the meal-kit delivery business is an incredibly challenging business. I've done my share of distribution center tours, but only Blue Apron required the hairnet, the gloves, the lab coat, oh, and the warm clothing, because the distribution center was refrigerated to preserve the fresh food. So Blue Apron had to master an unusually complex set of operational logistics right from the beginning. Then it had to get the marketing/customer acquisition right. And the product development. That's a lot to get right, so it needed an extremely talented management team in it for the long haul—perhaps not cofounders who stepped down within five months of the IPO. Granted, they had been with the company for five years prior to that. But that clearly wasn't enough. It reminds me of the takeaway from *Outliers*, the classic book by Malcolm Gladwell. To really excel at something, you need 10 years or 10,000 hours. To this day, I'm not sure whether members of the Blue Apron management team were capable of pulling off meal-kit delivery success. I just know they cut out after "only" five years, and that was probably the best signal there was to cut your losses on that investment.

ZULILY—HARD TO KEEP FASHION IN FASHION

Here's another one where I didn't wrap myself in stock-picking glory.

On November 15, 2013, Zulily, a flash-sales e-commerce site geared toward young mothers and young children, IPO'd at $22 per share, above its filing range of $18–$20, raising $250 million. Shares quickly almost doubled to reach $41, giving the company a market cap of almost $5 billion. Zulily's founders were Mark Vadon and Darrell Cavens, previous founders and executives at Blue Nile, the successful online jewelry store. Their cred was one of the reasons Zulily was an eagerly anticipated IPO.

Less than two years later, in August 2015, Zulily was acquired by Liberty Interactive's QVC for approximately $19 per share, an almost 50% premium to where the stock was then trading, but at a discount to the IPO price, meaning the stock had materially underperformed during its brief public market history. What happened? And what's the stock-picking lesson? Let's turn to one of the analysts who covered the stock. Me.

Although perhaps not a household name like some other tech executives, Mark Vadon is a fascinating example of an entrepreneur who lives and breathes his business. In 1999, he founded Blue Nile because of a frustrating experience he had finding the right diamond engagement ring for his fiancée. He found the process of shopping for a diamond ring in retail stores intimidating, unpleasant, and overly complex; he thought the Internet could provide a better way. Vadon helped build Blue Nile into one of the largest fine jewelry retailers in the world. The company went public in May 2004 and saw its stock rise 39% on its first day of trading. Although NILE never sustained a multibillion-dollar market cap, it was a publicly traded asset for 13 years before being acquired by private equity firms Bain Capital and Bow Street in 2017 for approximately $500 million.

In 2009, Mark Vadon and fellow Blue Nile executive Darrell Cavens founded Zulily, featuring clothing, footwear, toys, and home products, primarily for young mothers and children.

As I mentioned earlier, Vadon started Blue Nile out of a frustrating personal experience. He and Cavens started Zulily when Mark's wife became pregnant with their first child, and they became overwhelmed with the amount of supplies they needed to acquire for the baby. Just as he thought the Internet would provide an apt marketplace for jewelry, Vadon thought the Internet might provide a better way for consumers to find and buy maternity clothes and supplies for babies and young children.

When in mid-2013 my employer asked me to assess whether there might be public market interest in Vadon and Cavens's latest venture, I eagerly took on the assignment. I knew the founders well, had seen them operate at Blue Nile, and thought the market opportunity could be attractive. I was especially focused on the pluses of the management team. I had come to consider Vadon and Cavens wicked smart, obsessed with their business, extremely hardworking, and understated and humble in their approach—characteristics I had started to look for in great management teams.

Unlike with Blue Apron, I didn't initiate coverage of Zulily with a Buy. Instead, with the shares still close to 80% above their IPO price, I initiated coverage with a Sector Perform rating, arguing that a somewhat aggressive valuation offset what appeared to be a truly disruptive online business model, a substantial $300 billion+ market opportunity, and a highly talented and experienced management team. Valuation kept me on the sidelines.

I kept tracking Zulily, highlighting for investors all the positives about the company, but warning them away due to its valuation (4x price to sales). In an earnings note published six months later, I even put as the title: "Still Waiting . . . For an Attractive Entry Point."

But I did finally pull the trigger. On June 26, 2014, post a 50% correction in Zulily shares (from an early 2014 peak of almost $75 down to approximately $40), I upgraded the stock to Buy with a $50 price target. Even though the share price was almost double the IPO price, I thought the 50% correction allowed me to look smart, to look like I was not chasing the stock. I also had some new survey data that clearly showed Zulily to be the leading flash-sales site with high customer satisfaction. About six months later, however, in February 2015, I downgraded the shares of Zulily to Hold, with the stock price down to $19.89—about 50% below where I had upgraded it to Buy. Sigh. I had upgraded Zulily to Buy to take advantage of a 50% correction, only to step in front of another 50% correction. And what happened after that? Another 50% correction (or close to it), with Zulily shares retreating down to below $12 (Figure 1.2). Sigh.

What happened? And what are the stock-picking lessons? At the risk of gross oversimplification, I'm going to go with customer value proposition. It just wasn't robust enough to maintain the company's fundamental momentum. And that's the lesson here—customer value proposition trumps TAMs and business models. You get the customer value prop right, and it can offset a lot of issues and challenges. You get it wrong, and it can also offset a lot of positives, such as large market opportunities and good business models (highly profitable or highly capital efficient).

And what were the customer value proposition issues at Zulily? Shipping speed and return policy. To be specific, in early 2014 customers of Zulily were looking at average order-to-ship times of 13 days. That means it took almost two weeks from the time customers ordered the product to when it shipped. Then they had to tack on two to three days for the package to actually reach their doorstep.

FIGURE 1.2 ZU: Fashion Is Fickle . . . and Hard to Model

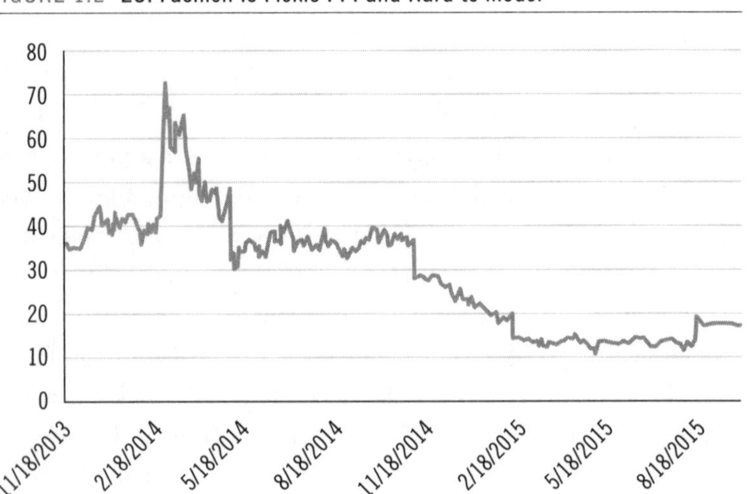

That's over two weeks. That's not Internet speed. And the return policy? There was none. Zulily had a "no returns" policy for several years. Were these major issues for the company? This is a hard one to answer with certainty, but the educated guess has to be that they were. Survey work I ran in mid-2014 listed these as the two biggest features that customers disliked about Zulily. Satisfaction scores were high, however, according to the same survey. But this was a survey of existing customers. You couldn't effectively survey non-customers—at least I couldn't—so you couldn't be sure how new cohorts would react. Turns out there were about 5 million satisfied customers of Zulily, but probably not a lot more, given the shipping speed and return policy. In the December quarter of 2014, Zulily's customer count reached 4.9 million, and it didn't rise from there. Two quarters later, its revenue growth slowed to an anemic 4% year-over-year—versus the 100%+ it had generated just two years prior.

Zulily had an impressive business model—stable and high gross margins, an inventory-light model, and a solid negative working capital cycle. Not carrying material inventory meant that Zulily didn't have to tie up as much capital as other retail companies did. Negative working capital meant Zulily collected cash from its customers long before it had to pay its suppliers. All of this was great for Zulily's P&L and cash flow statement. But the long shipping times and no returns policy that produced this business model weren't such a hot deal for most mass market consumers. That's why Zulily didn't become a mass market brand. That's why the growth stopped cold in 2015. And that's why Zulily got sold to QVC in 2015.

GROUPON—FROM GROUP HUG TO GROSS-OUT

The 10-year chart for Groupon does not look great. It just doesn't. If Peter Lynch made money on the long side on that stock, he would have had to be nimble as hell. (See Figure 1.3.)

FIGURE 1.3 GRPN: From Group Think to GRPN Sink

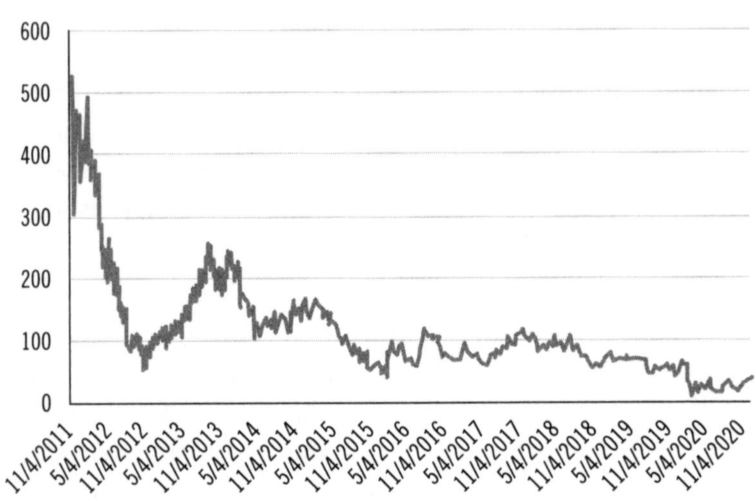

As with Blue Apron, Groupon did a reverse stock split—1-for-20 in June 2020. This right here might be a worthy investing lesson. When a company even considers doing a reverse stock split, run for the hills! In the Internet sector, that might have been a great lesson. Except it would have caused you to miss Priceline.com, which executed a 1-for-6 reverse split in 2003 and then became the single best performing S&P 500 stock over a five-year period. But more on Priceline later.

In what was the biggest US initial public offering since Google back in 2004, Groupon IPO'd on November 4, 2011, at $20 ($400 post-split) and soared 30% to peak at $26 ($523 post-split) within two weeks. There were plenty of peaks and valleys over the next decade, but the clear long-term trend was down, and shares currently (early 2021) trade around $1.70 ($34 post-split). That's a bad deal.

I assumed coverage of Groupon on February 27, 2013, with a Hold or a Sector Perform rating and a $5.00 (pre-split) price target. The stock had already corrected massively (down over 80%) since its IPO. The next day, the company's founder and CEO Andrew

Mason was fired. He issued a letter to Groupon employees with the explanation:

> After four and a half intense and wonderful years as CEO of Groupon, I've decided that I'd like to spend more time with my family. Just kidding—I was fired today. If you're wondering why . . . you haven't been paying attention. From controversial metrics in our S1 to our material weakness to two quarters of missing our own expectations and a stock price that's hovering around one quarter of our listing price, the events of the last year and a half speak for themselves. As CEO, I am accountable.

As a quick aside, the candor in Mason's letter was impressive. And his willingness to publicly take full responsibility was impressive. And rare.

Mason had developed a reputation for being irreverent, funny, reckless, and arguably genius-like. The letter demonstrated the first three adjectives. The fact that Mason had helped develop the highly innovative Groupon business model from scratch demonstrated the fourth.

I, for one, believed Mason was genius-like—in part because I had been introduced to Andrew two years earlier by the Groupon CFO, who had just joined the company after a lengthy stint at Amazon and whom I knew reasonably well. And that CFO told me that Mason was the only executive he knew that reminded him of Jeff Bezos. That was extremely high praise, and I took it seriously. Plus, Groupon was an innovative business model. It offered local merchants a smart and quick customer acquisition tool, and it offered local consumers a way to save money on a host of different services.

At the core of Groupon was the Daily Deal. At the beginning of the company's history, consumers were offered one promotional deal a day—for example, 25% off a pizza and pasta lunch for four or 30% off flowers at the local florist—*if* enough consumers signed up for the deal that day. So there were a lot of great moving parts—savings for consumers, customer acquisition for local merchants (the "coupons" could be treated as marketing or advertising spend to bring in new customers), and social gamification (the deal only worked if enough people participated, which incentivized individuals to tell their friends and so on). Over time, Groupon dramatically expanded its offerings, its product lines, and its markets. It eventually overstretched and mis-executed, which caused its market cap and share price to grind down over the years. But the original Groupon idea was highly innovative and genius-like.

And highly successful! Groupon was founded in 2008, and by 2011 it was generating $1.6 billion in revenue. Groupon was likely the fastest company in history in reaching this mark. Amazing! And people noticed. In 2010, Google reportedly offered $6 billion for the company, an offer that Mason and the Groupon board snubbed. (Groupon in early 2021 carried a market cap of $1.1 billion. Coulda shoulda woulda.)

So what went wrong? And what's the stock-picking lesson?

Fundamentally, Groupon overstretched. Dramatically. Both in terms of markets served and in terms of services offered. In late 2010, Groupon was available in 250 cities in North America, Europe, Asia, and South America. By early 2015, Groupon was available in 500 cities worldwide and offered 425,000 active deals, expanding into international markets both organically and via acquisitions. Later, the company would find itself exiting from many of these international markets, laying off over a thousand sales and customer service employees as it did. In November 2013, the company acquired Korean ticket and e-commerce company Ticket Monster for $260 million, only to have to sell off a majority stake less than 18 months later. A part of these international setbacks was due to substantial competition. At one point, there were 7,000 copycat Groupon businesses around the world. But another part of the setbacks was the result of simple market overreach.

To compound the challenge, Groupon also aggressively entered into a variety of new categories, including Groupon Goods, which focused on discounted merchandise and required the company to develop Amazon-like distribution and logistics expertise. You can probably guess how that turned out. The company also launched Groupon Getaways, which put Groupon in competition with Priceline.com, Expedia, and other travel companies for leisure travel dollars; GrouponLive, which pitted Groupon against TicketMaster and other companies in the event ticketing market; and Groupon To Go, a food delivery service, a segment that it would take another five years and arguably a Covid-19 crisis to prove out the unit economics of. And that proof came from DoorDash, not Groupon To Go. And there was at least one more—restaurant reservations, a segment Groupon entered via acquisition of the company Savored. This segment already had an established, well-operating leader in OpenTable.

And throughout much of this time, Groupon was acting without an effective CEO. After Andrew Mason stepped down as CEO in 2013, it was almost three years before a new full-time CEO was announced—Rich Williams, who came from Amazon. Groupon's cofounder, Eric Lefkofsky, had stepped in as interim CEO on the firing of Mason. He was named CEO a few months later, but as he later acknowledged, Lefkofsky did not have the management and operational skills required to take Groupon to the next level. And given the company's dramatic market and product expansions, Groupon needed those management and operational skills. The company announced that it wanted to be "the starting point for Mobile Commerce," but it simply didn't have the skill to pull off that big of a goal.

That was my call, too, when I downgraded the shares of Groupon to Sell in early 2014, writing:

> We view GRPN's goal of becoming the "starting point for (all) Mobile Commerce" to be excessively ambitious and undermining of the company's potential to win the Local Commerce/Services market. The challenge is that the Goods and Travel markets that GRPN wants to succeed in are extremely competitive with very well-entrenched competitors—AMZN, EBAY, PCLN, EXPE. We may be overly pessimistic on the company's ability to succeed in this transition—but we also believe that even if it does succeed, the required duration of this transition makes buying GRPN shares now a risky deal.

Over the next few years, Groupon shares remained volatile, and I switched my rating back and forth between Sell and Hold or Sector Underperform and Sector Perform, based largely on fundamental concerns. Turns out that Groupon could never consistently execute well against that goal of being "the starting point for Mobile Commerce." In part because some other companies were already achieving that goal—Amazon and Google, to name two. And in part because that goal required extraordinarily skillful execution that Groupon management could never quite deliver on.

And Groupon's stock never really performed well. Even the most nimble of investors or traders would have had a tough time making money on the long side of GRPN. For some quick comparisons, since its November 2011 IPO, Groupon has returned a negative 7% versus an 825% return for the S&P 500. Over the last five years, Groupon has returned a negative 32% versus a 90% return for the S&P 500. And over the last year, Groupon has returned a negative 19% versus a 14% return for the S&P 500. Peter, I really hope you didn't buy Groupon.

The lesson? There will always be blood in the market. But picking the wrong companies will definitely increase your chances of spilling some of it too.

If you invest in the stock market, you will lose money from time to time. Being a good stock-picker involves being both a good fundamentalist—correctly forecasting revenues and profits—and a good psychologist—correctly guessing what multiples the market will place on those revenues and profits. It's very, very hard to get both of those right most of the time. Then there are always market shock events—think Covid-19 pandemic in early 2020—that are impossible to forecast and can undermine the best-laid stock-picking plans. Investing requires grit.

You will also lose money from time to time because you will almost certainly make some bad stock calls. I had been professionally analyzing stocks for almost 15 years when I got Zulily wrong, and I knew that management team well. What I didn't appreciate well enough was how its customer value proposition limited its TAM and its growth outlook. I had been professionally analyzing stocks for almost 20 years when I got Blue Apron wrong, largely because I either overestimated the abilities of that management team or underestimated the challenges the company faced. I may have gotten Groupon largely right, but its unprecedented growth and highly innovative business model attracted a lot of market interest and investor capital. You can't get every stock call right, and even "sure thing" stocks can go down 70%, 80%, 90%.

LESSON 2

There Will Be Blood . . . Even When You Pick the Best Stocks

Be ready to endure material pullbacks, even with best-in-class companies and stocks. Patience will be rewarded, but you will almost certainly face major, painful pullbacks along the way, even with stocks of the companies with the most compelling fundamentals. Best-in-class stocks aren't immune from major sell-offs.

Amazon, Facebook, Google, and Netflix have been amazing stocks over the last 1, 2, 5, 10, and 15 years. They have been ten-baggers—multiple ten-baggers. Patient investors who bought and held these stocks made outstanding returns on their investments. But their patience was tested. At times sorely. At times dramatically. And that's the key lesson here. Even the best stocks can suck at times. They don't teach you this in business school. Well, they don't teach you to describe stocks as "sucking." But it is true. So brace yourself.

Here are the stories that generated this lesson.

FACEBOOK—SELF-INFLICTED WOUNDS

Over the last several years, Facebook has been one of the most controversial stocks in the Internet sector, but not because of its fundamentals. For 35 straight quarters, Facebook generated at least 30% year-over-year revenue growth up through the September quarter of 2019. That is very-rare-air super premium growth. And it did this while maintaining well over 40% operating margins, which are intrinsically robust margins. That 30% revenue growth + 40% operating margin meant Facebook sported a Crucial Combo (revenue growth + operating or EBITDA margin) of 70%+ for multiple years. These were fundamentally impressive results—among the strongest you could find in the Internet sector or the tech sector or in any other sector. And for the free cash flow (FCF) fans out there, Facebook generated at least $10 billion in FCF every year from 2016 to 2020. Impressive.

But no doubt about it, Facebook has been one of the most controversial stocks in the Internet sector. Why? In large part because Facebook is ubiquitous. By the end of 2020, more than 3.2 billion humans used one of Facebook's services (Facebook, Instagram, WhatsApp) on a monthly basis. That's 41.026 percent of the entire human population. Nothing other than Google is as widely used by so much of the human population. And this ubiquity itself has been controversial. How did Facebook become so large? Just how influential and powerful has Facebook become? And exactly who is in charge of this massive platform? What if Mark Zuckerberg were to be succeeded by Lex Luthor? What if Mark Zuckerberg secretly *is* Lex Luthor? Call it the curse of ubiquity.

There are other reasons Facebook has been so controversial. Some of the content shared on its platform has been deeply disturbing. On March 15, 2019, Brenton Tarrant livestreamed on Facebook his mass murder of 51 innocent civilians in Christchurch, New Zealand. And his video went viral, with 1.5 million related posts within 24 hours. The mass murder, the livestreaming, and the reposting were all deeply disturbing. And they highlight the controversial nature of Facebook because they highlight the controversial nature of humanity. If you establish an open mic night on the town commons—or an open cam night—you bet you're going to hear and see disturbing things, regardless of how many resources the company has put into content moderation.

And the company has put a *lot* of resources into content moderation—tens of millions of dollars and tens of thousands of employees. Which has served to create even more controversy around Facebook. Who makes the decisions over which content should be moderated? What about all the borderline political propaganda that is part and parcel of competitive, at times divisive, political campaigns? Who should make the calls as to what's accurate and what is inaccurate? As Republican Senator Ted Cruz challenged Twitter CEO Jack Dorsey in a recent congressional hearing: "Who elected you?!" The implied criticism holds for Zuckerberg, too.

There have also been legitimate issues around Facebook's lack of sufficient focus on protecting its users' privacy. In April 2020, a federal court approved a $5 billion settlement between the Federal Trade Commission and Facebook arising from the FTC's assertion that the Cambridge Analytica scandal, in which data on 87 million Facebook users was used by a political consultancy that worked on President Trump's 2016 election campaign, violated an earlier 2012 agreement between Facebook and the FTC to protect user privacy.

All of which leads to the June 2018 quarter, one of the greatest self-inflicted share price wounds in tech history that I have witnessed, and the lesson of how even the best stocks can suck at times.

From July 25, 2018, to December 24, 2018, Facebook shares corrected a massive 43%, falling from $218 to $124. This was after rising 20% from the beginning of that year and 86% over the prior 18 months. FB shares would eventually recover to that $218 high by early 2020 and then dramatically rise above it in the latter part of the year. But that 43% correction was massive and painful. And it was almost entirely self-inflicted.

On July 25, 2018, Facebook announced its June quarter earnings, and its stock tanked (Figure 2.1). Here are the two key parts of that earnings call that did the damage (emphasis added).

Mark Zuckerberg:

> Looking ahead, we will continue to invest heavily in security and privacy because we have a responsibility to keep people safe. But as I've said on past calls, *we're investing so much in security that it will significantly impact our profitability.* We're starting to see that this quarter. But in addition to this, we also have a responsibility to keep building services that bring people closer together in new ways as well. In light of increased investment in security, we could choose to decrease our investment in new product areas, but we're not going to—because that wouldn't be the right way to serve our community and because we run this company for the long term, not for the next quarter. Dave will talk about this in a few minutes.

"Dave" was David Wehner, Facebook's CFO, who a few minutes later said:

> Our total revenue growth rate decelerated approximately 7 percentage points in Q2 compared to Q1. *Our total revenue growth rates will continue to decelerate in the second half of 2018, and we expect our revenue growth rates to decline by high single digit percentages from prior quarters sequentially in both Q3 and Q4.* . . . We continue to expect that full-year 2018 total expenses will grow in the range of 50–60% compared to last year. In addition to increases in core product development and infrastructure, this growth is driven by increasing investments in areas like safety and security, AR/VR, marketing, and content acquisition. *Looking beyond 2018, we anticipate that total expense growth will exceed revenue growth in 2019. Over the next several years, we would anticipate that our operating margins will trend towards the mid-30s on a percentage basis.*

FIGURE 2.1 FB: The Facebook Faceplant

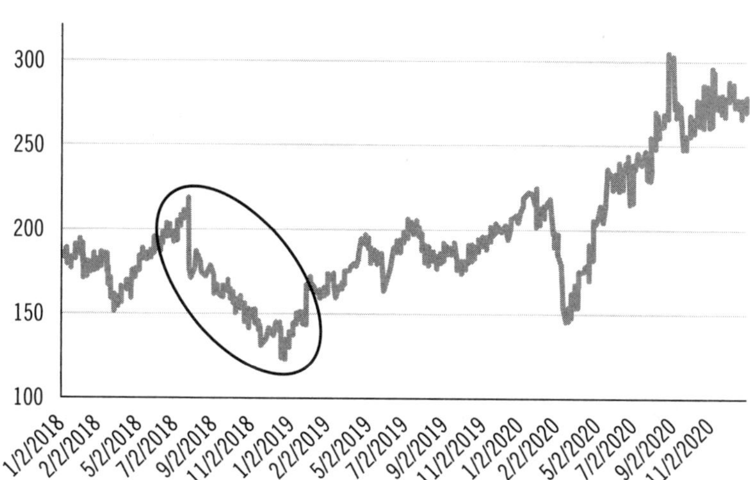

In my almost 25 years of covering tech stocks and listening to countless earnings calls, I had never seen a management team so fundamentally change the Street's outlook for its earnings growth. I later concluded that this was one of the long-term smartest things I had seen a management team do. But that was a later conclusion. And the near-term impact was dramatic and negative. Instead of the Street's assumption that Facebook was a 30%+ EPS grower going into 2019, management was implicitly guiding analysts like me to single-digit percentage EPS growth, at best. In terms of the numbers, prior to the July 25 EPS call, the Street had been assuming 30%-ish revenue growth and expanding operating margins in 2019, which equated to that 30%+ EPS growth. Great, premium growth. Instead, post that earnings call, the Street was modeling 20%-ish revenue growth with materially declining operating margins, which equated to almost no EPS growth in 2019. Which for investors meant a *much* lower multiple. A dramatic derating. And that's exactly what happened.

For some quick context, Facebook's new financial guidance still implied a robust business model—20%-ish revenue growth and mid-30s% operating margin. That would be a 55% Crucial Combo, for a company generating over $50 billion a year in revenue. Very few S&P 500 companies screen that well. But it was a material change from what the market had expected going into the June quarter earnings call. And for those keeping track, Facebook's dour outlook was never actually achieved. Revenue growth in 2019 actually came in at 30%. And operating margin, excluding some one-time legal expenses, came in at 41%. But the market didn't know this in July 2018.

In hindsight, Facebook was reacting to some of the highly public controversy around its platform and trying to convince investors (and the public) that it would invest whatever it took to ensure the safety of its platform. It needed to do this. The #deleteFacebook movement was real. But Facebook was also signaling that it wanted to invest substantially in areas like augmented reality/virtual reality and in content for its new Facebook Watch (mini-YouTube) platform. Which meant that these were also offensive investments—not just defensive ones—the company was making. Facebook was going to become less profitable temporarily in part because it wanted to develop new revenue streams, which is exactly what patient, long-term investors want a good management team to do. But near term (as in five months), this created a lot of pain and a lot of dislocation in Facebook's share price.

One of the most important takeaways I hope you'll get from this book is to look for DHQ (dislocated high-quality) opportunities. These occur when the stocks of high-quality companies become dislocated and trade off aggressively, due to either overall market corrections (such as the Covid-19 crisis in the spring of 2020), market misperceptions, company missteps, or concrete steps by managements that reduce near-term earnings (the Facebook example). I'll dive into DHQs in the tenth lesson, but I'll highlight here that even the best companies' stocks can get dislocated from time to time. Can suck from time to time. And sometimes for self-inflicted reasons.

NFLX—SUBSCRIBER MISSES AND THE DISNEY DEATH STAR

Even before the spread of Covid-19 virus, the world was undergoing a dramatic shift in video entertainment consumption, and Netflix as a company and NFLX as a stock were arguably the two greatest beneficiaries of this shift. The world was going streaming, as more and more consumers preferred streaming's superior value proposition—almost any movie or TV show on almost any device at any time—all at a reasonable monthly subscription price of $8.99 (the rough equivalent of four large coffees at Starbucks). And the clear streaming leader was Netflix, which went from having 75 million global subscribers at the end of 2015 to 111 million at the end of 2017 to over 200 million at the end of 2020.

And Netflix shares followed suit, surging from $111 to $531 (up over 375%) over that five-year period, four times better than the S&P 500, which rose 93% over that same period. But this dramatic rise came with a lot of volatility, including two dramatic corrections. The first was when Netflix shares cratered 44% from $417 on June 20, 2018, to $234 on December 24, 2018. The second was when Netflix shares crashed 34% from $385 on May 3, 2019, to $255 on September 24, 2019. (See Figure 2.2.) Even this great five-year stock performance had dramatic corrections—i.e., sucked—which sorely tested investors and analysts (like me) who were Bullish on Netflix shares.

That 40% NFLX correction starting in mid-2018 was massive. The cause was a June quarter subs miss against elevated expectations. "Subs miss" means that Netflix missed the Street's and its own guidance for subscriber adds for the June quarter. In the United States,

FIGURE 2.2 **NFLX: An Action Movie with a Little Too Much Action**

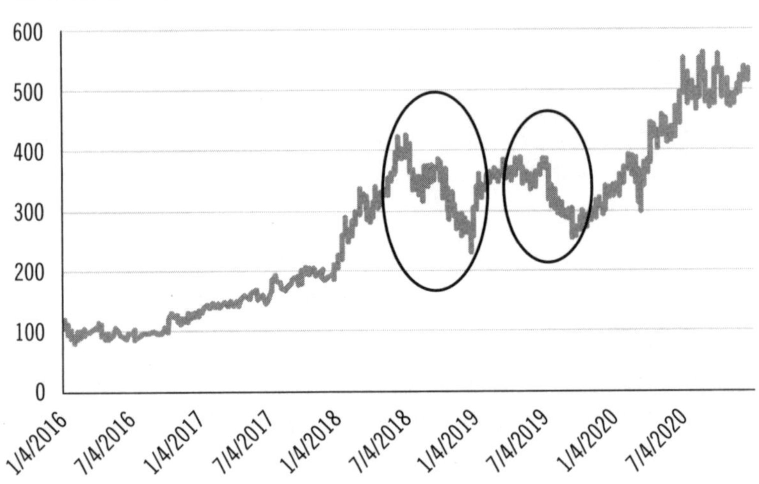

Netflix added 674,000 new subscribers, but guidance had called for and the Street was expecting 1.2 million. So Netflix essentially came in almost 50% below expectations on its most important metric. And in international markets, Netflix added 4.5 million new subscribers, but guidance had called for and the Street was expecting at least 5.0 million. Fundamentally, little had changed as the company's 40% revenue growth and 12% operating margin results for the quarter were consistent with the prior quarter, but a subs miss was a subs miss. Actually, it was more, because the company had beaten subscriber adds guidance and expectations the prior four quarters and because the stock had almost doubled (from $210 to $411) over the first six months of 2018. Expectations were, indeed, elevated.

One quarter later, Netflix handily beat its subscriber adds guidance and Street estimates, and the stock began to recover, although a general sell-off in tech stocks (actually, in all stocks) in the fourth quarter temporarily capped NFLX upside. Arguably more important, Netflix ended up adding more new subscribers in 2018 than it had added in 2017, suggesting that adoption of streaming was still in its early days globally. But the 40% correction was real . . . and really painful.

What caused the subs miss that June quarter? At least four things. First, the World Cup that summer likely caused a slowdown in subscriber adds in Europe. Europeans *love* watching soccer . . . er, football. Second, Netflix didn't benefit from the launch of any major new shows that quarter, as it had earlier in the year with the highly popular *13 Reasons Why*. Third, the June quarter was and typically is the slowest growth quarter of the year for Netflix (except during Covid-19 pandemic in 2020), as streaming has to compete with outdoor activities during the warm, long summer days. And fourth, forecasting subscriber adds—and revenue and profits—is an inherently challenging task. It *is* forecasting the future. And you're never going to get that right all the time.

Imagine being the person at Netflix responsible for generating the company's guidance. I'll take Netflix management at its word that the subscriber guidance it gives to the Street every quarter is its own internal forecast. It's possible it's a sandbagged, conservative forecast, but the not insignificant number of times over the last five years that Netflix has missed its own guidance lends credence to the idea that it's likely an honest midpoint internal forecast. (My tracking showed that Netflix came in below its revenue and subscriber guidance about one-third of the time during that period.)

So imagine being the person at Netflix responsible for forecasting exactly how many new subscribers Netflix was going to add over the next 90 days in over 150 countries around the world. Needing to factor in things like the state of the economy in each market, the potential attraction of new content slates (both by Netflix and by local competitors), the overall level of broadband and streaming adoption, the weather (remember the impact of warm, long summer days), and so on. This must be almost impossible to do with any real precision. So imagine being that person.

I didn't have to, because I met him in May 2018 when I brought a group of investors to Netflix's headquarters in Los Gatos, California.

This was part of a bus tour of technology companies in Silicon Valley called Rallies in the Valley that I arranged twice a year. On this rally, we actually met with the person who ran Netflix's forecasting group. He didn't disclose any details about that quarter's progress, but instead fielded a series of questions from investors on how he and his team did their forecasting. I and the investors walked out of that meeting with increased confidence that Netflix had a thorough and detailed process behind its forecasting and, therefore, that the odds of a major subs miss were small. Sixty days later . . . oops!

The 32% correction in mid-2019 was also massive, and a subs miss was the culprit again. But there was also fear of the Disney Death Star—also known as the pending launch of the Disney+ streaming service. Netflix shares crashed 32% from $385 on April 29, 2019, to $263 on September 23, 2019. Netflix shares traded off on both its March quarter EPS results (reported in mid-April) and its June quarter results (reported in mid-July). Those June quarter results actually led to the stock's biggest one-day sell-off (10%) in three years. What happened wasn't just that Netflix missed its subscriber growth guidance and Street expectations. It missed them badly. Worse, for the first time in almost a decade Netflix reported a decline in US subscribers, with its subscriber base declining 130,000 from March to June. International subs also came in light during the quarter.

The factors that caused the June 2018 quarter miss were largely at play here—lack of a robust new content slate, summer seasonality, the inherent challenge of forecasting a global consumer subscription business where users can sign up and sign off at a click's notice. But there were two new plausible factors that worked to spook the stock down substantially for several months. First, earlier in the year Netflix had implemented another price increase—its fourth in the prior five years—though this one was more aggressive, because it was the first time Netflix had raised the price of its basic streaming plan—from $7.99 per month to $8.99. Second, Disney had announced in mid-April that it would soon be launching its

Disney+ streaming service, and the launch date was officially set for November 12. Both of these factors were quickly retrofitted by investors to explain the June 2019 quarter subs miss, pressuring Netflix's stock price down on the concern that Netflix's fundamentals would be permanently impacted.

As it turned out, Netflix was able to successfully implement its price increase. And the launch of Disney+ didn't have a sustainably negative impact on Netflix's subscriber growth. Netflix shares traded up solidly on its September quarter EPS results, thanks to much stronger than expected international sub growth. And then the Covid-19 lockdowns helped generate Netflix's two strongest subscriber adds quarters ever in the March and June quarters of 2020. And the stock achieved new highs that it largely maintained by the end of the year. Consumers were apparently willing to sign up for more than one streaming service—given the low subscription costs (four cups of coffee) and the exclusive, differentiated content on each service.

But all this is getting ahead of ourselves. Yes, the Netflix stock price corrections created great DHQ opportunities for investors. But this is the warning part of the book. And the lesson here is that even the best stocks (NFLX up 375% over the last five years) can suck at times (corrections of 32% and 40%).

GOOGL—SOME THINGS REMAIN A MYSTERY

Google's stock has been a steady performer over the last five years, rising approximately 140% from the beginning of 2016 ($731) to the end of 2020 ($1,735). That compares to the S&P 500 rising 93% over that time. That's doing more than 50% better than the market. That's great outperformance.

Google's stock has been a steady performer because its fundamentals have performed steadily. Excluding two quarters in 2014 and one in 2019, Google generated 20%+ revenue growth for 50 straight quarters up to and including Q4 2019. That's 12½ years! Then Covid-19 pandemic hit. But that track record was extraordinarily impressive, especially for a company of Google's size—$162 billion in revenue in 2019, which makes Google one of the 10 biggest companies in the world ranked by revenue. The bigger a company is, the harder it is to maintain premium growth rates. A growth rate of 20% on a $1 billion revenue base requires adding $200 million in new revenue. A growth rate of 20% on a $162 billion revenue base requires adding $32 billion in new revenue, which is more than the GDP of 100 different countries on this planet. Another way to think about it is that in most years, global GDP growth is in the 2–5% range. So 20% revenue growth implies growth 4x to 10x faster than the global economy.

I've made the point. A growth rate of 20% is impressive. And Google consistently reported that. Until it didn't. In the March quarter of 2019. Which led to a sizable 20% correction from April 29 ($1,296) to June 3 ($1,039). Figure 2.3 shows what happened.

FIGURE 2.3 GOOGL: What Happened to Your Revenue Growth?

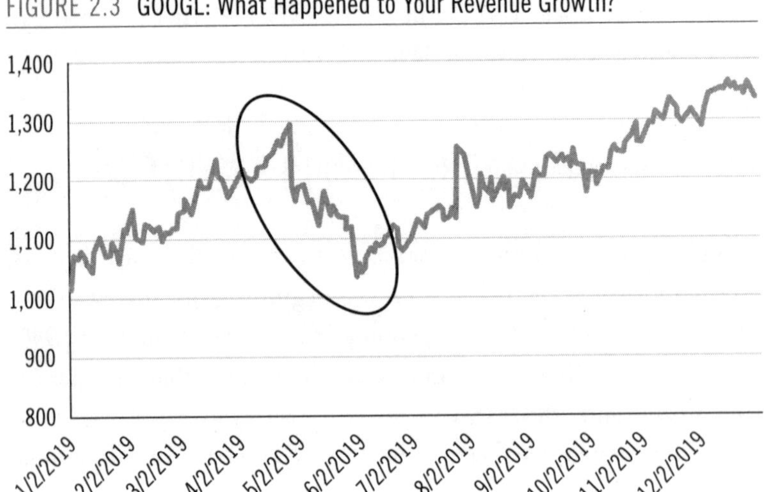

Actually, to this day, I still don't know what exactly happened. With the March 2019 EPS results, Google printed its first sub-20% (19% to be exact) revenue growth quarter in almost four years. Google has never provided detailed guidance, but the Street had assumed that growth would remain consistent at Google as it had for a long time. So the revenue growth deceleration—from 23% in the December quarter of 2018 to 19% in the March quarter—was a negative surprise, and the top-line results missed Street expectations. The stock promptly dropped 7% the next day to $1,199 (a very big drop for a large cap company like Google and its largest one-day correction in some time) and then continued to correct for the next five weeks. For some quick context, that 7% one-day correction amounted to a loss of $59 billion in market cap! That's more than the market cap of 75% of the S&P 500. Losing $59 billion in market cap is like losing a GM or a Dollar General or a DuPont or a Waste Management. It's a *lot* of market cap.

Reading the company's earnings press release, you would have thought nothing was amiss. The very first paragraph from the release stated:

> "We delivered robust growth led by mobile search, YouTube, and Cloud with Alphabet revenues of $36.3 billion, up 17% versus last year, or 19% on a constant currency basis," said Ruth Porat, Chief Financial Officer of Alphabet and Google. "We remain focused on, and excited by, the significant growth opportunities across our businesses."

Nothing to look at here! Yet the Street and its Google analysts spent the next several months trying to figure out what happened, until Google printed its June quarter results in late July and quickly reverted to 22% year-over-year revenue growth, causing the stock to march right back up to all-time highs and continue to climb until Covid-19. A clear DHQ opportunity, but again I am getting ahead of myself.

Even with the benefit of hindsight and reviewing numerous statements by Google management and the company's financial trends, it's still unclear to me what happened in the March 2019 quarter. To its credit—or discredit—Google management, when pressed on the March quarter results, consistently and simplistically stated that the results were within its expectations. When I look back, it appears that Google's Other Revenue segment, which includes its Cloud Computing segment, weakened a bit that March quarter, and both the Latin American and European region results looked soft. But it's hard to come up with a clear compelling reason why Google's revenue growth streak broke that quarter. Perhaps just the random vagaries of different end markets and product changes. We may never know.

But what we do know is that Google's stock, which has been a solid outperformer over a five-year period reflecting impressive fundamentals (up 140%), materially corrected for a notable period of time (20% for six weeks). Even the best stocks can suck at times.

AMZN—HOW YOU CAN LOSE MONEY ON A STOCK THAT HAS RISEN 183,000%

You can type into Google: "How much would I have now if I had invested $1,000 in *name your stock* at its IPO?" It's a fun exercise. Do this with AMZN, and you'll see links that will get you close to the right answer. Or simply pull up AMZN's stock price chart on Google Finance and click on MAX: 183,292%. That's how much Amazon has soared since its IPO (as of early 2021). So if you had invested $1,000 at the time of the IPO, you would now have $183,292,000. And chances are you wouldn't bother reading this book.

AMZN's share price performance since its May 1997 IPO has been utterly amazing. That 183,292% return up through early 2021 is more than 2x that of Apple (88,000% since its IPO), and

Apple's IPO was 16 years prior to Amazon's. It's not as phenomenal as Microsoft's return (up 223,000% since its IPO), but Microsoft's IPO was 11 years prior to Amazon's.

Since the last day of the twentieth century, AMZN has risen from $76.13 to over $3,100 today—4,300%, a 43-bagger. That's AMZNing! And if you had bought and held AMZN over that entire time frame, you would have done phenomenally well. But you also would have been phenomenally insane. Because for the first several years of this century, Amazon's fundamental outlook was uncertain. During the dot-com bust (2001–2003), revenue growth in some segments slowed down to single-digit percentage growth, as the company had to rein in almost all growth investments/spend to reach profitability. That's why the stock dramatically declined from $76.13 at the beginning of 2000 down to below $6.00 in the fall of 2001 (down 92%).

I dimly recall only one investor—a European fund manager—being interested in possibly buying AMZN that fall. I wish I could remember his name, and I hope he has long retired (very successfully) from the business. His argument to me at the time was that Amazon was trading cheaper than Walmart on a price-to-sales basis, and if retail really was going to move online, Amazon would eventually be able to generate much faster growth than Walmart and thus trade at a much higher multiple. It was a simple investment thesis, and a decisively accurate one too.

But there's no question that Amazon was a highly speculative investment idea for many years after its 1997 IPO. There were so many unknowns, including: Would retail really move online? Would Amazon be the market leader if and when it did? Could the business model actually generate profits? Was the Amazon management team good enough to figure this all out and execute well?

The intriguing question is: When did Amazon become a "reasonably sane" growth stock? When did it morph from being a speculative investment on the future of Internet retail to being a growth investment (still risky, but not speculative) on the future of one of the Internet's largest platforms? My answer is 2006–2007, because that's when Amazon launched both Amazon Web Services (AWS), its cloud offering, and the Amazon Kindle, its e-reader. Although I was skeptical at the time and viewed AWS as a limited, commodity-esque business, AWS eventually became arguably the most important growth engine at Amazon, and today it accounts for arguably half of the company's market cap. The first version of the Kindle was clunky and awkward. But even with that first version, you could get the idea—the win—of being able to acquire almost any book in an instant. On-demand books! Kind of like the wow factor behind video streaming that Netflix introduced a few years later.

And the so-what of these two launches is that they proved that Amazon could be much more than a retail company. It could be an enterprise solutions company and a device/product company as well. The 2006–2007 period was also when Amazon generated $1 billion or more in net income in back-to-back years, proving that its core retail business could be materially profitable despite low operating margins.

I'll get back to the full Amazon story later. I'll just make the point that Amazon has been a fundamentally attractive company—in terms of premium revenue growth and consistent profits—for going on 15 years now, which explains why its stock has performed so well over that period—up 7,200% since the beginning of 2006. Over the five-year period 2016–2020, AMZN surged 441%—almost 5x better than the S&P 500's 93% return.

But nothing lasts forever. Trees don't grow to the sky. And even the best stocks can suck at times. From August 31 to December 21 of 2018, AMZN shares corrected 32%, from $2,013 to $1,377. (See Figure 2.4.) The other examples in this lesson have all involved specific missteps by the companies (Facebook, Google, and Netflix)—such as an EPS miss. That wasn't the case here. Instead, Amazon shares got caught up in a broad trade down across the market (the

FIGURE 2.4 AMZN: Nobody Is Immune to a Sell-Off

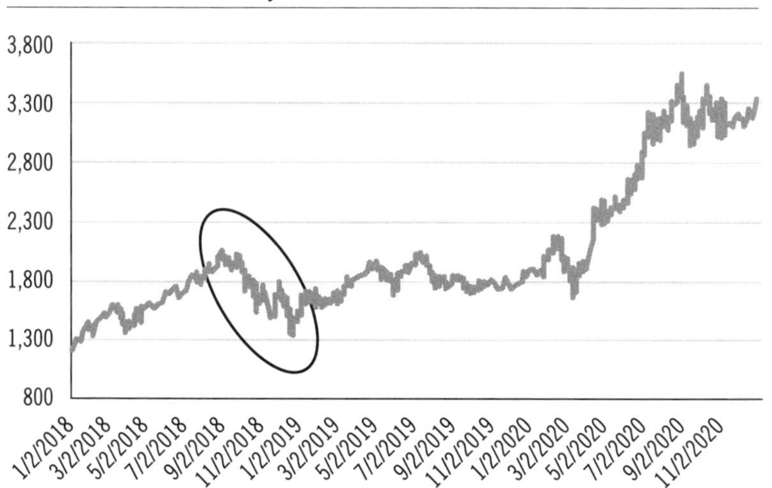

S&P 500 down 17% over that time) and more so across tech stocks (NASDAQ down 22%).

Market sell-offs happen. That particular one in late 2018 was caused by President Trump's trade war with China, a slowdown in global economic growth, and concerns that the Federal Reserve was raising interest rates too quickly. These factors weren't specifically linked to Amazon. Yet that market sell-off led to a material sell-off in Amazon shares. Amazon Bulls were sorely tested. And they learned the lesson that even the best stocks can suck at times.

There's also a basic point here that near-term stock price movements can sometimes be meaningless. Amazon shares traded off 32% over four months in late 2018. In late July, after strong Amazon June quarter earnings results, I titled my EPS note: "Scale & Profits & A Path To $1T." $1T as in $1 trillion in market cap. It was the first time I had placed a $1 trillion market cap price target on any company. But given the size and scale of Amazon at that point ($208 billion revenue run rate), and the very consistent premium revenue growth (26%) and rising and record-high operating margins (6%), I believed Amazon would achieve the $1 trillion level within the next 12 months. It ended up reaching that level 35 days later. Then began the 32% correction, meaning Amazon shed $320 billion in market cap in four months—the equivalent of a GM, a Dollar General, a DuPont, and a Waste Management combined.

But nothing changed fundamentally for Amazon during those four months. Its revenue growth in the September and December quarters remained solidly in the 20%+ range. Its operating margin remained solidly in the mid-single-digit percentage range. Financial results for both quarters were in line with or above Street expectations. Essentially, nothing changed in the fundamental growth outlook for Amazon. Yet the stock lost one-third of its value.

Sometimes stock movements become unhinged—or dislocated—from company fundamentals, even with the best of companies. That's what this Amazon example shows. And that's why it's often best to ignore short-term volatility in stocks. Those stock moves are sometimes truly without meaning. Think long term; win long term. And perhaps nowhere is this clearer than when it comes to trading around earnings.

Even best-in-class stocks aren't immune from company-specific sell-offs. Facebook, Google, and Netflix—three of the best performing stocks of 2015–2020—all experienced major corrections (from 20% to 40%) during that period. In the case of Netflix, it was twice in a 12-month period. Despite fundamentals that were at times dramatically better than those of other tech stocks—and 95%+ of the S&P 500—these stocks experienced major setbacks, before recovering to continue to materially outperform the market.

Even best-in-class stocks aren't immune from broad market sell-offs. In late 2018, in the wake of a broad market correction tied to trade war concerns, global GDP growth, and rising interest rates, AMZN lost a third of its value, despite no change in its estimates or growth outlook. Be ready to endure material pullbacks, even with best-in-class companies and stocks. There will be blood, for reasons that can sometimes be totally out of the control of specific companies.

LESSON 3

Don't Play Quarters

Don't play quarters, because successfully trading around quarters requires both an accurate read of fundamentals and (more importantly) a correct assessment of near-term expectations, a tricky task for individual (and most professional) investors to pull off. Trades around quarters can be misleading. Stay focused on the long term and ignore short-term stock price fluctuations.

Over the years one of the questions I have least liked receiving from investors has been: "Should I buy XYZ stock in front of the quarter?" There's nothing wrong with the question per se, especially for funds that are heavily involved in tech stocks and are looking for ideas on how to position portfolios to best manage volatility and risk. Also, for fund managers who want to build a full position in a stock, but don't want to do it all at once or are looking for ideal valuation-based entry points, these quarter questions make sense.

But too often I find the question to really be: "Should I buy XYZ stock in front of the quarter for a quick pop so that I can sell it for a nice tidy short-term gain right after?" This is the question I don't like receiving, for several reasons.

First, getting the EPS trade right is often much more of an expectations call than a fundamentals call. You not only have to be reasonably accurate in estimating whether Street estimates will be missed, made, or beaten; you also have to be reasonably accurate in determining what the expectations for the quarter are—whether a "beat" will be enough of a beat to cause the stock to trade up.

Second, short-term stock movements are rarely linked to material changes in company fundamentals. Even when those movements occur right around material company fundamental events—like quarterly EPS reports—the trades can often be dislocated from the fundamentals. Stocks can go up on fundamentally weak results and down on fundamentally strong results. And focusing on these trades can cause you to miss the big picture *and* the big investment opportunity.

Third, especially for retail investors, when you are making a bet just on one quarter's results, you are making a bet with a dramatic data disadvantage. Professional institutional investing funds often pay for access to sources like credit card data, third-party web traffic data, user surveys, and expert networks that a retail investor will almost never be able to afford. They can often have a much better idea of what quarterly financial results a company is likely to report—and what the market expectations are—than any retail investor can have.

Fourth, it's inherently difficult to "call quarters." I can still recall one of the most seasoned hedge fund analysts I know declare: "You could tell me in advance what the earnings and the guidance are going to be, and I still wouldn't know which way the stock would react to the print."

All of which leads to my simple advice to retail investors: Don't play quarters. Which is another way of saying: Don't be distracted by short-term stock volatility.

I fully understand the appeal of "the EPS trade." Making a 10% return in 24 hours by guessing correctly that Apple or Tesla or Peloton will trade up or down when it releases its quarterly earnings results is instant financial gratification. But it can also often mean instant financial loss. And again, it can lead to some major missed investment opportunities.

Table 3.1 shows an example from Amazon. Between January 1, 2015, and December 31, 2018, AMZN traded up 386%—almost 100% a year—from $309 to $1,502. Over that entire period, the S&P 500 rose 22%. AMZN was an Incredible Long over those four years. And over those four years, Amazon had 16 earnings releases. On four of those releases, AMZN shares spiked 10% or more in one

TABLE 3.1 Playing the Amazon Quarters

EPS	Earnings Date	Closing Price	Price Change 1 Day	Price Change 3 Days
1Q:15	4/23/2015	$389.99	14%	10%
2Q:15	7/23/2015	$482.18	10%	9%
3Q:15	10/22/2015	$563.91	6%	8%
4Q:15	1/28/2016	$635.35	–8%	–13%
1Q:16	4/28/2016	$602.00	10%	12%
2Q:16	7/28/2016	$752.61	1%	1%
3Q:16	10/27/2016	$818.36	–5%	–4%
4Q:16	2/2/2017	$839.95	–4%	–3%
1Q:17	4/26/2017	$909.29	1%	4%
2Q:17	7/27/2017	$1,046.00	–2%	–5%
3Q:17	10/26/2017	$972.43	13%	14%
4Q:17	2/1/2018	$1,390.00	3%	4%
1Q:18	4/26/2018	$1,517.96	4%	4%
2Q:18	7/26/2018	$1,808.00	1%	–2%
3Q:18	10/25/2108	$1,782.17	–8%	–14%
4Q:18	1/31/2019	$1,718.73	–5%	–3%

day. So you could have "played" the stock for those four pops, or you could have simply stayed invested. You would have made a lot more money staying invested. Oh, and by playing the quarters, you could also have lost money on four quarters when AMZN shares traded off materially.

I really hope that this example and table will pound through the point that playing quarters is a fool's errand.

So do quarters matter? Of course they do. I know there's a strong correlation between a year's four quarters of financial results and its annual results. About 100%. No, exactly 100%. But rarely does one quarter fully confirm or refute an investment thesis. As an analyst with a Buy recommendation on a stock, my hope is that three out of every four quarters will largely confirm my Long thesis. That for those three quarters, the customer metrics and revenue and profit results come in at least in line with my and Street expectations. And on the miss quarter or the sloppy quarter or the disappointing quarter, my job is to assess whether the results mark a temporary or a permanent change to my Long thesis. Did the company miss the top-line estimates because a product launch slipped by a quarter (in the case of software or an app company like Adobe or Snap) or because there was a calendar change in holiday travel schedules (e.g., Easter timing) that hadn't been thoughtfully enough considered by Street analysts? This latter happened with online travel companies like Priceline and Expedia far too often over the almost 25 years I tracked them.

Over time, I came to realize that although volatility around EPS results was often high, it was almost always higher than the fundamental change in a company's financial outlook. The stock may have traded off 10% on an estimate's miss, but long-term estimates did not decline 10%. The stock move was almost always exaggerated versus the fundamentals move, which created DHQ opportunities.

The key point of this lesson is: Quarters are hard to predict, and the trades around quarters can be misleading. Stay focused on the long term and ignore short-term stock price fluctuations. Plenty of great financial books will advise you to avoid short-term trading and invest in stocks for the long run. That's my advice too. I'm just making the advice more graphic, more memorable, and, frankly, more actionable, because I *know* how strong the demand is for these short-term quarter trades. I've got the call logs to prove it.

THE EXPECTATIONS GAME . . . OR WHEN A BEAT IS NOT ENOUGH—SNAPCHAT

The March quarter 2019 earnings results of Snap (first known as Snapchat) provide a great example of how playing a quarter would have meant missing a great investment opportunity. On April 23, 2019, Snap reported its March quarter results, posting revenue of $320 million that was $14 million or 5% above Street expectations. Revenue growth also accelerated, from 36% year-over-year in the December quarter to 39% in the March quarter. So revenue trends were getting stronger. Snap's EBITDA loss was also lower/better than expected—$123 million actual versus $144 million expected. And the EBITDA loss was $100 million lower than it was in the March 2018 quarter, so profit/loss trends were also improving. Finally, the company's most important user metric (DAUs or daily average users) came in better than expected—190 million users actual versus 187 million expected by the Street. DAUs grew 4 million from the prior quarter, the biggest increase in a year. So not only were Snap's March quarter results better than expected all around, but they also showed fundamental improvement. What could go wrong?

The stock. Snap traded off 6% the next day and continued to decline the following two days, shedding 10% in all. That's a sizable correction. And if you had played it for the quarter on the belief that results would be better than expected and fundamentals were improving, you would have been completely right, but 10% down on your position. And out of frustration likely sold the stock and locked in your losses. Two months later you might have looked again to see how Snap's stock price was doing and been shocked to see that it had soared 38%. And at the end of the year, you would have seen that Snap's share price reached $15.89, up a monstrous 174% on the year. And you would have been speechless and frustrated, having allowed a botched quarter trade to cause you to miss a great investment opportunity. By the way, Snap ended 2020 at $50, for another 198% return.

Now, one reason you might have played Snap for the 2019 March quarter was because you saw one Street analyst upgrade the shares of Snap to Outperform on April 5, about three weeks before the quarter print. That analyst was me. But first let me tell you the story of Snapchat.

Snapchat was founded in 2011 by Evan Spiegel and Bobby Murphy. In 2016, the company renamed itself Snap. Also that year, Snap launched smart glasses known as Spectacles, which had very limited functionality but added to the innovative allure of the company. Along the way, Snap reportedly turned down acquisition offers from Facebook (in 2013 for $3 billion) and Google (in 2016 for $30 billion). In rebuffing Facebook's reported $3 billion bid, Spiegel said: "Trading that [his company's assets] for some short-term gain isn't very interesting." Which turned out to be prescient (Snap's market cap in mid-2021 was north of $100 billion), as well as reasonably good investment advice in general. By the end of 2016, Snap had 144 million DAUs, was generating $400 million in annual revenue, and was growing that revenue 590% year-over-year. Snap was on a roll!

On March 2, 2017, the company went public on the NYSE under the ticker SNAP, trading up 44% on its first day to a high of $26.05 and gaining a $33 billion market cap. That turned out to be the peak—for almost three years! SNAP traded down 81%

over the next two years, bottoming out at $4.99 in late December 2018, with a market cap of $8 billion. This was still well above the Facebook $3 billion bid—so good rebuff call there, Evan—but well below the Google $30 billion bid—hmmm, maybe that bid wasn't so uninteresting after all . . . SNAP's share price eventually recovered to its $26 first-day trading level in July 2020. By the end of 2020, SNAP had reached $50 and sported a $70 billion market cap. What a roller coaster!

I first met Snapchat management about a year prior to its IPO. The company had recently hired a new chief strategy officer named Imran Khan, whom I had known and competed against for many years as he was J.P. Morgan's lead Internet analyst. I met with him and the company's new CFO Drew Vollero at their Venice Beach headquarters. Yes, Venice Beach. In hindsight, red flag number one. Not that there's anything wrong with Venice Beach. It's a fun, exciting, stimulating place—great place to get a tattoo, and Saint Mark is the city's patron saint. But the way the headquarters were constructed was just . . . odd. The main entrance was secretive. No signs. Just an unmarked door on a Venice Beach side street guarded by security agents sporting secret service–style earphones. At that time, Snap owned several similar buildings all around Venice Beach—all unmarked, all secretive. You might guess that such an unusual work structure would lead to a dysfunctional corporate culture. Given the volatile fundamental performance and stock price performance of Snap over its first two to three years as a public company, you would be proved right.

I first met Evan Spiegel during the analyst pre-IPO organizational meeting held at another one of those unmarked buildings. He looked young because he was young. Twenty-six-years old at the time. One of the youngest self-made billionaires ever. He was also short and very thin, wearing skinny jeans and a plain black-gray shirt. Could have easily passed as a college or grad student or as a young starving artist. He snuck into that meeting for about 45 minutes of Q&A with the analysts. It was only a brief appearance, but he came across as highly intelligent and preternaturally calm, thoughtfully fielding a broad array of pointed questions from Wall Street's "best and brightest" about his product visions and the company's strategy. The balance of the day was spent listening to and questioning the rest of Snap's management team. The Spectacles smart glasses had just been launched and were available for sale to all the gathered Street analysts. I bought two pairs for my then teenage sons, who never even opened the boxes. And they were rabid Snap users. Red flag number two.

About three weeks after SNAP's IPO, I initiated research coverage with an Outperform rating and a $31 price target, with the stock at $22.74. And I proceeded to get the stock wrong for the next two years as I vacillated between Buy and Hold recommendations while the stock sank 81%, to $4.99 in December 2018. Perhaps that sinking should have been clear just from the company's first public earnings report, when its shares collapsed 21% in one day due to a miss versus Street revenue and EBITDA estimates.

The Long thesis in my initial SNAP Outperform recommendation revolved around the company's industry-leading growth rate, its unique and strong appeal to millennials (survey work showed Snap to be very popular with younger users), its relatively good product innovation track record (the fact that Facebook sought to aggressively copy Snap's feature innovations spoke volumes about how good product development was at Snap), and its potentially large market opportunity (a close to $1 trillion global advertising market). That thesis eventually turned out to be right, but it was about two years premature.

In the meantime, the 81% two-year correction in SNAP shares post its IPO beautifully highlighted many of the key investment lessons I had come to learn (though I sometimes forgot):

- **First, the extreme importance of a good and stable management team.** Over that period SNAP lost not one but two CFOs and also saw its VP of marketing and chief strategy officer step down. That volatility in management, I believe, was a key factor behind the volatility in the company's financial results over the next two years.

- **Second, the key importance of product innovation.** While Snap successfully rolled out many new product features during this period, including Snap Maps, the company screwed up its biggest product innovation—the redesign of its app for the Android platform. That screwed-up redesign, which went through several user-irritating iterations before coming out right and helped cause a decline in Snap DAUs in mid-2018, dogged the company's fundamentals.
- **Third, the immense value of large TAMs (total addressable markets).** The key reason Snap had to redesign its app for the Android platform was because it simply didn't work as well on Android smartphones as it did on Apple iPhones. The user experience was slower and kludgier—on some Android devices the phone's camera didn't integrate seamlessly with the Snap app. And the Snap Android app didn't work as well as the Snap iPhone app because the company didn't devote nearly as many resources to it as it did to the iPhone platform. That was a problem when the company tried to expand to international markets, because outside the United States, the Android platform is much more popular than the Apple platform. It's an Android world, not an Apple world. (The Android operating system powers over 70% of global smartphones.) So until Snap got its app to work well on Android devices, its addressable market opportunity was geographically limited.
- **Fourth, stock prices really do follow fundamentals.** At the risk of oversimplification, SNAP shares cratered from $26.05 in March 2017 to $4.99 in December 2018 as revenue growth consistently decelerated from 286% year-over-year

> in the March quarter of 2017 to 36% in the December quarter of 2018, and the forward price-to-sales (P/S) multiple declined from over 20x to under 5x. The lower the growth, the lower the multiple. And when Snap's revenue growth began to reaccelerate in the March quarter of 2019, its P/S multiple expanded and its stock rose. (See Figure 3.1.)

So that's the story of Snap, at least from a Wall Street perspective and at least until its turn into a successful investment vehicle (aka—a rising stock). I upgraded SNAP to Outperform on April 5, 2019, based on four factors: early evidence that Android platform improvements were finally—finally!—gaining traction, the company's longstanding high level of product innovation, recent positive takeaways from a Snap developer/partner conference, and my belief that Snap may have reached a fundamentals inflection point.

Over the next two years, fundamentals did improve—revenue growth accelerated, gross margins expanded, and free cash flow losses materially declined. The SNAP Long thesis was proved

FIGURE 3.1 Learning How to SNAP Out of It

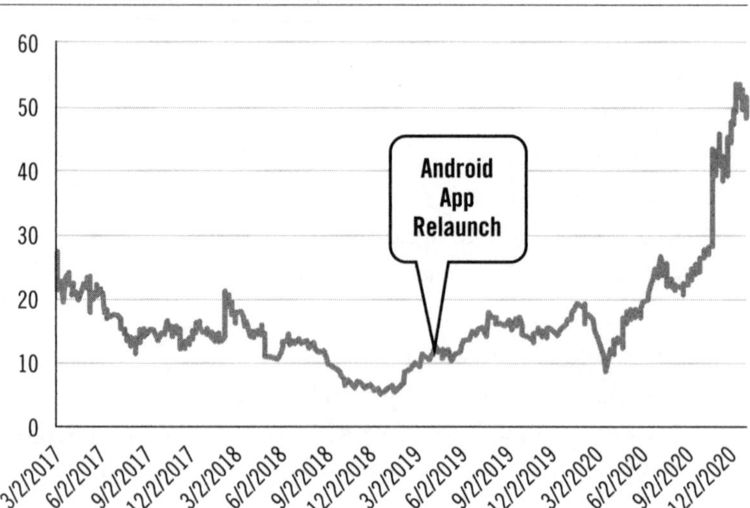

correct. And the stock soared—up 174% in 2019 and another 198% in 2020. But it didn't trade up every quarter. On that March 2019 quarter—despite both a fundamentals improvement and a Street estimates beat—it traded off 10%. It also traded off on both the September and December 2019 quarter EPS results. But the investment worked and worked well. The quarter trades were the noise. And if you had been able to tune out that noise, you would have heard great fundamental music and benefited from one of the tech sector's best performing stocks over the two-year period.

And finally, getting to the key question: Why exactly did SNAP trade off 10% on that March 2019 quarter? There are two answers. First, it was an expectations correction. Going into that print, SNAP shares had skyrocketed 107% since the beginning of the year. Whisper expectations were high. In the earnings game that is often played on the Street, the company was expected to beat Street estimates. By how much is hard to know. Given that revenue came in 5% above the Street, but the stock traded off 10%, clearly the stock "needed" more than 5% upside. It is hard to know exactly where the "expectations bar" has been set. For retail investors, it's close to impossible. One simple rule of thumb is if a stock is trading up aggressively going into earnings—say, up 107% since the beginning of the year—when the S&P 500 is up only 17% during that same time—then you can be pretty certain that expectations are high for those EPS results, and a "beat" may not be enough to get a stock to trade higher.

The second of the two answers might be the more useful one. Near-term stock price movements—even when tied to clearly fundamental events like quarterly earnings releases—can be meaningless. Short-term price action can often just be a distraction. It's almost impossible to forecast the direction of a particular stock over a couple of days. And fixating on that near-term stock movement may well cause you to miss the long-term great investment opportunity. *That's* the best lesson from the March 2019 SNAP quarter.

DO YOU WANT TO TRADE, OR DO YOU WANT TO INVEST?—CHEWY

The July 2020 quarter earnings results of Chewy (ticker: CHWY) also provide a great example of how playing a quarter would have meant missing a great investment opportunity. On September 10, Chewy reported its July quarter results, posting revenue of $1.7 billion that was $60 million or 4% above Street expectations. Revenue growth also accelerated, from 46% year-over-year in the April quarter to 47% in the July quarter. So revenue trends were getting stronger. I really should amplify this point. Revenue trends were robust—very few companies can grow 46% year-over-year, especially on a revenue base of $1.6 billion. For the July quarter, gross margin also reached a record high, as did EBITDA, which came in nicely better than Street estimates. And Chewy added a record-high 1.6 million customers to reach 16.6 million customers. The July quarter results were better than expected and fundamentally and intrinsically stronger—faster revenue growth, higher gross margins, more EBITDA, many more customers. What could go wrong?

You know the answer. The stock. Just like the previous Snap example. The next day, CHWY shares traded down 10%, from $59.69 to $53.81, and then stayed in a tight range between $53 and $56 for the rest of the month. If you had bought Chewy for the quarter trade, you would have been frustrated. Maybe you waited a few weeks for the market to come to its senses and realize that fundamentals were improving at Chewy. But nothing happened. So you sold your Chewy shares. You pointedly ignored tracking CHWY for the next few months, but then glanced at it briefly over the winter holidays and were stunned by the fact that CHWY ended the year at $89.89, 50% above where it traded on September 10. The last time you felt *this* frustrated was when you tried to potty-train your goldendoodle.

What happened? Well, first let me tell you the story of Chewy. No, first let me tell you the story of Pets.com.

Pets.com was a true dog. There weren't enough pooper scoopers to pick up the mess that company and that stock (IPET) left behind. The bankers, analysts, and investors who were involved in that public offering should have been sent to the doghouse . . . permanently. OK, enough of the bad jokes.

Pets.com IPO'd in February 2000 at $11 and traded up almost 30% to $14. (IPO trades can be so deceiving.) Pets.com went public with a lifetime revenue of $6 million—$6 million! That's the entire amount of revenue it had generated up through its IPO. And that's because it had only been in operation for 12 months. It raised $83 million in its IPO, reaching a market cap of $300 million. And that's all she wrote. Despite a memorable Super Bowl commercial (a $1.2 million ad that brought national fame to the Sock Puppet—one of which I keep in my office as a useful warning), Pets.com went belly-up nine months later, with its stock at $0.19 the day of the bankruptcy announcement.

Pets.com was one of the most egregious examples of the excesses and the folly of the dot-com bubble. Kozmo was another. Kozmo offered free one-hour delivery of "videos, games, DVDs, music, mags, books, food, basics, and more." Kozmo did better than Pets.com. It lasted three years before going bust. With the tremendous visibility of hindsight, Pets.com and Kozmo had a lasting impact on tech investing because: (1) they helped create an almost permanent Wall of Worry that new tech companies are still climbing today, and (2) they paved the way for Chewy ($40 billion market cap as of mid-2021) and DoorDash ($60 billion market cap as of mid-2021). I'm serious. Though you'll have to bear with me for a few paragraphs.

So here comes Chewy with its IPO at $22 in June 2019. On the first day of trading, Chewy jumped 59% to $35. It then proceeded to trade off 35% before reaching $23 in late November. It didn't recover to that $35 level until March of 2020. And yes, comparisons with Pets.com were abundant. An article on CNBC's website the day of the Chewy IPO couldn't help but point out that Chewy was joining a long list of unprofitable companies (including Uber, Pinterest, and Survey Monkey) that were going public and that the percentage of companies going public that were unprofitable was "topping numbers seen even in the Dot-Com Bubble."

But Chewy was and is different from Pets.com. Not in its market opportunity or in its basic customer value proposition. But in its scale (definitely) and in its management team (almost definitely). Whereas Pets.com went public with $6 million in trailing 12-month revenue, Chewy went public with $3.5 billion in trailing revenue—which would be 583 times bigger than Pets.com. Also, Chewy was and is a fundamentally sound business—not in terms of net income (it is still unprofitable)—but in terms of revenue and profit potential, which is what tech investors should focus on.

Briefly, Chewy was founded in 2011 by Ryan Cohen and Michael Day. The company grew aggressively over the years, hiring employees and executives from Amazon (smart move), PetSmart, and Whole Foods, and reached $2 billion in revenue and approximately 50 percent of US online pet food sales by 2017. Along the way, it received funding from several savvy private investors, including Mark Vadon of Blue Nile and Zulily fame. Chewy considered going public in 2017 but then decided to sell itself to PetSmart for $3.4 billion, at the time the largest-ever acquisition of an e-commerce company. Two years later, the company went public.

I first met Chewy management at the company's headquarters in Dania Beach, Florida, in 2017. This is perhaps not where you would expect a tech company to be located, although Magic Leap, the augmented reality company, was located very close by. I met with Chewy's then CFO (a former Amazon finance specialist who would soon depart) and his colleague Mario Marte (who would later become CFO). A quick one-hour meeting gave me a great overview of the company, its market opportunity, and how it was competing with Amazon. I came back to my offices and relayed to my colleagues my belief that Chewy would be a good IPO candidate. A few months later, Chewy sold itself to PetSmart. Oh well.

Two years later, however, I was back in Florida for a dinner with senior management and a day of meetings with the full management team. The IPO was on! In Lesson 8, one of the 10 timeless stock-picking lessons, I'll explore the key importance of management, and that dinner and those meetings gave me great insight into management, especially CEO Sumit Singh, who had joined the company in 2017. Sumit struck me as exceptionally smart, hardworking, and highly detailed. The last characteristic was perhaps the most striking. In a series of calls and meetings over the following two-year period, I became most impressed with Sumit's unusually detailed knowledge of every part of Chewy's business—marketing, logistics, product plans, and so on. Often, I meet CEOs who are impressive on vision but not on operations. Sometimes it's the opposite. There's no one formula for a perfect CEO. It depends on the needs of the company and the industry.

Getting back to Chewy's stock, it finally recovered to its IPO price in March 2020. And then . . . the Covid-19 crisis occurred. Which actually gave Chewy a major boost and helped cause its share price to rise 103% up into its July quarter earnings release on September 10. Most companies were negatively impacted by the spread of Covid-19 virus, especially companies in the restaurant, travel, physical retail, and live events sectors. Chewy was not. Like children, pets need to be fed and cared for, pandemic or not. And physical retail stores were shuttered for weeks and months. That was Chewy's opportunity. Not only that, but with people forced to shelter in place, the desire for in-home companionship rose, and pet adoption in the United States increased materially. Per a report in *USA Today*, the community adoption rate for pets jumped from 64% in 2019 to 73% in 2020, and shelter euthanasia declined 43%, due to exceptionally strong demand for foster pets.

This all led to Chewy having record customer adds in its April and July quarters (over 1.5 million new customers in each quarter). And to accelerating revenue growth. And record gross and EBITDA margins. And yet the stock traded off 10% on the July quarter print. (See Figure 3.2.) Why? As with Snap's March 2019 quarter, it was due to expectations. When a stock rises 103% on the year, you just know that expectations are high. And the chances of an expectations miss and an expectations correction are high. Be prepared for that. But also be prepared for a stock to continue outperforming as the company's fundamentals continue to strengthen. This really is the point of the next lesson—stocks follow fundamentals over the medium-to-long term. The point of this lesson is that near term they often don't, but don't let that distract you from the stock price potential of improving fundamentals. Learning somewhat from my SNAP mistakes, I initiated coverage of CHWY shortly after its IPO with a Hold rating. I upgraded what I believed to be a good fundamental story several months later in February 2020. And stuck with it while it rose that 103%, despite the trading volatility around its earnings.

FIGURE 3.2 **CHWY: Who Let the Dogs Out?**

WHEN THE EARNINGS STORY ISN'T THE EARNINGS STORY—UBER

Uber was a failed IPO. At least, that has been the view of most market participants since its May 2019 IPO. Much of the criticism around Uber (as a publicly traded stock) has revolved around its valuation, or its "fantasy valuation," as several commentators over the past year have referred to it. In 2018, the year prior to its IPO, Uber's free cash flow was negative $2 billion. And that free cash flow loss more than doubled to $4.9 billion in 2019. The net income loss tallied more than $8 billion in 2019 . . . for a $75 billion market cap IPO! Fantasy valuation indeed! But this isn't the lesson for a discussion about valuation, and why traditional valuation metrics caused you to miss UBER's 65% stock rise in 2020 (despite Covid-19), and why they could well cause you to miss ongoing upside to UBER shares. That's Lesson 9.

For now, what is key is that Uber—like Snap, Chewy, and many other tech companies—did sell off aggressively after its IPO "pop." Uber's IPO was priced at $45 per share and traded off 7% on its IPO day to under $42. Under increasing concerns about its lack of profitability, Uber's stock continued to trade off until it reached $26.94 on November 6, 40% below its IPO price. It traded off 15% after its June quarter earnings were released in early August, and it traded off another 13% after its September quarter earnings release on November 4. (See Figure 3.3.)

The key thing about that November 4 EPS release is that it contained fundamentally good news for UBER investors. On the number they most cared about: EBITDA. September quarter EBITDA loss came in at $585 million, still a dramatically high number, but a result that was 30% better than Street estimates. You rarely see that much of a delta between actual results and Street estimates. Further, Uber management lowered its 2019 EBITDA loss guidance by $250 million, meaning its expected EBITDA loss would be $250 million

FIGURE 3.3 UBER: A Rocky Ride

better/lower than previously expected. And for the first time ever, it officially guided to achieving EBITDA profitability in 2021. This was great news for a company and a stock that had been dogged by profitability concerns.

As a quick side note, famed investor Charlie Munger (vice chairman of Warren Buffett's Berkshire Hathaway conglomerate) has been widely quoted as referring to EBITDA as "bull*@!t earnings," and he is right. EBITDA isn't earnings. It's earnings before interest, taxes, depreciation, amortization, and other below-the-operating-income-line items. Just like operating income isn't earnings. It's earnings before interest, taxes, and other below-the-operating-income-line items. Just like gross profit isn't earnings. It's earnings before operating expenses, interest, taxes, depreciation, amortization, and other below-the-operating-income-line items. The point is that all these profitability measures are linked to earnings. Almost invariably—though not always—an improvement in one of these measures is a positive indicator for earnings—either currently or in the future. So yes, Uber's September quarter 2019 EBITDA results were a distinct fundamental positive.

Given that Uber shares traded off 13% over the next two days, clearly something was amiss. Something was, but it wasn't fundamentals. Introducing the lockup expiration.

November 6, two days after the September quarter earnings release, was the first day that Uber insiders, including early investors and employees, were allowed to sell their UBER stock. This was exactly 180 days after the IPO date and was consistent with how other IPOs were handled. Approximately 750 million UBER shares were no longer restricted for sale on November 6. The purpose of these lockup expirations has long been to provide greater stability for IPOs by preventing company insiders (many of whom have held their shares for years) from dumping their shares on new investors in the weeks and months immediately post an IPO, thus pressuring down the now public share price. It's basic supply-and-demand theory. Restrict supply, and prices will hold or rise. Which also means that when that supply is eventually released, as with a lockup expiration, prices will hold or fall. It happens almost every time: trading pressure around lockup expirations.

And that's exactly what happened to UBER shares on November 4, 5, and 6—and for the next week or so—*despite* the fundamentally positive profitability news from the September quarter. Eventually, however, UBER shares began to rally. And rally mightily—up 51% until late February—due to that positive profitability news. Which was reinforced by the company's December quarter EPS release. So fundamentals do drive stocks. But near term, fundamentals and stocks can be highly dislocated even when it comes to fundamentally key events like earnings—sometimes because of expectations, and sometimes because of events like lockup expirations that have nothing to do with fundamentals.

Don't play quarters. Successfully trading around quarters requires both an accurate read of fundamentals and a correct assessment of near-term expectations, a tricky task for individual (and most professional) investors to pull off. Trades around quarters can also be misleading and can cause investors to miss long-term fundamental and stock trends. Between 2015 and 2018, AMZN rocketed up 386%, with 4 of the 16 quarters generating a material 10%+ one-day pop and 4 quarters generating a material 5%+ one-day slide. Staying invested in a strong fundamentals name and ignoring short-term stock fluctuations can be highly profitable.

Quarter trades are strongly determined by expectations. Fundamentals may be clearly improving (revenue growth acceleration and operating margin expansion), but stocks can still trade down on these results if "whisper" expectations aren't met. This is what happened to Snap with the March 2019 quarter and Chewy with the April 2020 quarter. There may also be unusual events—like IPO lockup expirations—that cause near-term stock movements that are disjointed versus fundamental trends. This is what happened with Uber in November 2019. Don't let this dissuade you from investing, but do let it dissuade you from short-term trading. From overreacting to near-term stock fluctuations. *Don't play quarters.*

Revenue Matters More Than Anything

Over the long term, fundamentals move stocks, and for high-growth tech stocks, the fundamentals that matter most are revenue, revenue, and revenue. Companies that consistently generate 20%+ top-line growth can potentially provide good stock returns, almost regardless of their near-term profitability. The 20% revenue growth "rule": Only about 2% of the S&P 500 have been able to consistently generate 20%+ top-line growth for five years, but these stocks have usually materially outperformed the market. So look for consistent 20%+ revenue growth as one fundamental tell of a high-quality, high-growth tech stock.

A long-tenured Street tech analyst once confided in me: "Lucky for us, markets are inefficient. Or else we'd be out of a job." I've thought about this comment and its implications many times over the years. And I've reached the conclusion that that analyst was wrong. And for the record, that analyst is no longer working on the Street—though he has been CFO of at least four public Internet companies.

The market that I have tracked for roughly a quarter of a century has been extremely efficient at incorporating and rapidly reacting to every bit of new information and data that has been presented to it. That's true efficiency. The inefficiency lies in the fact that the market always seems to give extra weight to the most recent datapoint, regardless of how reliable the particular source has been in the past. (I think the pseudoscientific term for this is "recency bias.") And the market always seems to equal-weight all the datapoints coming in at the same time, even when some are patently more robust, more reliable than others—at least to my eyes.

The best example I can think of is Netflix and the third-party services that over the years claimed the ability to accurately forecast for paying institutional investor clients how many new subscribers the company would report in any one quarter. Over time, it increasingly felt to me that the third-party services were just as likely to get the forecast wrong as they were to get it right. I remember one firm in particular that had a name with the word "Park" in it. And when "Park" would provide its weekly update on whether Netflix's quarter sub count was coming in hot or cold, Netflix shares would respond. Netflix shares down 2% today? "Park" must be forecasting a subs miss. Netflix shares up 3% today? "Park" must be calling for a subs beat! But "Park" was never able to consistently call the quarters. Its estimates at times turned out to be wildly and widely off. I started calling the firm "South Park." And "Park" eventually stopped making subs forecasts. I believe its clients demanded refunds.

The lesson for now is that fundamentals really do drive stocks. And as an investor, you should focus on fundamentals. And particularly, revenue and key customer metrics. Hence the title of this lesson.

WHY REVENUE MATTERS MORE THAN ANYTHING

In *One Up on Wall Street*, Peter Lynch advised investors to focus on three key financial metrics: earnings, earnings, and earnings. My advice for tech investors is to focus on three different financial metrics: revenue, revenue, and revenue.

Now before The Wharton Business School at the University of Pennsylvania calls to revoke my MBA, I want to acknowledge that earnings matter. As does free cash flow. I don't know of any sophisticated market investor who runs DR (discounted revenue) models. They all run DCF (discounted cash flow) models based on years of projections of revenue and cash flows discounted back to the present to determine reasonable current value.

But you can't generate earnings or cash flow if you don't first generate revenue. Yes, there are many companies that generate revenue and don't generate earnings or cash flow. They are called unprofitable companies. And if they never generate earnings or cash flow, they won't stay in business. Or if they never demonstrate the potential to generate earnings or cash flow, investors won't buy their stock. But I don't know of a single tech company that ever generated earnings or cash flow without first generating revenue.

So revenue is a leading indicator, if you will, of earnings and cash flow. This is one reason why tech investors should focus primarily on revenue, along with leading customer metrics, which will vary from company to company.

The second reason is that public market investors tend to reward—pay a higher multiple for—companies that generate earnings through revenue growth as opposed to other ways. Simplistically, there are three ways companies can generate earnings: grow revenue, reduce operating costs, or engage in "financial engineering." And by "financial engineering," I mean things like selling loss-generating assets, reducing tax rates through a shuffling of profits toward lower-tax locations, generating one-time gains by selling investment stakes, sharing buybacks, better positioning the cash and equivalents on a company's balance sheet to generate higher investment income, and the like.

Maybe this is the realization of the simple maxim "The greater the effort, the greater the return." "Financial engineering" is easy. There are armies of consultants who can help a company better execute on tax and asset strategies. They advertise on TV. And there are somewhat easy ways to reduce costs—laying off employees (not really easy), cutting back on marketing campaigns, reducing funding for new R&D projects, and so on. But growing revenue is hard. In tech, it involves successfully innovating new features and new products, expanding into new geographic markets, growing a customer base, raising prices (risky), and so on. That's why companies that can do the hardest thing—grow revenue—tend to be more rewarded by investors (i.e., get a higher multiple, whether it be on revenue, earnings, or free cash flow).

Almost every institutional investor will be familiar with something like Figure 4.1, which compares valuation multiples (in this

FIGURE 4.1 Pro Tip: The Link Between Revenue Growth and Valuation

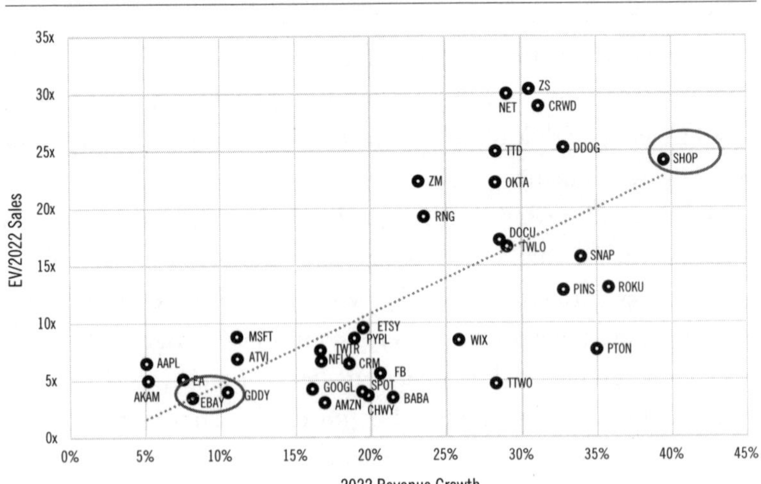

case enterprise value to sales, which is similar to price to sales or market cap to sales, only adjusted for the cash and debt on the company's balance sheet) with the expected revenue growth of the company. On this chart are the stock tickers for about 30 of the leading technology stocks in early 2021. The relationship isn't perfect, but generally the higher the revenue growth, the higher the multiple. So EBAY (eBay) is expected to grow its revenue approximately 7% in 2022 and trades at an EV/sales multiple of 4x. Whereas SHOP (Shopify, the Canadian Internet services company) is expected to grow its revenue around 40% in 2022 and trades at an EV/sales multiple of about 25x. The basic point comes through in this figure: The higher the growth, the higher the multiple, all other things held reasonably equal.

Tech investing requires a different mindset. Traditional financial textbooks will focus their readers' attention on earnings, maximizing of profits, share buybacks, and dividends. Tech investors need to think differently because tech investors are focused on growth. So when companies begin to aggressively ramp up profitability levels, the skeptical tech investor should ask: "Don't you have growth initiatives to invest behind?" And when companies begin to pay a dividend, the critical tech investor should ask: "That's it? You've run out of ideas to grow your business, so you're retiring and returning cash to shareholders?" By the way, there's nothing wrong with either of these moves, and at the appropriate time, they are absolutely the right move. But when it's an appropriate time for a company to do take these steps, well, that's the exact time a tech investor may not want to be around.

One of the earnings growth strategies that I didn't mention above, but is used quite often, is M&A or acquisitions. I would still put this in the "financial engineering" camp, though I realize that is clearly cheapening the term. As a rule, I would argue that organic revenue growth—driven by increased unit sales, new product offerings, geographic market expansion, or price increases—is more impressive and should be worth more to tech investors than acquired growth. But I have seen several examples of acquisitions that created enormous financial value and helped drive stock prices higher over the medium-to-long term. Probably the best acquisitions I tracked over the last 25 years include eBay for PayPal in 2002, Priceline for Bookings.nl in 2005, Google for YouTube in 2006, and Facebook for Instagram in 2012. I could also mention Yahoo! for Overture in 2003, which gave Yahoo!, then the leading digital media company, a substantial lead in the emerging search industry, a lead it subsequently squandered to Google. And I could list Yahoo! for Alibaba in 2005, which wasn't an acquisition per se but rather an investment. Yahoo! bought 30% of Alibaba for $1 billion. That 30% stake would have been worth as much at $250 billion in late 2020. A theoretical 250x return!

I'm only highlighting here the good acquisitions. Some bad ones get called out later in the book. But the more I reflect on the good acquisitions, the more I am struck by how much of the shareholder value created in the tech sector has been driven by organic revenue growth. As of February 2021, Amazon has amassed a $1.6 trillion market cap (one of the largest in the world), and although it has acquired many companies along the way, none have contributed a material amount (10%+) to the company's market cap. The jury is still out (way out) on its biggest acquisition, the 2017 $14 billion acquisition of Whole Foods. YouTube is a big deal for Google, but it's hard to ascribe more than a quarter of Google's current market cap to that asset. And YouTube's success has come largely because Google invested an enormous amount of capital and talent and resources into YouTube. I'm truly not sure YouTube could have survived on its own, especially given the legal challenges it was being swamped by at the time of its acquisition by Google.

The third and most important reason why tech investors should primarily focus on revenue is because that's what the market does—not just near term but long term, too. I've got three clear examples to prove the point. The first is the sad story of two of the leading pioneers of the Internet era, each of which maintained impressive profitability levels (arguably overearning) only to miss out on some of the sector's biggest growth trends, eventually leaving billions of market cap on the table. We're talking Yahoo! and eBay. The second is the spectacular and then rather ordinary story—in terms of revenue and share price—of Priceline.com, the global giant of online travel. And third is the company that created over $150 billion in market cap and upended the entire entertainment industry purely through revenue and subscriber growth, all the while going almost a decade generating higher and higher cash flow losses. Yup, Netflix.

Here's a cheat sheet summary of those three stories, covered in depth below. eBay and Yahoo! essentially failed as long-term stocks, because despite substantial and consistent profitability over prolonged periods of time, neither was able to maintain consistent, premium top-line growth. The contrast is stark with the example of Priceline, which performed phenomenally well as a long-term stock, not because it had substantial and consistent profitability (though it had this), but because it was able to sustain premium top-line growth (in this case, bookings) for over a decade. And the contrast is starkest with Netflix, which performed phenomenally well as a long-term stock, not because it had substantial and consistent profitability (it went almost an entire decade without generating free cash flow), but solely because it was able to sustain premium revenue and subscriber growth for over a decade. Revenue matters more than anything else for tech stocks.

EBAY AND YAHOO!

It's distinctly possible that some younger readers of this book will have never used either eBay or Yahoo! Believe me, young'uns, people your age 20 years ago used Yahoo! and eBay aggressively—and considered those companies cool, too!

Between 1998 and 2003, four major Internet companies dominated the landscape—Amazon, AOL, eBay, and Yahoo! And I'm pretty sure that an informal poll of investors back then would not have selected Amazon as the biggest long-term winner. If investors had been told one of these four companies would be sporting a trillion-dollar market cap 20 years later, I am certain that investors would *not* have selected Amazon as that company. The skepticism around Amazon, especially after 2000, was *so* great.

Here's the jaw-dropping comparison: At the end of December 1999, AOL boasted a market cap of $193 billion, about 2x that of Yahoo! ($97 billion), 6x that of Amazon ($34 billion), and 24x that of eBay ($8 billion).

Twenty years later, Amazon emerged as the 800-pound gorilla of the group. Which would make eBay a 20-pound gorilla (its current market cap is 1/40 that of Amazon). And AOL and Yahoo! each 2-pound gorillas, as each was acquired by Verizon for approximately $4.5 billion (1/357 that of Amazon) in 2015 and 2017.

Back during the dot-com boom, there was a major tech conference sponsored annually by a now defunct magazine called *The Industry Standard*. The 1999 conference, held at the swanky Ritz-Carlton resort near Laguna Beach, featured a panel with senior execs from each of the leading Internet companies at the time. And I vividly recall a senior Yahoo! exec on that panel taunting the other panelists that one of their companies would likely no longer exist 20 years down the road. It's hard to make predictions. Especially about the future.

For this lesson, I want to focus on the stocks that didn't succeed as well, which is putting it mildly. And I want to get at the point that revenue matters more than anything else for tech stocks. eBay and Yahoo! failed as long-term stocks because despite substantial and consistent profitability over prolonged periods of time, neither was able to maintain consistent premium top-line growth.

eBay

eBay went public on September 24, 1998, at $18 and shot up 168% on its first day to reach over $47 with a $2 billion market cap. One of the reasons eBay shares shot up so dramatically on its first day of trading was that a highly influential analyst placed a Buy recommendation on those shares that very same morning. It was my boss, Mary Meeker, then the Internet analyst at Morgan Stanley. At the time, this was a highly unusual event. Regulations barred analysts at the syndicate banks from initiating research coverage for 40 days post the IPO. Since Morgan Stanley wasn't part of the syndicate, these regulations didn't apply to Mary. But the idea that an analyst not involved in the syndicate would initiate coverage the same day as the IPO—and initiate with a Buy—was unheard of. The event was so surprising that a friend who worked on the Capital Markets desk at Goldman Sachs, which was the lead underwriter for the eBay IPO, called me at home early that morning to confirm what my boss had done. He woke me up, because I had pulled close to an all-nighter the night before helping publish that initiation report.

Over the next 15 years, there were five splits of eBay shares, so the split-adjusted IPO price of eBay was $0.32. Over the next six years, in the face of the massive NASDAQ sell-off and the dot-com bust, eBay soared 5,100% (a 51-bagger) to reach $24.48 and a market cap of $32 billion by the end of 2004 (Figure 4.2). eBay was one of only a handful of tech companies to see its stock materially outperform during that time period.

And that amazing stock outperformance was driven by amazing fundamentals (Table 4.1). Over the five-year period 2000–2004, eBay averaged over 70% revenue growth, in part thanks to the strategically savvy acquisition of PayPal in 2002. Its most important customer metric—gross merchandise value (GMV), the total value of all goods and services bought and sold on the platform—also averaged close to 70% over the five years. Growth did decelerate,

FIGURE 4.2 The EBAY Rocketship (1998–2004)

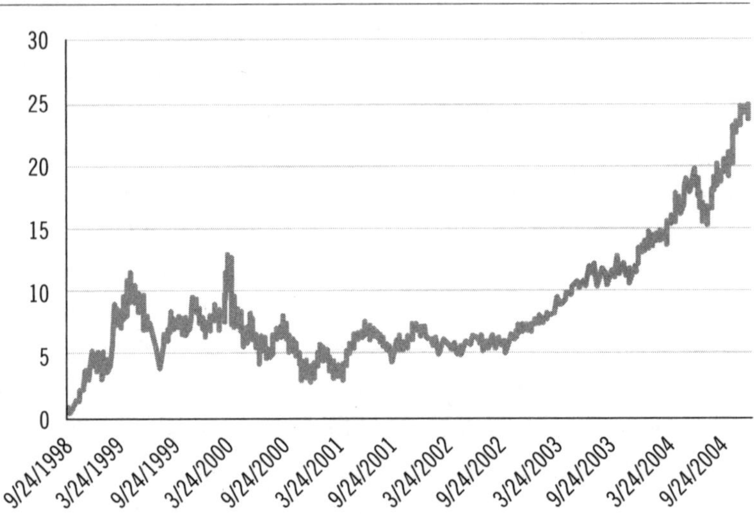

TABLE 4.1 The Fundamentals Behind the eBay Rocketship

($MM)	2000	2001	2002	2003	2004
GMV	**5,414**	**9,318**	**14,868**	**23,779**	**34,168**
Y/Y Growth	93%	72%	60%	60%	44%
Revenue	**431**	**749**	**1,214**	**2,165**	**3,271**
Y/Y Growth (Organic)	88%	74%	62%	78%	51%
EBITDA	**83**	**229**	**436**	**796**	**1,330**
Margin	19%	31%	36%	37%	41%

but only modestly. And profitability levels were high, with the company printing 41% EBITDA margins in 2004.

Then things began to change. In late 2005, eBay announced the surprise acquisition of Skype, an Internet communications company, for approximately $3 billion. Synergies at the time of the deal were unclear, and they became less clear over time, with eBay forced to take a $1.4 billion write-down of the Skype asset only two years later. Only later did the interpretation start to gain credence that

Skype may have been something of a Hail Mary acquisition by a company increasingly concerned by a potential material deceleration in its core business. And that's exactly what happened.

GMV was the key customer metric for eBay. eBay's Marketplace or commission revenue—and a large part of its PayPal revenue—was directly tied to GMV. If GMV growth accelerated, revenue growth accelerated. But if GMV growth decelerated, revenue growth decelerated. And that's what happened. Every year prior to 2006, eBay's GMV growth was 30% or greater. But starting in 2006, eBay's GMV growth descended to 18%, then 13% in 2007 and 1% in 2008, before declining 4% in 2009, during the Great Financial Crisis. It recovered somewhat after the GFC and reached 11% growth in 2011, but that was only one of three double-digit growth rate years (10% in 2012, 11% in 2013) eBay experienced until the Covid-19 crisis in 2020. And with that deceleration in growth came the end of the amazing stock run that eBay had generated through 2004, despite eBay maintaining a consistent high level of profitability over the next decade. Revenue—and customer metrics—matters more than anything else for tech stocks. (See Table 4.2.)

Figure 4.3 shows what happened to eBay's share price over this decade: nothing. Literally, nothing. EBAY closed the first trading day of 2005 at $24.01, and it closed the first trading day of 2015 at $23.66. Ten years. Nothing. Meanwhile, over that same time frame, the S&P 500 rose 71%, and AMZN rose 593%. The whys here are extremely important, and I'll get to those. But the key stock-picking so-what here is that the market was willing to keep bidding up the premium revenue grower (Amazon's revenue growth exceeded 20% every year between 2005 and 2015) and refused to bid up the non-premium grower (eBay). For 10 years. Despite its high profitability. Revenue—and customer metrics—matters more than anything else for tech stocks.

TABLE 4.2 How the eBay Rocketship Ran Out of Fuel

Year	GMV ($MM)	Y/Y Growth	Revenue ($MM)	Y/Y Growth (Organic)	EBITDA ($MM)	Margin
2004	34,168	44%	3,271	51%	1,330	41%
2005	44,299	30%	4,552	39%	1,833	40%
2006	52,473	18%	5,970	31%	2,290	38%
2007	59,353	13%	7,672	29%	2,914	38%
2008	59,650	1%	8,541	11%	3,200	37%
2009	57,207	–4%	8,727	2%	3,049	35%
2010	61,819	8%	9,156	5%	3,242	35%
2011	68,634	11%	11,652	27%	3,846	33%
2012	75,376	10%	14,071	21%	4,599	33%
2013	83,330	11%	16,047	14%	5,807	36%
2014	82,954	0%	8,790	–6%	3,647	41%
2015	81,718	–1%	8,592	–2%	3,568	42%

FIGURE 4.3 EBAY: From $25 to $25 in 10 Years

Yahoo!

Now, let's look at Yahoo! Yahoo! was the OIG—original Internet gangster! Its cofounders were savvy enough to put an ! at the end of the company name! How can a company with an ! as its last character not succeed!?

Yahoo! was the dominant Internet company for most of the 1990s dot-com boom. It was founded by Jerry Yang and David Filo in 1994 and went public about two years later, skyrocketing 150% on its first day of trading. (BTW, two years is an extraordinarily short time to go from founding to IPO.) Yahoo! quickly launched into international markets, beginning with the United Kingdom in late 2016, and then proceeded to acquire a series of companies, including GeoCities and Broadcast.com, for a combined $11 billion, all in stock. No cash—in hindsight, a bit of a tell that YHOO's management and board realized their share price might be a tad overinflated. In December 1999, Yahoo! was added to the S&P 500, which helped cause YHOO shares to more than double that December quarter, reaching a market cap of close to $100 billion and a P/E ratio of over 1,000x. (The S&P 500 "mega pop" was very similar to the one Tesla experienced when it was added in December 2020. Over the years, S&P 500 inclusion has consistently been one of the biggest trading catalysts the tech stocks I have tracked have experienced.) In early January 2000, YHOO shares peaked at $475, meaning the stock had soared 3,550% since its IPO.

In April 2000, shortly after the March 2000 NASDAQ peak, the movie *Frequency*, starring Dennis Quaid and Jim Caviezel, was released. It was a popular, action-packed movie involving a serial killer and a time warp between 1969 and 1999. At one point during the movie, the main 1999 character attempts to give his 1969 childhood friend a financial tip, telling him to pay attention to "Yahoo!" The 1969 child apparently has good recall, because in the final 1999 scene he is shown driving a very expensive car with "1 YAHOO" on the license plate. Yahoo! became part of the popular zeitgeist in the way that few companies ever do. That's how much of an OIG Yahoo! was.

But that was it for Yahoo! Sixteen years later, Verizon bought Yahoo! for $4.8 billion in cash, one-twentieth the value that the public markets briefly ascribed to it in early 2000. $95 billion in market value gone up in smoke (Figure 4.4). Was this just a case of public markets gone wild? My emphatic answer is *no*! For over those 16 years, while Yahoo! shed $95 billion in market cap, Google added $500 billion, and Facebook added $350 billion. In other words, the public markets were willing over those 16 years to bestow $800 billion–$900 billion in market value to two better Yahoo!s—two companies that through outstanding product development and excellent execution were able to become the leading Internet advertising platforms of 2016, just as Yahoo! had been the leading Internet ad platform of 2000.

The above recount of Yahoo! does no justice at all to the history of that company. But I did warn up front that this book is not a history text. Instead, I am looking to draw stock-picking lessons from some of the biggest tech stories of the last 25 years. One thing is clear about YHOO: It never had profitability problems. Every single year between 2000 and 2015, Yahoo! generated robust EBITDA margins—an intrinsically high 33% average over those 15 years. Yes, there was a fair amount of volatility around those margins, but in only one year were margins very low. That year was 2001, when in the wake of the dot-com crash, Yahoo's revenue declined 35% to $717 million and the company's EBITDA margin sank to 6%. And even in that year, Yahoo! still managed to generate around $21 million in free cash flow. Yahoo! also generated robust levels in almost every other year, with the two negative years impacted by one-time events such as tax charges related to its Alibaba investment stake.

So it wasn't profitability that kept tech investors away from Yahoo! Instead, it was the inability of the company to regain premium revenue growth (20%+) after 2006. Matching up Figure 4.4 and the fundamentals in Table 4.3 makes the point crystal clear.

FIGURE 4.4 The History of Yahoo! as Seen Through Its Stock Price

TABLE 4.3 How Yahoo! Lost Its !

Year	Net Revenue ($MM)	Y/Y Growth	EBITDA ($MM)	Margin	Free Cash Flow ($MM)
2000	1,110	88%	411	37%	415
2001	717	–35%	44	6%	21
2002	953	33%	206	22%	251
2003	1,473	55%	477	32%	311
2004	2,600	77%	1,032	40%	844
2005	3,696	42%	1,557	42%	1,302
2006	4,560	23%	1,906	42%	682
2007	5,113	12%	1,927	38%	1,317
2008	5,399	6%	1,805	33%	1,205
2009	4,682	–13%	1,691	36%	877
2010	4,588	–2%	1,710	37%	526
2011	4,381	–5%	1,655	38%	731
2012	4,468	2%	1,676	38%	–787
2013	4,522	1%	1,564	35%	857
2014	4,719	4%	1,362	29%	521
2015	4,934	5%	943	19%	–2,926

Between 2002 and 2006, as Yahoo! recovered from the dot-com crash and generated premium revenue growth, its stock outperformed strongly, rising 383% from the beginning of 2003 to the end of 2005. But similar to eBay, its stock held essentially flat over the next 10 years, rising from $41 at the beginning of 2006 to only $50 at the beginning of 2015—about 20% share price appreciation over that entire 10-year period, with potential M&A catalysts (the failed bid by Microsoft for Yahoo!) being the biggest share price driver near the end of that period, not fundamental revenue growth. Not once in that 10-year period did Yahoo! ever consistently reclaim premium revenue growth. And tech investors want revenue growth.

PRICELINE

On April 15, 2013, *Barron's* published a cover story titled "End of the Line for Priceline," which featured a cartoon of Priceline pitchman William Shatner (aka the original and best Captain Kirk) on a high wire about to slip on a banana peel. The article pointed out that Priceline (PCLN) at that time was the single best performing stock in the S&P 500 over the trailing five years, having risen 519%. The stock had also risen a fantastic 100-fold since 2003.

Barron's warned, however, that PCLN's best days were behind it. Direct competition from Expedia, Orbitz, and Travelocity as well as indirect competition from Google would squeeze Priceline's profit margins. The magazine also argued that Priceline's expansion into Asia and Latin America at the time was highly risky and these were less profitable markets. *Barron's* concluded that PCLN could fall 20% or more.

At the time I was one of the most prominent Bulls on PCLN on the Street. So prominent that I felt compelled to write a report in defense of Priceline that weekend. My 11-page report was published that Sunday night, and I went on my firm's institutional sales call that Monday morning at 7:15 ET (4:15 PT . . . gulp) to argue why the *Barron's* story was wrong, to defend PCLN's shares, and to reiterate my $900 price target. Nobody listened. PCLN shares fell 4% that Monday from $743 to $711, then proceeded to decline further, falling to $684 by that Friday, for an 8% correction.

To its credit, *Barron's* published my rebuttal in its online magazine that week. Also to its credit, *Barron's* wrote a follow-on piece approximately two years later with the heading "Priceline Stock: Dominant, Growing and Undervalued." By that time (June 4, 2015), PCLN shares had reached $1,186, up 60% since the *Barron's* cover story. And PCLN shares continued to soar, rising another 83% to $2,171 by March 2018. So over the 14 years between the end of 2003 and the beginning of 2018, PCLN shares rose over 120x. Extremely impressive. When Jeff Boyd, the longstanding CEO of Priceline, retired near the end of 2013, I gave him a gift during an investor conference I cohosted in New York. (For the record, the value of the gift was consistent with SEC regulations.) The gift was a fishing pole (Jeff is an avid fisherman). And on that pole was engraved: "To Jeffrey Boyd: Congratulations, Mr. 100-Bagger!"

So what's the lesson here, and what did PCLN Bulls get right and *Barron's* get wrong? Focus on the revenue and the key customer metrics.

Take a look at the PCLN stock price in Figure 4.5. (In early 2018, the company changed its name to Booking Holdings and its ticker to BKNG.) This is about as beautiful a chart as any stock Bull could ever hope to see in his or her lifetime.

Now look at Table 4.4, which shows gross bookings, room nights, and profitability for every year from 2004 to 2017. For an online travel company like Priceline, gross bookings represent the total value of the travel services purchased by customers—airplane tickets, hotel stays, rental cars, and so on. It's not revenue, as Priceline only recorded as revenue the commission it generated from the sale of these travel services. But gross bookings is the key

FIGURE 4.5 The PCLN 100-Bagger Move

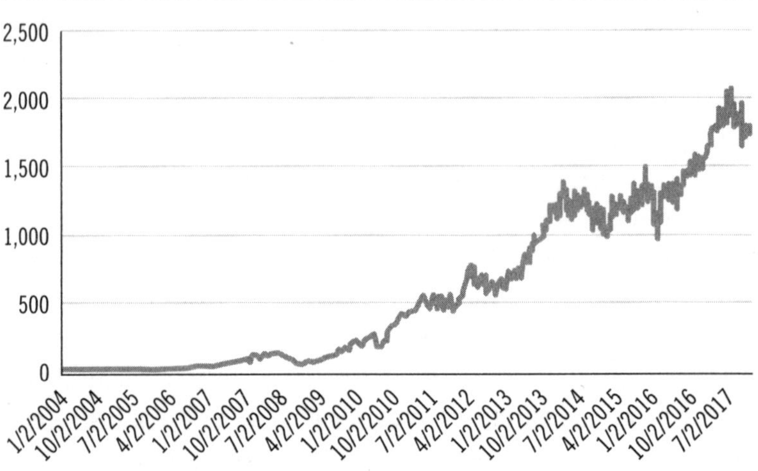

TABLE 4.4 The Drivers of the PCLN 100-Bagger Move

Year	Gross Bookings ($MM)	Y/Y Growth	Room Nights (000)	Y/Y Growth	EBITDA ($MM)	Margin
2004	1,676	52%	7,771	36%	48	5%
2005	2,227	33%	11,759	51%	69	7%
2006	3,320	49%	18,651	59%	109	10%
2007	4,829	45%	27,777	49%	228	16%
2008	7,400	53%	40,814	47%	374	20%
2009	9,310	32%	60,912	49%	553	24%
2010	13,646	50%	92,752	52%	902	29%
2011	21,658	53%	141,500	53%	1,510	35%
2012	28,456	37%	197,500	40%	1,978	38%
2013	39,172	38%	270,500	37%	2,684	40%
2014	50,061	29%	343,520	27%	3,281	39%
2015	55,528	24%	432,400	26%	3,779	41%
2016	68,087	25%	556,500	29%	4,406	41%
2017	81,226	19%	673,100	21%	5,141	41%

top-line measure that the Street has always focused on with online travel companies like Priceline. And room nights were the key customer metric for Priceline, as lodging room night stays were by far the most frequently purchased item on Priceline.

What comes though so clearly from the table is how exceptional Priceline's top-line growth and customer metrics were for so long. Over this 14-year period, Priceline averaged almost 40% bookings growth each and every year. That growth is something like 10x that of global GDP growth and something like 8x that of global travel growth. That growth was utterly extraordinary, and it drove stock price performance that was utterly extraordinary.

Yes, there were other factors that drove that extraordinary stock price performance. Two in particular. First, throughout that time Priceline was a consistently highly profitable company, averaging close to 30% EBITDA margins over that 14-year period. And second, PCLN's valuation was consistently "reasonable" over that time period. It traded at P/E multiples that were often a premium (15x–25x) to the overall market (15x–20x), but ones that were consistently at a discount to the company's growth rates. For example, it would trade at a 20x P/E multiple but would be generating 30%+ EPS growth. That meant PCLN had one of the most attractive growth-adjusted valuations in tech for a substantial period, because tech stocks generally trade at a P/E multiple in line with or at a premium to their growth rates—for example, generate 20% earnings growth and trade at a 30x P/E.

To be clear, there were key factors that drove that extraordinary top-line growth, two in particular. I'll devote a lesson to each of these later, as they are two of my key lessons. The first factor that helped drive that extraordinary top-line growth for so long was an enormous TAM (total addressable market), because Priceline was competing in a global travel market that was well over $1.5 trillion in size. Which meant that even after all those years of amazing growth, Priceline in 2017 still only accounted for perhaps 5% of total global travel bookings. Meaning that it could still maintain premium growth for years to come. The second factor was an exceptionally high-quality management team. Not every management team can be great. The PCLN management team, however, was well above average, but I'll get to this in Lesson 8, "M Is for Management."

The key point here is that revenue matters more than anything else when it comes to driving tech stocks. That the PCLN lesson.

But wait, we're not finished. Because there's more to the story and more to this point. Some of the best evidence of how important revenue growth is to stock price performance happened with Priceline/Booking after 2018.

Recall I earlier referenced the spectacular and then rather ordinary story—in terms of revenue and share price—of Priceline.com, the global giant of online travel. Now feast your eyes on Figure 4.6, which tracks PCLN/BKNG stock price from the beginning of 2017 to the end of 2019. What's gone is the super-charging, pulse-raising, wall-framing PCLN/BKNG Bull chart. It's been replaced with a fine but ordinary BKNG chart, with the stock up 39%, pretty much in line with the performance of the S&P 500, which rose 43% over that three-year period.

FIGURE 4.6 **BKNG: A Fine but Ordinary Stock Chart**

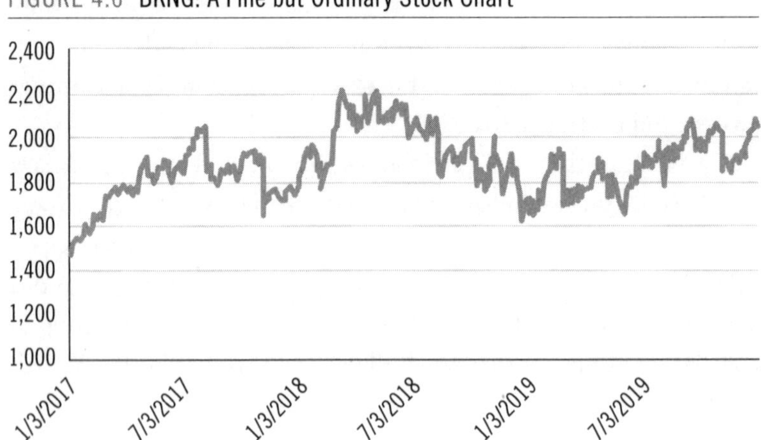

And now look at the fundamentals of Priceline from 2015 to 2020 in Table 4.5. Throughout all five years, the company remained highly, unusually profitable—41% or 42% EBITDA margins each and every year. For context, 40%+ EBITDA margins in tech are more the exception than the rule. What did change is the top line. See how gross bookings consistently slowed to 8% by 2019, along with room nights down to 11%? The takeaway? When the revenue growth leaves the premium category—which I somewhat arbitrarily, but with a lot of experience, define as 20%+—that's when the dramatic stock outperformance ends.

TABLE 4.5 What Happens When the Music/Growth Stops . . .

($MM)	2015	2016	2017	2018	2019
Gross Bookings	**55,528**	**68,087**	**81,226**	**92,731**	**96,443**
Y/Y Growth	24%	25%	19%	13%	8%
Room Night (000)	**432,400**	**556,600**	**673,100**	**759,600**	**844,000**
Y/Y Growth	26%	29%	21%	13%	11%
EBITDA	**3,779**	**4,406**	**5,141**	**6,045**	**6,180**
Margin	41%	41%	41%	42%	41%

I want to wrap up this PCLN stock-picking section with four key points:

First, when you come across a company that has consistently generated premium revenue growth for a reasonably long period of time—at least five or six quarters—then you have come across what could well be a very good stock going forward. Worried that you missed the big move already? Don't be. Instead, look at the quarters of evidence as the proof you were looking for that the premium growth can be sustained. Look at the PCLN experience. You could have first looked at the stock in early 2007, seen the 40% average top-line growth of the preceding 3 years, and decided it was too late. And *missed* the next 11 years of stock outperformance! And you could have looked at the stock in early 2011, seen the 40% average top-line growth of the preceding 7 years, and decided it was too late. And *missed* the next 7 years of stock outperformance. And you could have looked at the stock in early 2015, seen the 40% average top-line growth of the preceding 11 years, and decided it was too late. And *missed* the next 3 years of stock outperformance. Sometimes, past performance *is* an indicator of future performance.

Second, you want to watch out for signs of dramatic revenue growth deceleration. Growth rates cut in half—that's dramatic. You find a company growing its top line at a consistent 30% level. Then in three or four quarters that growth gets clipped to 15%. That's a red flag. True, 15% growth is intrinsically impressive. But not as the immediate next step after 30% growth, which raises questions about market share losses, market saturation, and management mis-execution. All growth rates fade eventually. There is a large numbers law. It's the rate of the fade that matters. And a 50% cut or reduction in a short period (three or four quarters) is a major concern.

Third, just because growth rates taper off below 20% doesn't mean you will face a "tech wreck" or a major stock correction. PCLN's growth did fade below 20%. It fell from 19% in 2017 down to 8% in 2019. But this was over three years. And the "tech wreck" turned out to be a stock that traded in line with the market over those three years. After rising 120x over the previous 14 years. That's what I would call a soft landing after an intergalactic flight!

Fourth, it was helpful to be able to buy PCLN when for so many years it traded at a discount to its growth rate. You find a tech company trading at a discount to a premium growth rate, that's definitely a company worth investigating—for example, a 30% revenue grower trading at a 20x P/E.

But even with good companies that are premium revenue growers, there can still be an amazing Long opportunity, even if there is no valuation support at all. Let me introduce you to a DVD rental company based in Los Gatos, California . . .

NETFLIX

Netflix IPO'd in May 2002. It posted its first full year of material positive free cash flow (defined as over $1 billion) in 2020. Just think about that for a minute: 18 years without material positive free cash flow. And its stock soared 42,000% over that time. (See Figure 4.7.)

FIGURE 4.7 **NFLX: What a 42,000% Performance Looks Like**

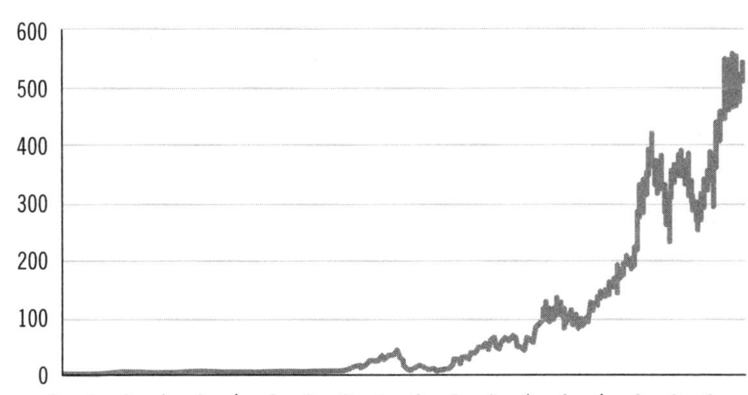

Clearly, NFLX shares surged on something other than near-term free cash flow projections. On what? Revenue and subscribers is what. The astounding rise in Netflix's share price is a perfect example of what often drives tech stocks—revenue growth and key customer metrics. In Netflix's case, the key customer metric has always been the number of paid subscribers—the number of people in the United States and then around the world who pay a monthly subscription fee of around $9 to stream Netflix to their heart's delight.

OK, I'm getting ahead of myself. Netflix was solely a DVD rental company for the first five years of its public life. And streaming wasn't a material part of its offering for a few years after that. In many ways, Netflix is a broad example of the positive lessons for how to invest in tech stocks. Netflix always faced a broad TAM—global consumer spending on entertainment runs over $400 billion a year. Netflix has been extraordinarily effective at product development—who do you think invented streaming? And Netflix has been run by one of the best management teams in tech—led by an impressive founder/CEO (Reed Hastings), with deep technical skills, long-term vision, and the courage to take steps that he believed would be beneficial long term but knew would be unpopular near term.

If memory serves, I first met Reed Hastings in late 1998 at a startup conference at the Marriott Hotel next to SFO airport. A large number of startups or reasonably young private companies were pitching their business plans to a group of investors. I don't remember details of Reed's presentation, other than that the room where he presented was full, and awareness of the Netflix DVD service was very high among the investors. Netflix had already been identified as one of the more promising new tech companies in Silicon Valley.

Over the course of the next 25 years, I hosted dozens of meetings with Reed and other members of Netflix management, including many with Barry McCarthy, who served as the company's CFO for almost a dozen years. A very recent book on Netflix's corporate culture describes McCarthy as "a little moody." All I know is that if an analyst or an investor asked him a simplistic or poorly thought-out question—which happened quite a bit, including from this analyst—McCarthy would occasionally stare at the questioner in disbelief, roll his eyes, or simply drop his head into his arms on the table in resignation.

Reed may have had a similar attitude at times. Actually, I know that he did. I once brought to his office three veteran portfolio managers from one of the largest investment funds on the East Coast. We met him in one of the company's conference rooms (each named after a different movie), where he was waiting by himself to meet with our group. No handlers, no assistants, just Reed. He started off by saying that he rarely did these meetings, but he fully realized the value of meeting with smart, savvy independent investors, who would hopefully challenge his thinking and give him new ideas to ponder. Reed was enthusiastic. The lead portfolio manager then began by asking a general question about Netflix's market opportunity. Which caused Reed to stare back in silence and then express: "You came all the way out here for this meeting, and *that's* the best question you could start the meeting with?!"

The rest of the meeting went fine, and that fund did end up taking a sizable stake in NFLX, generating an outstanding return on that investment. I would think that for that portfolio manager, the outstanding return more than made up for a few awkward minutes. And to be clear, I think Reed Hastings and the rest of the Netflix management team are among the best I have tracked over the last 25 years. And Barry McCarthy succeeded not only at Netflix, but also at Spotify, where he served as that company's CFO during its IPO.

To get back to the fundamentals story, Netflix can boast one of the most impressive growth streaks in tech, having generated 20%+ revenue growth for eight straight years—back through 2013. And that streak actually underrepresents the real growth story at Netflix, because it includes DVD rental revenue, which has steadily declined since at least 2012, when it accounted for almost one-third of Netflix's total revenue. Netflix's streaming revenue growth streak has been driven by closer to 30% for eight straight years.

That is almost unprecedented growth. Again, global GDP growth is more in the low-to-mid-single-digit range. And the median revenue growth of the S&P 500 companies over the last 20 years has been 5–7%. So we're talking about core revenue growth 4x to 6x that of the 500 leading companies in the world. Damn impressive.

As has been the subscriber growth. In fact, the number of new Netflix subscribers grew at an accelerated rate every year from 2012 to 2020, with the exception of one year (2019). In 2012, Netflix added 10 million new subscribers. In 2020, it added close to 35 million, with the effects of the Covid-19 pandemic driving record sub adds in the first half of 2020.

This almost unprecedented revenue and key customer metric growth is exactly what drove NFLX shares and made them the best performing stock of the decade. It certainly wasn't near-term free cash flow, because that actually became more and more negative throughout the period. As Table 4.6 shows, Netflix posted $67 million in negative free cash flow in 2012. In 2016, the free cash flow loss rose to $1.7 billion. And by 2019, the free cash flow loss reached $3.2 billion.

TABLE 4.6 The Fundamental Story of Netflix over a Decade

Year	Total Revenue ($MM)	Y/Y Growth	Streaming Revenue ($MM)	Y/Y Growth	Sub Adds (MM)	Free Cash Flow (Loss ($MM)
2012	3,609	13%	2,472	—	10	–67
2013	4,375	21%	3,464	40%	11	–22
2014	5,505	26%	4,739	37%	13	–128
2015	6,780	23%	6,134	29%	17	–919
2016	8,831	30%	8,288	35%	19	–1,659
2017	11,693	32%	11,242	36%	24	–2,013
2018	15,794	35%	15,429	37%	29	–2,893
2019	20,156	28%	19,859	29%	28	–3,162
2020	24,996	24%	24,757	25%	37	1,929

This was extraordinary! NFLX shares kept rising—and rising dramatically—despite rising and record-high free cash flow losses. Value investors were rolling over in their graves. Over and over.

Did Netflix investors really lose their grip on financial reality? No, because they were willing and able to extrapolate from revenue growth and subscriber growth trends, concluding that Netflix would eventually be generating dramatic amounts of free cash flow. They could also see rising operating margin trends and growing

GAAP earnings and see profit potential and thus stick with a stock that was consistently trading at a P/E multiple well above 50x.

The key point here is that revenue and customer metrics matter more than anything else when it comes to driving tech stocks. That's the NFLX lesson. It's the same as the PCLN lesson, except even stronger, because, unlike with Priceline, there was arguably no near-term valuation support as free cash flow losses were rising aggressively.

I'll wrap up this NFLX stock-picking section with three key points:

First, as with Priceline, when you come across a company that has consistently generated premium revenue growth—which I would define as 20%+—for a reasonably long period—at least five or six quarters—then you have come across what could well be a very good stock going forward. And you don't need to worry about missing the big move. Especially with subscription businesses like Netflix.

Second, subscription businesses are wonderful because when they are reasonably successful, two things happen. First, they provide an enormous amount of revenue visibility—as more and more customers stick with the service, more and more of any period's revenue is "known" at the beginning of the period. Netflix ended 2017 with 110 million paying subscribers. That meant that if Netflix was reasonably able to retain those subs, it would be able to generate 2018 revenue of $11.9 billion (110 million subs x $9 per month x 12 months), before adding any new subs or implementing any GCIs (growth curve initiatives). The second thing that happens with a successful subscription business is that marketing expenses can show leverage—that is, they decline as a percentage of revenue. Because marketing expenses are primarily focused on bringing in new subscribers. And as the base of subscribers gets older and more tenured, the marketing dollars needed against the total base is less.

Third, public markets can be long term in outlook. Many savvy investors in Silicon Valley would disagree with this statement, but I believe examples like Netflix and Amazon prove the point. There's no way the public markets would have given NFLX a $100 billion+ market cap going into 2020 in the face of clearly rising free cash flow losses if the market wasn't looking ahead many years to the positive free cash flows Netflix would generate with its revenue and customer base. Yes, stocks react sharply to all sorts of short-term catalysts, but the valuation frameworks that largely support them are long term. And they are first led by revenue and customer metrics. These, more than anything else, are what drive tech stocks.

GROWTH CURVE INITIATIVES

I want to quickly pivot to the GCIs (growth curve initiatives) mentioned earlier. In the PCLN section, I warned about the impact on stock prices of material revenue growth deceleration. Here, I'm going to go the other way and talk about the impact of revenue growth acceleration, which is almost always a positive catalyst for stocks. The simple reality is that growth accelerates; multiples re-rate—they go higher. When earnings growth accelerates, the P/E multiple expands. Usually, so does the P/S ratio (the price-to-sales ratio).

Depending on the driver of that earnings growth acceleration, the multiple can re-rate a little or a lot. This ties back to the prior discussion of the three ways of driving earnings: growing revenue, reducing operating costs, or engaging in "financial engineering." The market will be most impressed by an earnings growth acceleration that is driven by accelerating revenue growth, because that is the hardest of the three ways. And what drives accelerating revenue growth is GCIs.

So what are GCIs? These are steps that companies take to drive new top-line growth. Steps that companies take to bend the growth curve back up—to cause revenue growth to accelerate. Some of the most powerful steps I have witnessed have involved price increases, geographic market expansion, and new product introductions. And the example I want to give you of this is, again, Netflix, at the end of 2017 and early 2018. Back when we had that visibility into $11.9 billion in 2018 revenue. When Netflix successfully implemented all three of those GCIs, which caused its revenue to accelerate, its operating margins to expand, it's multiple to re-rate, and its stock to soar 98% in six months. (See Figure 4.8.)

FIGURE 4.8 The Impact of GCIs on NFLX's Stock Price

Figure 4.8 was the end result. But Figure 4.9 peels back the onion, where we see the re-rating. From January 1, 2018, to July 1, 2018, NFLX's EV-to-sales multiple expanded from 7x to 13x.

FIGURE 4.9 The Impact of GCIs on NFLX's Valuation

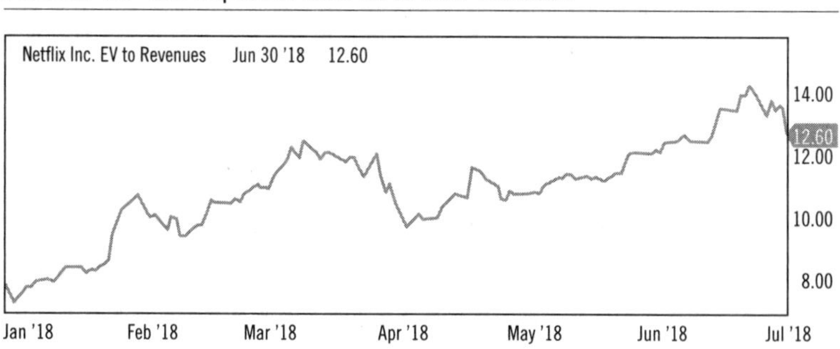

The Impact of GCIs on NFLX's Valuation

In early 2018, NFLX's re-rating was driven by revenue growth acceleration and operating margin expansion (Table 4.7). Total revenue growth accelerated from 33% in the December 2017 quarter to 40% in the March and June 2018 quarters. Streaming revenue growth accelerated to 43% in those two quarters, the fastest growth in five years! And operating margin also jumped to a record-high 12% in those two quarters, versus 4% in 2016 and 7% in 2017. The sweet thing about revenue growth acceleration is that it can lead to operating margin expansion, because the revenue will scale against fixed costs. Successful price increases are especially sweet, because the revenue unit generates more revenue, but the costs of delivering that unit are unchanged. That's why price increases can be considered "pure margin"—the extra revenue flows right down to the bottom line. *If*, that is, the price increases are successful—if the increases don't cause customers to cancel en masse.

TABLE 4.7 The Q1:18 Netflix Inflection Point

($MM)	Q3:17	Q4:17	Q1:18	Q2:18
Total Revenue	**2,985**	**3,286**	**3,701**	**3,907**
Y/Y Growth	30%	33%	40%	40%
Streaming Revenue	**2,875**	**3,181**	**3,602**	**3,814**
Y/Y Growth	33%	35%	43%	43%
Operating Margin	**7%**	**7%**	**12%**	**12%**

Another way to think about these inflection points is what I call the *earnings growth aperture*. There's earnings growth driven by consistent revenue growth and stable operating margins. The aperture is open. Then there's earnings growth driven by accelerating revenue growth and stable operating margins. The aperture is open wider. Finally, there's earnings growth driven by accelerating revenue growth and expanding operating margins. This is when the earnings growth aperture is its most open. And stocks react positively to this. If you invest ahead of this or during it, you could well have very good returns.

That's why you want to be on the lookout for GCIs—steps that companies are taking to bend up those growth curves. Is a new product line or a new key feature being rolled out? Is the company entering into material new international markets for the first time? Or is the company implementing a new price increase or a premium tier offering that looks promising? These are what you should be keeping an eye out for.

At the beginning of 2018, Netflix had these. In the fall of 2017, Netflix raised the price of its standard plan (two simultaneous users) by 10% (from $9.99 to $10.99) and the price of its premium plan (four simultaneous users) by 17% (from $11.99 to $13.99), while maintaining the price of its basic plan at $7.99. It had implemented a somewhat similar price increase two years earlier, and that had been successful—new subscriber growth didn't slow, and existing customer churn didn't rise appreciably. The fall 2017 price increase was equally successful. Netflix was also accelerating the launch of its original shows, including new seasons of *13 Reasons Why*, *Santa Clarita Diet*, and *The Unbreakable Kimmy Schmidt*, along with new international shows like *The Rain* in Denmark and *3%* in Brazil. Further, Netflix was rolling out new distribution partnerships with T-Mobile, Sky, and Comcast. And finally, Netflix was aggressively expanding into Asian markets. There you have it—GCIs up the wazoo!

Again, look for growth curve initiatives. Because if they are successful, they can lead to revenue growth acceleration, which many more times than not, the market will reward with a higher share price.

A QUICK WORD ON COMPS

Pro tip. For those looking for consistent revenue growth trends, the Covid-19 crisis creates some challenges. Companies with exposure to travel demand (e.g., Airbnb, Booking, and Expedia) or to ride-sharing (e.g., Lyft and Uber) or to advertising revenue (e.g., Google and Twitter) suffered a material year-over-year decline in their revenue for part or all of 2020. Whereas companies that were clear work-from-home (WFH) or live-from-home (LFH) winners—such as Amazon, Etsy, Netflix, Peloton, and Zoom—experienced material revenue growth acceleration for part or all of 2020.

This created issues for investors looking for consistent revenue growth rates in 2020 and in 2021. The "Covid-19 losers" will report impressive revenue recovery or acceleration in 2021, while the "Covid-19 winners" will report alarming revenue deceleration. The key in both circumstances will be to normalize results. The Covid-19 crisis was a black swan event. Just as one should back out one-time unusual expenses and gains from EPS results to get an accurate view of profitability trends, one should normalize for the dramatic impact on growth rates that the pandemic has wrought.

There are two ways to do this. One is to look at a two-year stack for revenue growth—add the year-over-year revenue growth of any one quarter to the year-over-year revenue growth of the prior year's similar quarter, and then track this over a period of time to see if there are any major changes. Here's a simple example with Amazon. In the March quarter of 2020, Amazon reported 26% year-over-year revenue growth. Then the Covid-19 crisis kicked that growth rate up to 40% year-over-year in the June quarter of 2020, as physical stores were closed and demand surged to online retailers like Amazon. This makes it likely that Amazon, because of tough comps, will see revenue growth deceleration from the March quarter of 2021 to the June quarter. Hypothetically, let's say Amazon's growth decelerates from 40% in the March 2021 quarter to 24% in the June quarter. This looks like material deceleration. But on a two-year stack basis, growth is actually going from 66% (26% + 40%) to 64% (40% + 24%). That implies a lot of consistency in Amazon's comps-adjusted revenue growth—a good sign.

The other way to do this is simply to line up the rate of deceleration that Amazon experiences in the June 2021 quarter with the rate of acceleration in the June 2020 quarter. If the rate of deceleration is consistent with the prior year's rate of acceleration, then Amazon's comps-adjusted growth rate is consistent. So in the above example, Amazon reports a hypothetical 16% deceleration from the March 2021 quarter (40% year-over-year growth) to 24% in the June quarter. But that is reasonably close to the 14% acceleration Amazon reported from the March quarter of 2020 (26% year-over-year growth) to the June quarter (40%). Conclusion? Amazon's comps-adjusted revenue growth remains consistent.

SOME EVIDENCE BEHIND THE 20% REVENUE "RULE"

I put "rule" in quotation marks for a reason. I want to caveat the heck out of the idea that a good stock-picking strategy involves simply finding companies with 20% revenue growth and then buying them.

The history of Internet stocks certainly gives credence to the idea that premium revenue growth—or the lack thereof—is a key driver of high-growth tech stocks. Of course, earnings matter. But my experience has taught me that earnings growth powered primarily by revenue growth carries more weight with tech investors than that powered by margin expansion or "financial engineering." And for good reasons. Revenue growth is hard. Premium revenue growth is harder. And consistent premium revenue growth is hardest of all.

The importance of revenue growth to stock performance comes through in the eBay, Yahoo!, Priceline/Booking, and Netflix histories in this lesson. The stock market history of Amazon and Google (covered in detail later in the book) also support the idea that premium revenue growth is a key driver of tech stocks. These two companies have pulled off the almost unprecedented feat of generating

20% consistent revenue growth for a full decade *after* achieving a $25 billion revenue run rate. Only one other company in history has matched this feat—Apple. And all three stocks have been extraordinary long-term winners. Facebook is potentially on a path to achieve this feat, and its stock has also been a great long-term winner.

I also believe there is some reasonable market evidence from the last 20 to 30 years that consistent 20%+ top-line growth is a decent fundamental tell of a high-quality tech stock. First, this is scarce, rare-air growth. This is about three or four times faster than the median revenue growth of the S&P 500 companies. Based on a review of the revenue results of the S&P 500 companies since 1994, on average only about 2% of these companies in any one year have been able to report consistent 20% revenue growth in each of the previous five years. That's only about 10 of the S&P 500 companies in any one year, and these companies are widely considered the highest-quality companies in the land. To make a key distinction, in any one year, approximately 15% of the S&P 500 have reported 20%+ revenue growth. But in any one year, only approximately 2% have been able to report consistent 20%+ revenue growth over the preceding five years.

Second, it turns out that companies with consistent (five-year) 20%+ revenue growth tend to outperform companies that don't meet this condition, and sometimes by substantial amounts. Over 2010 to 2020, the consistent 20+ revenue growers (the 20%-ers) outperformed in 8 of the 11 years (or 73% of the time) and by a median 52% over the whole period. Taking the analysis back further, from 1994 to 2020, the 20%-ers outperformed in 15 of the 27 years (or 56% of the time), underperformed in 8 of the years (30% of the time), and performed in line with the other stocks in 4 of the years (15% of the time). The median outperformance for the 20%-ers over the whole period was 12%. (See Table 4.8.)

TABLE 4.8 The 20%-ers Outrun the Rest of the Pack

Period	Outperform	Underperform	In-Line	Median % of Outperformance
1994–2000	15 Years	8 Years	4 Years	12%
% of Total	56%	30%	15%	
2010–2020	8 Years	3 Years	0 Years	52%
% of Total	73%	27%	0%	

Note: Performance measures the average one-year forward stock returns of the S&P 500 constituents that have generated 20%+ revenue growth in each of the prior five years (the 20%-ers) against those who have not.

Again, I am putting "rule" in quotation marks. I believe consistent 20%+ revenue growth is a good fundamental tell of a high-quality tech stock. But it's a tell—an output—of the key drivers of high-quality, high-growth tech stocks, which is the subject of the next four lessons. The 20% revenue growth "rule" should never be used in isolation.

LESSON WRAP-UP

Over the long term, fundamentals really do move stocks, and for tech stocks, the fundamentals that matter most are revenue, revenue, and revenue. Companies that consistently generate 20%+ top-line growth—either in revenue or in their key customer metric—these are companies that can potentially provide good stock returns, almost regardless of their near-term profitability outlooks. That's the 20% revenue growth "rule." Consistent 20%+ top-line growth—what I would label premium revenue growth—is three to four times faster than that of the S&P 500 and hard to sustain. It can often reflect large market opportunities, relentless and successful product innovation, compelling value propositions, and top-quality management teams. This is exactly what you want to be looking for in good long-term investing opportunities. As a start, look for companies that have generated 20%+ growth for five or six quarters in a row. Past performance can sometimes be an indicator of future performance.

Companies with sharply decelerating revenue growth—for example, revenue growth rates that get cut in half over three or four quarters—are likely to work poorly as Longs, especially if that deceleration is driven by market share losses, market saturation, or management mis-execution. When that deceleration is driven by major black swan events like the Covid-19 crisis, it's a different matter. Conversely, stocks of companies that are successfully executing GCIs (growth curve initiatives) and generating revenue growth acceleration can be good outperformers. Growth curve initiatives in particular are useful for investors because they can provide great catalysts for stock price appreciation. When GCIs such as new product launches, geographic market expansion, and price increases work, they can lead to revenue growth acceleration and often margin expansion, opening up the earnings growth aperture and leading to a re-rating in the stock's multiple. Look for GCIs.

Successful tech investing doesn't mean being oblivious to profits. Profitless growth creates no value in the long run. But the history of many of the leading tech companies over the last two decades demonstrates that revenue growth—especially premium revenue growth—is a good indicator of future profitability. Either the company will start getting leverage against largely fixed costs (G&A, building expenses, some R&D), or its growing scale will allow its unit economics to improve, as the company gains leverage against its suppliers and through increased experience and scale becomes more efficient at managing its costs.

LESSON 5

It Don't Mean a Thing, If It Ain't Got That Product Swing

Successful product innovation is one of the biggest drivers of fundamentals, especially revenue growth, and that's what drives stocks. Successful product innovation can generate entirely new revenue streams and enhance existing revenue streams. Successful product innovation is spottable, especially with consumer-focused tech companies. And product innovation is a repeatable offense—management teams that generate one or two impressive product innovations likely have the ability to continue to generate more innovations, because they have processes in place or a culture that fosters successful product innovation.

If fundamentals are what drive stocks over the long term, and the most important fundamental for tech stocks is revenue, what drives revenue? I'll go with four key drivers: relentless product innovation, large market opportunities, compelling value propositions, and excellent management. In this lesson, we look at product innovation.

Product innovation covers a lot of things. One of the most obvious examples is the new version of the iPhone that Apple has brought out pretty much annually since it first introduced the product back in June 2007. Another not so obvious example is the monthly software updates that Tesla has released for its cars since it introduced the Tesla Roadster in 2008. This lesson will cover a range of examples of product innovation—most successful, but some not—and show how they helped drive revenue and stock performance.

I'll also make the simple point that product innovation can be assessed by most people, because much of the most substantial product innovation of the last two decades has been consumer oriented. It has been focused on improving an existing—or creating a new—consumer experience. And you are a consumer. So you can and will decide for yourself which innovations are amazing, which so-so, and which bad.

And if you come across a product or a service that you think is really great or materially improved, you may well have come across a great stock. At least, you'll have some incentive to start doing homework on a stock.

It's a small example, but one of the reasons I became so Bulled up on Stitch Fix (SFIX) shares in early 2020 was because I was a customer. I was impressed by some of the new features the service was rolling out, especially Shop Your Colors and Shop Your Looks, which made it much easier for me to find clothing items I was interested in buying. This, combined with the stock being highly dislocated, made me believe that both fundamentals and stock price performance could materially inflect up. Yes, luck was involved, but SFIX shares did rally from $12 in April of 2020 to $70 by the end of the year, as customer metrics improved and the revenue growth outlook strengthened, thanks in part to those new features.

For a big example, I'd point to the 2006 launch of Amazon Web Services (AWS), the company's cloud computing offering, which goes down as one of the single most impressive, most impactful product innovations of this millennium (since 2000), along with those iPhone and Tesla launches. AWS is widely known and widely regarded by tech investors today. Though that was far from the case when it was launched. Some tech observers (unfortunately, including me) were skeptical when Jeff Bezos first announced the AWS offering, which seemed like a diversion into a small, commodity-esque, uninteresting sector. That "diversion" arguably now accounts for half of Amazon's current $1.5 trillion market cap.

THE STORY OF AWS—CHANGING THE TICKER

Amazon has introduced many product innovations over the years. Some have failed, including its March 1999 launch of Auctions to take on eBay and its June 2014 launch of the Fire Phone, which received mixed critical reviews, little consumer interest, and a $170 million inventory write-down within 12 months.

Others have succeeded quite well, including Amazon Prime (its express shipping service, launched in 2005, that now has over 200 million subscribers worldwide), Amazon Subscribe & Save (an offering launched in 2007 that enables automatic reordering of a variety of household products), and one of my personal favorites—the Amazon Kindle (its e-reader device, which was launched in 2007 and became the category leader and helped the company hedge against the digital disintermediation of its physical book retail business).

For avid readers, Amazon Kindles have been a heaven-sent gift. The ability to download and access almost any book at any time was a huge breakthrough. The first-generation Kindles may have been kludgy and awkward, but they removed friction. They eliminated time between discovering a book and reading it.

This idea of removing friction has been key to much of the innovation we have seen on the Internet and across technology these last two decades. The faster, the easier, the cheaper it is to do something, the more consumers will do that thing. Shed microseconds off generating search results, and people will Google more. Make it simpler to access country music hits from the 1990s, and people will use Spotify more. Reduce the cost of purchasing a kids' basketball hoop for the swimming pool by increasing the speed of delivery (time is money after all), and people will use Amazon more. Reducing friction wins.

Anyway, the original Kindle reduced friction, and the potential for improvement was clear. In early 2008, I published the first report on Wall Street on the Kindle—what it was, what it signaled about innovation at Amazon, and what it meant for the AMZN P&L. I still recall one blogger trashing my analysis and suggesting that I "go back to Kindlegarten." I appreciated the wit.

Far and away the biggest and most successful product innovation at Amazon—other than this online retail thing—was the launch of AWS in 2006. My longstanding joke with professional investors has been that AWS was so momentous of a product innovation, they should have changed the stock ticker from AMZN to AWS. Investor clients chuckled. OK, only a few.

Around the time of the AWS launch, Jeff Bezos had publicly stated that AWS could be as big as the company's retail business one day. At the time, I thought the statement was ridiculous. In 2006, Amazon was generating over $10 billion a year in revenue and over $1 billion a year in operating income via its core retail business. No new "boring IT business" could achieve those levels. Well, AWS actually achieved over $1 billion in operating income by 2015 and over $10 billion in revenue by 2016 (Figure 5.1). By 2020, AWS was generating $45 billion in revenue and $14 billion in operating income, which was close to 20 percent the size of Amazon's retail revenue and 2x the size of Amazon's retail operating income. AWS was growing much faster than Amazon's retail business. AWS may have become the more appropriate ticker.

FIGURE 5.1 AWS: The Second Largest Software Company in the World

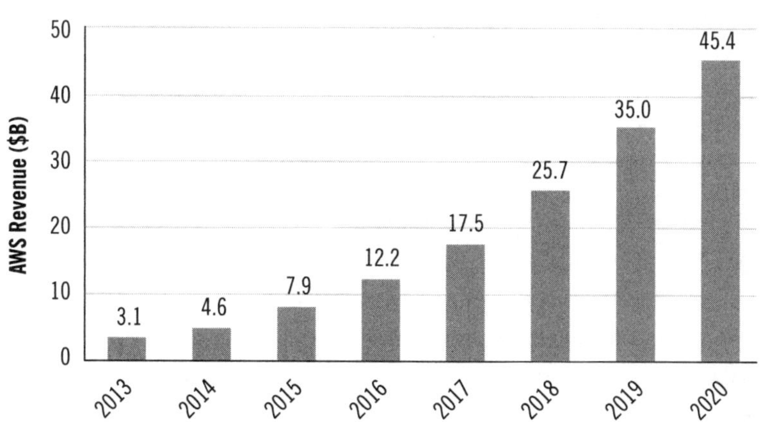

So what is AWS, and why was it so innovative? Amazon describes AWS as providing "a highly reliable, scalable, low-cost infrastructure platform in the cloud that powers hundreds of thousands of businesses in 190 countries around the world." In layperson's terms, AWS enables an outsourcing of a company's or an organization's IT department. All the servers and server racks and databases and wires and cords and doohickeys and the personnel that a business would use to store, analyze, and utilize its data (covering its products, its operations, and its customers) could be outsourced to AWS. Instead of needing substantial, up-front fixed capital expenditures, businesses could now pay for IT services on a pay-as-you-use basis.

AWS and cloud computing were absolutely revolutionary. They increased the speed and efficiency with which any organization could scale up. They allowed any company the ability to "spin up" onto Amazon's immense server infrastructure its applications and software solutions and make them available to consumers and enterprises worldwide. Without having to invest massively in its own infrastructure, saving substantial time and money and operational complexity. Companies that now use AWS include some of the largest digital organizations in the world: Facebook, LinkedIn, Netflix, Snap, and the CIA.

I sometimes refer to AWS and cloud computing as creating 19-year-old risk. They allow any 19-year-old with a great business idea to scale it up to tens of millions of customers without having to spend tens of millions of dollars on up-front infrastructure costs. In this sense, cloud computing has been a wonderful spur to competition and innovation across the technology landscape.

So did Amazon invent cloud computing? No. That was Joseph Carl Robnett Licklider in the 1960s, when he was working with ARPANET. According to Wikipedia, Amazon "popularized" cloud computing when it released its Elastic Compute Cloud product in 2006. I'd use the word "commercialized." Most investors would too. Especially since AWS came to generate more than 50 percent of the cloud computing industry's revenue and came to rank as the second largest software company in the world (behind only Microsoft).

The one-paragraph story of how AWS came to be goes as follows: Back in 2000, Amazon engineers were trying to launch a service that would allow companies like Target to build online shopping sites. They had a hard time doing it because common web infrastructure services (like database, storage, and compute capacity) didn't exist. And internal Amazon projects were always taking longer than expected because each team was building these services from scratch. Eventually, light bulbs went off, and management realized its internal needs and those of its enterprise customers were demonstrating the potential for a whole new market opportunity.

Let's look at the indicators that AMZN could be a good stock. I'd argue that those indicators began flashing bright green sometime around 2008. When the company had already demonstrated it could maintain 20%+ premium revenue growth—by 2008, it had already generated six straight years of 20%+ revenue growth. And when the company was proving that it could be highly innovative—having successfully launched at least two different new products or services—the

Kindle and AWS. You didn't have to guess just how large cloud computing was going to be. You just had to realize that this online retail company had launched through its own efforts (i.e., not through acquisitions) two new businesses that were dramatically different from its core business and that were starting to look successful.

An investor could have seen the signs that Amazon's core business (online retail) was a premium revenue grower and that the company was potentially generating other revenue streams. It was beginning to look like a *platform company*—a rare company that successfully generates multiple revenue streams. At the very least, Amazon was clearly demonstrating its ability to be innovative. When a management team shows that it has been innovative in the past, that's another good reason to stick with a stock, because that management team can be innovative again (and Amazon has been). Sometimes past performance is an indicator of future performance.

In terms of my stock-picking, I already had a Buy on AMZN going into 2008, but it was more of a tactical Buy—a rating that could change were AMZN shares to skyrocket above my price target. Somewhere during this period, AMZN became a core Long for me, which meant that it would take something truly drastic to get me to change my rating. Increasingly respecting the power of Amazon's platform, I became unlikely to let even a super aggressive valuation change my rating, although valuation did impact where AMZN stacked in my Buy list. Looking back, I may not have got the stack ranking right every year, but I absolutely got the Long call right. Long AMZN has been one of the best calls of my career.

THE STORY OF STREAMING—CHANGING THE MOVIE REEL

AWS is an amazing example of where product innovation created brand-new, robust revenue streams for a company. Streaming is an example of product innovation cannibalizing a company's core revenue stream but creating a dramatically stronger business. Consider Netflix.

From early on, Netflix cofounder Reed Hastings wanted the company to be a streaming service. But when the company was founded in 1997, the technology landscape just wouldn't support streaming. Perhaps the biggest gating factor was US household broadband adoption, which didn't reach 50 percent until 2007. Per the FCC, there were about 2.8 million US households in 2000 with access to advanced services, defined at the time as 200 Kbps. The typical recommended speed for streaming standard def video is 3 Mbps, over 15x greater than what advanced services allowed in 2000. So no one was going to be streaming *Traffic*, *Memento*, *Remember the Titans*, or *Unbreakable* in 2000. Accordingly, Netflix was exclusively a DVD-by-mail offering until 2007, the first year it offered streaming.

The DVD-by-mail business was a good business for Netflix. It allowed Netflix to generate $1.2 billion in revenue in 2007, with 7.3 million paid subscribers and a slender $67 million in net income. It was a good business but not a great one, and it was starting to slow materially. Netflix's revenue growth was cut by more than half, from 46% in 2006 to 21% in 2007. The growth would slow further to 13% in 2008. And 2007 was the first year in which Netflix's sub growth decelerated—it added only 1.2 million new subs that year, after adding 1.1 million in 2004, 1.5 million in 2005, and 2.1 million in 2006. NFLX shares traded like the company would soon be ex-growth—declining 5% in 2006 (versus the S&P 500 up 14%) and growing 3% in 2007 (versus the S&P 500 up 4%), ending the year at $3.80. Remember, NFLX shares are now well north of $500.

So streaming saved Netflix. But it's not that simple. First, Netflix management had to have the courage to embrace streaming, a business that would cannibalize growth at its core DVD business. And cannibalize it did. At the end of 2007, Netflix had roughly 7 million DVD subs. Today, it has less than 2 million DVD subs. Sure, streaming is a no-brainer today, but that wasn't the case back in 2007. Netflix had to switch gears from supporting a steady but slowing DVD business to investing heavily in a streaming offering with unproven mass market appeal, uncertain unit economics, and unstable technology infrastructure (the quality of the Netflix streaming service would be dependent on variables like the quality of an individual user's broadband connectivity and home Wi-Fi network). When Netflix first announced its streaming service, it warned the Street that it would require at least $40 million in investment spend, which was close to the entire net income the company posted in 2006. So this was a big bet by the company.

Then Netflix had to execute well on that bet. It had to develop a compelling offering—in terms of content selection, ease of use, reliability, and such. The initial offering had only about 1,000 titles (versus 70,000 available via DVD) and only worked on the most recent versions of Windows and Internet Explorer. Very limited. But did Netflix execute well on that bet? And did that bet pay off? Hell, yeah.

After fits and starts, Netflix became the leading global streaming company. It started generating 20%+ premium revenue growth for over a decade starting in 2009, with an accelerating number of new subscribers every year from 2009 to 2019—with the exception of 2011–2012, when a completely botched effort to materially raise fees and spin off its DVD business (the Qwikster catastrophe) stunted subscriber and revenue growth for 12 months (see Table 5.1). Harvard Business School was going to do a case study on the Qwikster disaster, but *Saturday Night Live* beat them to the punch with one of the greatest corporate spoof skits of all time. Netflix streaming became so successful that it caused arguably the world's greatest entertainment company (Disney) to completely upend its business model in search of streaming (Disney+). And NFLX became the single best performing stock of the decade.

TABLE 5.1 The Fundamental History of Netflix

Year	Total Revenue ($MM)	Y/Y Growth	Total Unique Subscribers (MM)	Net Sub Adds (MM)
2005	682	36%	4	2
2006	997	46%	6	2
2007	1,205	21%	7	1
2008	1,365	13%	9	2
2009	1,670	22%	12	3
2010	2,163	29%	20	8
2011	3,205	48%	26	6
2012	3,609	13%	35	9
2013	4,375	21%	44	9
2014	5,505	26%	57	13
2015	6,780	23%	75	17

Successful product innovation—in this case streaming—revived Netflix's fundamentals and its stock price. It did so by over time creating a vastly better consumer experience for enjoying video entertainment, offering subscribers instant, on-demand access via a broad range of devices to well over 10,000 titles, an increasing percentage of which were exclusive to Netflix. It also did this at an absurdly cheap price, with its basic offering remaining at $7.99 per month for multiple years. Eventually (in 2019), Netflix raised the basic monthly fee to $8.99, but that was still absurdly cheap. In most cities and towns in the United States, you couldn't go to a movie theater by yourself to watch one movie for less than $8.99. So for roughly the same price as one movie ticket, Netflix allowed you to watch two shows a day each day for the entire month and still have over 10,000 titles to go. (And obviously, you could binge-watch as many shows as you wanted in a day.)

Successful product innovation—i.e., streaming—also provided another enormous advantage to Netflix's fundamentals and stock price. It dramatically expanded its TAM (total addressable market) by making it much easier to expand internationally. As a DVD-by-mail service, Netflix had no success expanding outside the United States. Once streaming started gaining momentum in the US market, Netflix quickly pivoted to launching globally, beginning with Canada in 2010, Latin America in 2011, and Europe in 2012. Over time, Netflix found that its consumer adoption in international markets was as fast as or even faster than what it experienced in the United States. Today, over 60 percent of Netflix's subscribers are located outside the United States.

As an analyst, I have maintained a Buy on NFLX for the entire last decade. A great call! Again, I've had many bad ones. And there were also significant periods over the last decade when NFLX did not work as a Long. But three factors kept me long-term Bullish on the shares. The consistent premium revenue growth Netflix maintained, the example of excellent product innovation the company demonstrated with streaming, and extensive consumer survey work I did every quarter that indicated high levels of satisfaction among Netflix subscribers.

The key stock-picking point here is that two of these factors were viewable by the retail investor. The third—extensive consumer survey work—the retail investor could easily have developed through his or her own impression about the quality and value of the Netflix service. The cost of that research would have been just $7.99 a month, which allowed you to see for yourself how intuitive, easy to use, and entertaining the service was and how it was improving in terms of not only new shows, some of which were originals (e.g., *House of Cards*)—but also show discovery, personalization, and so on. You didn't need to know the mechanics of streaming—just as few people know how cellular signals are transmitted to their mobile phone. You just had to develop a reasonable belief that streaming could become popular and that Netflix was likely to be the leader in streaming for the foreseeable future. Successful product innovation can be a great indicator for a great stock.

THE STORY OF STITCH FIX—BRINGING PRODUCT INNOVATION BACK IN FASHION

Stitch Fix (SFIX) IPO'd on November 17, 2017, at $15. Through the beginning of 2021, it rallied up 291%, easily beating the market, which traded up 46% over this time. You would think SFIX has been a great Long over that three-year period. You would have thought wrong.

If you do a Google search for SFIX IPO, one of the first results you will see is a reference to "broken IPO." That's because its share price broke below its $15 IPO price on its second day of trading—down to $14.85. But that was only for a day. SFIX shares actually stayed above their $15 IPO price for the next 2½ years, generally trading in a range of $20–$30, with a few breakout moves above and below that range. (See Figure 5.2.)

Then the Covid-19 crisis hit, and SFIX shares plummeted from $29.37 on February 21, 2020, to $11.47 on April 2, down 67%, much worse than the 24% correction in the S&P 500 over that

FIGURE 5.2 The Story of SFIX

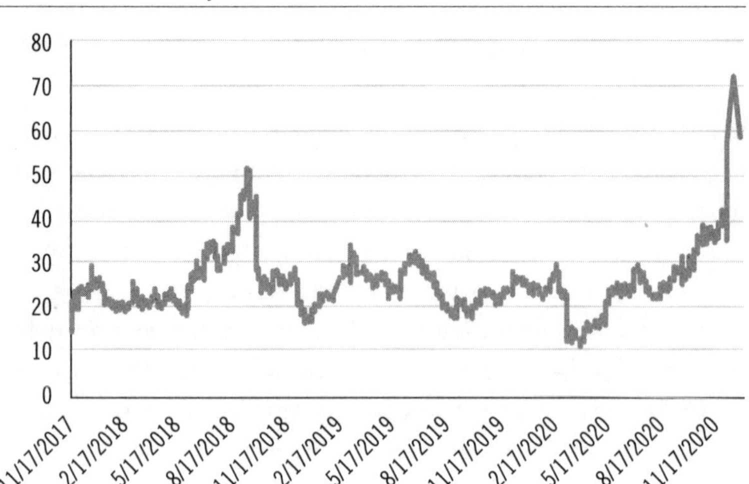

same period. Two factors caused SFIX to trade down so aggressively. First, the company experienced Covid-19 breakouts at three of its six distribution centers, at one point plunging it to 30 percent of its full capacity. Second, demand for its offering evaporated, as stay-in-place restrictions eviscerated consumer demand for premium fashion apparel: no need to "dress for success" if the only people around to impress were your spouse, the kids, the dog, and a few neighbors. And that April 2020 quarter ended up breaking what was at least a 14-quarter streak of 20%+ revenue growth. In that April quarter, Stitch Fix's revenue declined 9% year-over-year.

Here's the quick, key history of Stitch Fix. The company was cofounded in 2011 by Katrina Lake. Stitch Fix provides a personal styling service that sends individually picked clothing and accessories for a one-time styling fee. Customers fill out an online survey, and stylists use algorithmically generated results to help pick five items to send to the customer. The customer schedules a date to receive the items, which is referred to as a "Fix." Once the shipment is received, the customer has three days to choose to keep the items or return some or all of them. Customers choose the shipping frequency, such as every two weeks, once a month, or every two months.

I became a big fan of the service and the stock. For me, the service worked, because it helped me broaden my fashion wardrobe (an easy task) in a way that was convenient (items shipped to my home) and comfortable (which I never really felt walking around clothing stores—call it fashion insecurity). The stock seemed like a potential big winner, because it had already achieved impressive scale ($1 billion in annual revenue, 2 million active customers), profitability (two years of operating profitability at the time of the IPO), and most importantly, premium revenue growth (consistent 20%+ revenue growth for multiple years at the time of the IPO).

So I initiated with a Buy and a $29 target price in December 2017 and waited for the stock to do its thing. And waited. And waited. The stock did nothing. Well, it traded down 34% in 2018 and then traded up 50% in 2019, ending the year at $26, exactly where it began in 2018. So no move in two years, despite premium revenue growth throughout those two years.

What went wrong? The key customer metric. For five of the next six quarters beginning in early 2018, Stitch Fix reported a deceleration in the number of new customers it was adding each quarter. For example, in the July 2017 quarter, SFIX added 120,000 new customers. But in the July 2018 quarter, it added only 54,000 new customers. Revenue growth was consistent, but the customer growth wasn't. (See Table 5.2.) And eventually, that slowing new customer growth was going to drag down the revenue growth. That was the market's take on SFIX. It would take GCIs (growth curve initiatives) and substantial product innovation to change the market's mind. And that's what happened.

Beginning in early 2019, Stitch Fix embarked on two GCIs, expanding into the United Kingdom and launching a kids offering. Both would take some time to ramp up, and the UK initiative did face some delays and challenges in its first year. But both steps increased the company's long-term growth outlook and expanded its

TABLE 5.2 The Fundamental Story Behind SFIX

Fiscal Quarter	Total Revenue ($MM)	Y/Y Growth	Active Clients (000)	New Active Clients (000)
Jan '18	296	24%	2,508	112
Apr '18	317	29%	2,688	180
Jul '18	318	23%	2,742	54
Oct '18	366	24%	2,930	188
Jan '19	370	25%	2,961	31
Apr '19	409	29%	3,133	172
Jul '19	432	36%	3,236	103
Oct '19	445	21%	3,416	180
Jan '20	452	22%	3,465	49

TAM. They both involved tweaking and changing the core Stitch Fix offering. Then the company rolled out a series of personalization improvements that made the service . . . well . . . more personalized. The new improvements were grouped under something called *direct buy functionality*, which allowed users of the service to buy clothing directly from Stitch Fix without having to wait for the next Fix.

The Stitch Fix app and emails from the company would suggest items you might like to buy, based on what you had purchased from the company in the past. Items that would complement what you had already purchased (a shirt to go with those slacks), items that would mirror what you had already purchased (the same blouse, just in a different color), and items that would match or replace what you had already purchased. I know Katrina and crew were working on these innovations for some time, but I once found myself complaining to her that a pair of jeans I had bought on Stitch Fix had become my favorite, and yet the company didn't offer me an easy way to buy a backup pair. All Katrina said to me at the time was, "We're working on it."

These personalizations—these product improvements—started to add up, and in the July quarter of 2020, Stitch Fix added slightly more new customers (104,000) than it had added in the July quarter of 2019. And in the October quarter of 2020, Stitch Fix added 241,000 new customers, more than it had ever added in any one quarter. It wasn't Covid-19 relief that drove these new customers. Many parts of the United States were going back into lockdown mode as Covid-19 cases once again surged. Instead, it was the cumulative impact of these product innovations that improved success rates, retention rates, and overall customer satisfaction. Further, revenue growth reaccelerated, and the company guided to a recovery to 20%+ revenue growth for the fiscal year. And for the last six months of 2020, SFIX shares soared 136%.

Stitch Fix the company and SFIX the stock are very much a work in progress. In early March 2021, the company reported disappointing January quarter results, and the stock traded off over 20%. The company cited shipping delays and the need to further tweak its direct buy functionality before rolling it out to its entire customer base. What seems clear from Stitch Fix's history is that successful product innovation has been key to its fundamentals and its stock price and that *continued* successful product innovation will also be key to its fundamentals and its stock price.

SPOTIFY—ARE YOU LISTENING TO ME?

In a blog post in early 2019, Spotify (SPOT) founder and CEO Daniel Ek announced that audio—not just music—would be "the future of Spotify." He noted that Spotify was already one of the world's most used apps but he saw an opportunity "to reach beyond music to engage users in entirely new ways." Spotify was going after the podcasting market, and Ek's blog announced that Spotify was acquiring two podcasting companies (Gimlet and Anchor), with Spotify CFO Barry McCarthy (of Netflix fame) announcing the company's intention to spend $400 million to $500 million in total on podcast acquisitions in 2019.

So this was product innovation based heavily—though not entirely—on acquisition. In addition to the 2019 acquisitions, Spotify also paid a reported $100 million to bring highly popular podcaster Joe Rogan onto its platform in late 2020, along with sizable amounts for Bill Simmons, Michelle Obama, and Amy Schumer. The total bill was something close to $1 billion. Want some context for this? That $1 billion was more than the free cash flow Spotify had generated in 2016, 2017, 2018, and 2019 combined. Yes, this was a *Big* Bet. Kind of like Netflix and streaming.

Is this product innovation in the traditional sense? No. But from a Spotify consumer experience, it certainly was. For the same basic $9.99 a month, Spotify listeners could essentially get ad-free access to pretty much all recorded music plus a growing library of high-quality podcasts on a wide variety of topics—comedy, news and politics, true crime, celebrities, and so on. For most Spotify paid subscribers, they were getting more bang for their buck. Their Spotify experience was improving.

Did this product innovation work? Yes, but first let's briefly go through the setup.

Spotify was founded in Stockholm, Sweden, in 2006 by Daniel Ek and Martin Lorentzon. It expanded into the United Kingdom in 2009 and into the United States in 2011. It currently operates in almost every country around the world, save China, North Korea, and a handful of others. In 2011, Spotify announced that it had 1 million paying subscribers. By the end of 2020, that number was over 150 million, with total monthly active users (MAUs) around 350 million. Spotify is a freemium model, which means that it offers both a free ad-supported music streaming service and a paid subscription ad-free service. It is currently the largest music/audio service in the world, with arguably 2x more users than any other service.

Spotify IPO'd on April 3, 2018, with a reference price of $132. I initiated coverage in late March with a Buy rating and a $220 PT. (This was a direct listing versus a traditional IPO, so the research publishing rules were different.) The title of my initiation report was: "I SPOT the Sheriff," which in hindsight was a silly title. My simplified Long thesis was: Music is going streaming. Streaming is going global. Spotify is the global leader and has sustainable competitive advantages. SPOT's business model is inflecting up. And valuation is reasonable. And my price target implied almost 70% upside.

What happened to the stock for the next two years was pretty much nothing. Very similar to Stitch Fix (see Figure 5.3). From its IPO price of $132 in April 2018 to $140 in early April 2019 and back to $132 in early April 2020, SPOT basically had no change over two years. That means it slightly outperformed the S&P 500, which slipped 4% over those two years, thanks in large part to the

FIGURE 5.3 The SPOT Unlock—Brought to You by Product Innovation

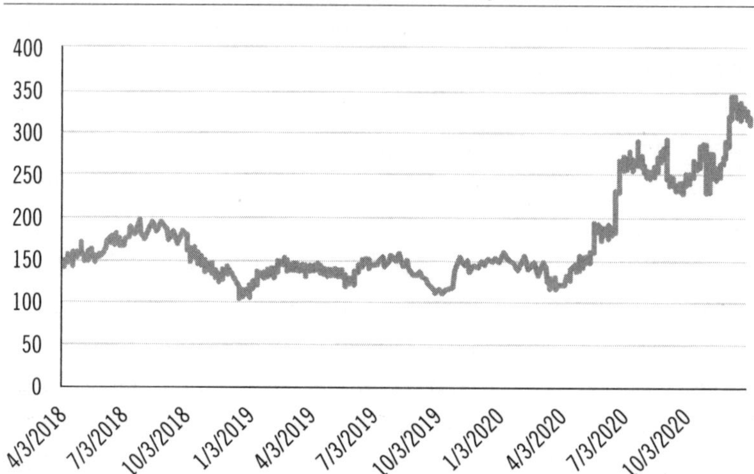

late February 2020 Covid-19 crash. But there was no material outperformance by SPOT, despite the fact that it had generated premium revenue growth (20%+) for at least four straight years. And it had generated accelerating new MAUs from 2016 to 2019, adding 32 million in 2016, 36 million in 2017, 48 million in 2018, and 64 million in 2019.

The stock was suffering under an overhang of pressures related to low gross margins, thanks in part to the stranglehold on industry economics that the major music labels had, and pressures related to declining ARPU (average revenue per user), thanks in part to strong Spotify user growth in poorer economic regions like Asia (where pricing was lower) and a mix shift to lower-revenue-generating family and student plans. What the stock needed was an unlock, and that's where product innovation and podcasting came in.

Although Spotify's significant podcasting initiatives began in early 2019, they didn't really start to impact the key customer metrics until 2020. Over the first three quarters of 2020, Spotify experienced increased subscriber retention and accelerating monthly average users, with the stock responding in kind, rising 109% in

2020, finally breaking through its August 2018 all-time high of $192 in June of 2020 and then soaring materially higher. Whereas there were clearly tech companies that benefited from Covid-19 conditions—Zoom, Netflix, and Amazon were three of the biggest winners—Spotify was not one of them. It didn't experience a major positive inflection in its revenue growth or in its key user metrics. But it did experience a notable improvement in its user metrics, thanks largely to the appeal of podcasting.

There's more to the story than just Spotify aggressively investing in podcasting product innovation and unlocking its stock. For one thing, Spotify's podcast investment timing was good. I had been running user surveys on online music and podcasting for eight years, and 2020 was the first year that substantially more than 50 percent of US online households listened to podcasts. Second, podcasting created an opportunity for the company to diversify its revenue streams somewhat—to generate more ad revenue—and to potentially improve its gross margin, as podcasting generated ad revenue that wouldn't need to be shared with the major music labels. Third, podcasting increased the overall value of the Spotify service, allowing the company to eventually increase its subscription fees to its users.

My personal exposure to the joys of podcasting came with the hit HBO series *Chernobyl*, which won the Golden Globe for Best Miniseries in early 2020. I found the five-part series totally riveting and learned that there was a five-hour podcast on the series, which I devoured on Spotify. At a November 2019 investment conference, I hosted outgoing SPOT CFO Barry McCarthy and incoming CFO Paul Vogel, breaking away from the Q&A transcript to let them and the audience know how much of a game changer that podcast had been for me. That experience—the thrill of the Chernobyl podcast—helped push SPOT high in my Buy List stack ranking for 2020.

So here's another example of just how powerful successful product innovation can be as a fundamental and as a stock catalyst, even if acquired. Keep your eyes and ears open, and you'll come across other examples that might well create good stock-picking opportunities.

Why Spotify Beat Pandora

In March 2021, Spotify carried a market cap of over $50 billion. In February 2019, Pandora was acquired by SiriusXM for $3.5 billion, meaning that Spotify reached a value almost 15x greater than what Pandora was acquired for two years ago. So Spotify won. Why? What are the investing lessons?

Spotify and Pandora are similar in several ways. They were both early music streaming pioneers. Pandora was founded in 2000, while Spotify was founded in 2006. They both faced the challenge of extracting economics in an industry with a concentrated supplier base—i.e., the three major music labels (Universal, Sony, and Warner Music) own the vast majority of modern recorded music rights. They also both faced stiff competition from the same three large technology platforms—Apple, Google, and Amazon. Finally, both combined ad-supported and paid subscription offerings to consumers, although Pandora leaned more heavily on its ad-supported offering, while Spotify leaned more heavily on its paid subscription offering.

Spotify and Pandora are different in several ways, however, and these differences probably help explain why Spotify won. First, Spotify has been better at product innovation, the key theme of this lesson. This is hard to demonstrate, but survey work I ran over the years certainly suggested that Spotify's features were preferred by consumers to Pandora's. What is demonstrable is the materially higher level of R&D spend at Spotify than at Pandora. Over 2016–2018, Spotify spent approximately 3x more on R&D than Pandora ($1.1 billion versus $350 million). Second, Spotify, in part due to its European roots, was always more global than Pandora. Pandora did briefly expand into Australia and New Zealand, but the company was for all intents and purposes a solely US company. Spotify ended up expanding into almost all international markets, except China and a small handful of other countries. Which meant that Spotify faced a larger TAM than Pandora, which in turn meant that it could better tap into scale benefits. Finally, Spotify benefited from a more consistent, founder-led management team. Cofounder Ek has remained CEO of Spotify throughout its existence. Over the five-year period 2013–2017, Pandora had five different CEOs.

So that's why Spotify won. And it suggests that relentless product innovation, large TAMs, and excellent management teams are key factors in company and stock success. Look for them.

WHAT HAPPENS WHEN YOU DON'T GET PRODUCT INNOVATION RIGHT—TWITTER

Pull up a stock chart of Twitter (TWTR) since its IPO, and you'll see a smile (Figure 5.4). You won't smile. You'll see a smile. You'll see the TWTR stock line start up on the left, curve downward for three

FIGURE 5.4 The TWTR Stock Chart Smile

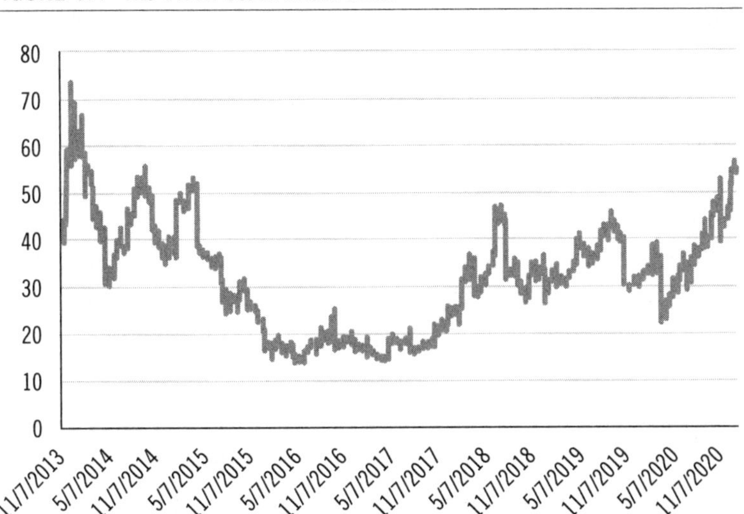

years, curve upward for three years, and return in late 2020 to the level where it was in early 2014. A bit crooked, but a smile nonetheless.

That smile can be interpreted several ways, but it doesn't suggest success for long-term investors who bought in at the IPO. Or bought a year later. Or a year after that. As with most stocks, there are cherry-picking opportunities. Buying TWTR in the mid-to-high teens it sustained for almost all of 2016 and 2017 and trading out of that position in mid-2018 or holding it for the second half 2020 Internet advertising stock rally would have generated market-beating returns. But what is particularly noteworthy about the stock chart history is the substantial period that TWTR was a broken IPO stock—the roughly four years from its IPO before it could sustain levels above its IPO price. And even then, not dramatically until the second half of 2020. There are several key reasons, but one has to do with unsuccessful product innovation. First, the quick stock history.

Twitter IPO'd on November 7, 2013, at $26 and soared 73% on its first trading day to close at almost $46. It continued to rise and reached $69 at the beginning of January, two months later. TWTR didn't see that price again for seven years. Nor, after it broke down to $38 in early May 2015 after unusually weak March quarter EPS results, would it see $46 again until briefly in mid-2018 and briefly again in mid-2019. Over the entirety of 2016 and 2017, TWTR was a "broken IPO," with its share price meaningfully below its $26 IPO price. TWTR ended 2020 at $54, up a bit less than 20% from its first day closing price of $46—over more than seven years. There must be a lesson in here somewhere.

There is, but some quick company background is useful. Twitter was founded in March 2006 by Jack Dorsey, Noah Glass, Biz Stone, and Evan Williams. Twitter is a microblogging and social networking service, which allows users to post and respond to comments with messages known as tweets. Some of those tweets became famous, such as when on May 1, 2011, Sohaib Athar tweeted: "Helicopter hovering above Abbottabad at 1am (is a rare event)," which marked the first live-blogging of the Osama bin Laden raid. Ellen DeGeneres tweeted a picture from the 2014 Oscars showing Brad Pitt, Meryl Streep, Bradley Cooper, and other famous celebs, and that pic was retweeted 3.1 million times. Tweets in March 2011 warned Japanese citizens about a massive 8.9 magnitude earthquake and what soon became the Fukushima disaster. President Donald Trump used Twitter for four straight years to dictate policy, including to sack senior administration officials.

Twitter helped shape the zeitgeist. It still does. Twitter now has over 200 million users. It has generated positive and substantial free cash flow for six straight years. Its revenue base has almost tripled since its IPO, from $1.4 billion in 2014 to a path to well over $4 billion in 2021. And yet there's still that disappointingly long smile.

Part of TWTR's challenge has been revenue. Similar to Snap's, throughout its first two years as a public company, Twitter's growth steadily decelerated—from 116% year-over-year in the December quarter of 2013 to 20% in the June quarter of 2016—which caused its price-to-sales ratio to steadily derate from 17x to 5x over that time. Growth continued to deteriorate after that June 2016 quarter and on an annual basis only exceeded 20% once (in 2018) with a shocking 3% revenue decline in 2017, before surging to 28% in the December quarter of 2020. Shocking because this was from a company competing in a secular growth industry (online advertising) that was growing at least 15% year-over-year, from a company that enjoyed global brand awareness, and from a company that had a large base of users.

For five years—from 2016 to 2020—Twitter consistently had the weakest fundamental results of all the major Internet advertising platform companies—Facebook, Google, Pinterest, and Snap. Not in terms of margins, but in terms of what investors most cared about—revenue growth. Over this time period, marketing spend was clearly migrating toward the Internet, but Twitter was last in line in terms of the major net ad platforms.

It's hard to blame any one factor for Twitter's fundamental and stock challenges over 2014–2019, but it's also hard not to pin at least part of the blame on weak product development at the company. And perhaps on the company's unusual management structure. These factors consistently kept me at either a Hold or a Sell on TWTR over the seven-year period, with the brief error of a Buy for six months post its IPO.

By "weak product development," I mean largely the tools that Twitter made available to advertisers to launch and manage advertising campaigns on the platform. Part of this may be due to the limited targetability of a platform that has always allowed its users to remain anonymous. Twitter could know me as @toptechstockpicker (*not* my real handle), but Facebook would know me as Mark Mahaney, with an enormous amount of demographic and psychographic detail to work with. Twitter's early pitch to marketers was that while Facebook had a user's social graph, Twitter had a user's interest graph—which bloggers and other Twitter users they were following. But that likely gave marketers only a limited understanding of its users. And Twitter didn't have the functionality to allow users to follow specific topics (such as venture capital, the Oscars, University of Maryland men's basketball) until late 2019.

To its credit, Twitter's management team acknowledged its product development shortcomings at its February 25, 2021, Analyst Day. CEO Jack Dorsey specifically acknowledged that the company was slow and not innovative enough:

> [W]e agree we haven't been innovative. This is very closely related to the critique of our slowness. If we can't ship code fast, we can't experiment and iterate, and every launch comes with massive expectation and cost. A few years ago it may have taken 6 months to a year to get a single feature or new product to our customers. While we are in a better position today, consistently bringing this down to under a few weeks is a goal of ours.

Twitter was also in the unfortunate position of being dramatically smaller (one-tenth the size) than Facebook and Google in terms of users, with no shot at competing on reach and frequency, which marketers care a *lot* about. Snap offered an interesting hold on the youth demographic. And Pinterest arguably had commercial intent—users were on Pinterest looking for house-decorating ideas, for example, in order to . . . you know . . . decorate their houses. All Twitter had was a lot of anonymous users, a fair amount of crude, nasty, negative commentary (until that was belatedly forced out), and this "interest graph." The upshot of all this was that Twitter had to execute flawlessly on product innovation, and the hard truth is that the company didn't.

Two recent examples come to mind. The first is when Twitter reported disappointing September quarter 2019 results, with revenue and operating income badly missing Street estimates, sending the stock down 20% in one day. Management blamed "revenue product issues," citing "bugs" that impacted Twitter's ability to target ads and to share data with its advertising partners. The second example occurred a year later, when Twitter reported mixed September quarter 2020 results, again sending the stock down 20% in one day. The biggest negative for the Street was a dramatic slowdown in user adds, but the company also disappointed by delaying until 2021 a key ad product improvement that investors were eagerly counting on to reaccelerate growth. Again, given its somewhat challenging position in the online advertising industry, Twitter had to execute flawlessly on product innovation, and it just wasn't doing that.

It's hard not to compare the product development, fundamentals, and share price challenges at Twitter with those at Snap (Table 5.3). Although Snap had its fair share of product development snafus early on (especially, integration challenges on Android devices), it has also rolled out a series of highly innovative features for both users and advertisers over the last few years that has created a much larger user base, along with consistently and dramatically faster

TABLE 5.3 Comparing Key Fundamentals at TWTR (*top*) and SNAP (*bottom*)

	2017	2018	2019	2020
Ad Revenue ($MM)	**2,100**	**2,617**	**2,993**	**3,207**
Y/Y Growth	–6%	24%	14%	7%
mDAU (MM)	**115**	**126**	**152**	**192**
Y/Y Growth	—	9%	21%	27%

	2017	2018	2019	2020
Total Revenue ($MM)	**825**	**1,180**	**1,716**	**2,506**
Y/Y Growth	104%	43%	45%	46%
mDAU (MM)	**176**	**188**	**205**	**245**
Y/Y Growth	22%	7%	9%	19%

mDAU = monetizable daily active users.

advertising revenue growth. It's the key reason SNAP's stock chart doesn't resemble an elongated smile, though it certainly shares the initial downward slope.

Has product innovation really been materially better at Snap than at Twitter? This is hard to prove, other than to point to the product issues that Twitter itself responsibly disclosed. I also believe this would be a hard call for a retail—or even a professional—investor to make. But there has been one tell about the strong product innovation at Snap that any investor could pick up on: the numerous examples of new features at Snap that have been copied by Facebook. From Snap-like geofilters and selfie masks to Snap's Stories feature to Snap's product orientation around the phone camera, there are numerous examples of Facebook following in Snap's footsteps. You can Google "What Snap features did Facebook copy" and find a series of published articles with other examples. This was not a secret. Nor was it illegal. Snap CEO Evan Spiegel took it all in stride, publicly stating that Facebook's copycatting "bothers my wife more than it bothers me." The takeaway for investors may well be that a reasonably good sign that a company is good at product innovation is when its competitors emulate its products. Imitation may well be the sincerest form of successful product innovation.

Twitter's checkered track record on product innovation may be due to its unusual management structure—the fact that Jack Dorsey, its CEO, is simultaneously the CEO of Twitter and Square. Now there are several examples of successful two-firm CEOs, such as Elon Musk, who has been extraordinarily innovative with Tesla. And Dorsey's other company, Square, has been enormously successful in the public markets. I also believe Dorsey deserves the highest of praise for cofounding two different successful businesses. He has to go down as one of the greatest entrepreneurs of our generation.

I recall a conversation I had with Dorsey during the mid-2015 Square IPO research analyst meeting. I specifically asked him how he could possibly balance the demands of being CEO of two companies at the same time. He looked me straight in the eye, warmly put his hand on my shoulder, and said: "I am extremely efficient with my time." I smiled and walked away thinking, "I'm pretty damn efficient with my time, too, working as a Wall Street analyst, raising four sons, trying to keep up with all the new Netflix series, but I don't think it's possible to run two S&P 500 companies simultaneously." I'd still lean in on the idea that a half-present CEO might have been one factor behind some of the product development challenges Twitter has experienced from time to time, but I admire Dorsey's success and confidence.

I'd like to close out this Twitter review with the observation that successful product innovation is not binary. A company may have a mixed track record of product innovation, but this doesn't have to be a permanent condition. In early 2021, Twitter is in fact showing tentative evidence of improved product innovation, thanks in part to a rebuilt ad server and a slew of reasonably new product features like Fleets (ephemeral stories), Spaces (live audio chats), a more robust Topics offering, and a new subscription product. If the company can get this right, these product innovations could well drive a fundamental inflection point and finally boost TWTR well above its IPO price.

Product innovation matters. Successful product innovation is one of the biggest drivers of fundamentals, especially revenue growth, and that's what drives stocks. Successful product innovation can generate entirely new revenue streams (Amazon with cloud computing), replace existing revenue streams (Netflix with DVDs and streaming), and enhance existing revenue streams and boost key customer metrics (Spotify with podcasting, plausibly Stitch Fix with direct buy functionality). Successful product innovation can be a significant driver of stock prices over time, if you can spot it.

Product innovation is spottable. Few public investors, including me, realized early on how revolutionary cloud computing would be, how sizable a market opportunity it presented. But cloud computing did become a widely reported-upon trend in the years after AWS was launched, and all an investor had to do was realize that this could be a material opportunity and that it was being led by a company initially famous for selling books online and conclude that Amazon was an innovative company. The cost of doing due diligence on Netflix's streaming innovation? $7.99. Some of the most interesting product innovation going on today is consumer-driven—think of gig economy companies like Airbnb, DoorDash, Lyft, and Uber that barely existed 10 years ago. You're a consumer. You can try out the services, and if you find one you really love, it could be the making of a great stock idea. Finally, when you see one company's innovations aggressively copied by others (Snap's features copied by Facebook), chances are that first company is a legitimate innovator.

Product innovation is a repeatable offense. A company or a management team that generates one or two impressive product innovations may well have the ability to continue to generate more innovations. When a company such as an Amazon "invents" online retail, cloud computing, and Kindles, it likely has the ability to innovate in other areas (like advertising revenue or Echo devices or cashier-less stores) because it has processes in place or a culture or a management team that fosters successful product innovation. If Netflix can successfully innovate on streaming, then it may well be able to successfully innovate on original content and then local-language original content—which is what it has done. Sometimes past success *is* an indicator of future performance.

LESSON 6

TAMs—The Bigger the Better

TAM matters. The bigger the total addressable market, the greater the opportunity for premium revenue growth, which is a major driver of tech and growth stocks. And TAMs can be expanded, by removing friction and by adding new use cases. Sometimes, TAMs are hard to ascertain, especially when a traditional industry is being disrupted. This requires creative new approaches to sizing market opportunities. Finally, large TAMs can help drive growth that can lead to scale, which has intrinsic benefits in the form of experience curves, unit economics advantages, competitive moats, and network effects. Scale wins. And large TAMs increase the opportunities for companies to tap into these scale benefits.

Total addressable market, or TAM, is the second key driver for revenue, the most important of the fundamentals, which in turn drives stocks. Here we go.

In finance there is a concept called the law of large numbers. This concept is a bastardized version of a statistics and probability theorem, and it essentially states that as companies get larger, their growth rates will inevitably slow. It makes total sense . . . but not always.

Here's a thought experiment. You have two companies. Company A is generating $10 billion a year in revenue; Company B is generating $100 billion. All things equal, which company will grow faster? The law of large numbers would tell you Company A. But what if Company A is competing in a $50 billion market, and Company B is competing in a $1 trillion market? So Company A accounts for 20% of its TAM, while company B accounts for 10%. You probably get the point. And you're probably arguing that the "all things equal" caveat was misleading.

The really key point is that while size certainly does impact growth rate potential, TAM is even more important. That's why Google (Company B) was able to sustain premium revenue growth (20%+) for so many years (10 years!), despite the fact that its revenue base approached and then exceeded $100 billion.

TAM is an extremely important factor to consider when investing because it helps determine revenue growth. It's one of the biggest lessons I learned over the years. And, yes, the bigger the better.

Professional investors know this well. That's exactly why almost every public company—and every private company looking to go public—starts off its investor pitch presentation with its TAM projections. The pitch onion usually gets peeled back like this:

1. We face this enormous $XYZ billion TAM.
2. We are the leader/one of the leaders competing against this enormous $XYZ billion TAM.
3. Here's a quick glimpse at our strategy for gaining even more share of that enormous $XYZ billion TAM.
4. Our technology stack is perfectly suited to support our growth plans against that enormous $XYZ billion TAM.

5. Our management team is chock-full of experienced rock stars, and we will prevail in our plans to win against that enormous $XYZ billion TAM.
6. Did we mention that we face this enormous $XYZ billion TAM?

So, yes, TAM is an important factor. It's also one that is "creatively" estimated, projected, and tabulated. The bigger the TAM a company can convincingly project, the more positively analysts and investors might consider that company's stock. I have also seen examples of when TAM is misunderstood or underappreciated. The key point for an investor is that understanding a company's TAM is a critical part of doing homework on a potential investment. Bigger TAMs create more revenue growth opportunities for companies and enable significant scale benefits.

GOOGLE—NOT A CONVENTIONAL COMPANY, NOT A CONVENTIONAL TAM

Google's S1 filing (its 2004 IPO document) began with a letter from its founders Sergey Brin and Larry Page. The first two sentences read: "Google is not a conventional company. We do not intend to become one."

Google largely lived up to this promise. It included the goals "don't be evil" and "make the world a better place" in its founders' letter. It promoted and maintained at its headquarters a college campus–like atmosphere of creativity and challenge, replete with gourmet cafes open day and night. Its first Analyst Day featured a presentation not by its CFO, George Reyes, but by its executive chef, Charlie Ayers. I criticized this in the investor report I published the morning after the event, to which the head of Google investor relations (Lise Buyer, now a good friend) heatedly responded: "What would you have had our CFO discuss?! You know we don't talk about short-term financial goals." To which I responded, "I dunno. How about long-term financial goals?!"

Google was unconventional in maintaining a long-term investment horizon. It never bothered to provide the Street with quarterly financial guidance. The management team was perfectly willing to experiment with intra-quarter search algorithm changes, even if that caused Street quarterly estimates to be missed. This long-term orientation turned out to be a major positive for Google investors.

What was also unconventional about Google was that it never really tried to spell out or estimate or quantify its TAM. Looking back on Google's S1 filing 18 years later, it's the one big missing piece. Look at the S1 of almost any major public online advertising company, and you'll see some reference to or a discussion of the global advertising market. The 2019 Pinterest S1, for example, refers to an $826 billion global advertising market in its Market Opportunity section. There's nothing like that in the Google S1.

I don't know why the Google S1 didn't concretely address the company's TAM. My guess is the management team either didn't feel it was necessary, given how much interest the offering was going to command, or honestly didn't know how to size the real market opportunity. How big was the market for a service that provided the world's information to the world's population? Or for a service that allowed any marketer anywhere to put its ad in front of a consumer looking for exactly what that marketer was hawking? The opportunity was enormous. And from almost the beginning, that created premium revenue growth opportunities for Google and helped drive the share price higher for years and years.

The Brief Story of Google

Google was founded by Page and Brin in 1998 while they were PhD students at Stanford University. Their bold goal was to instantly deliver relevant information on any topic for anybody anywhere in the world. They accomplished this—at least better than anyone else has been able to so far—by deploying a proprietary algorithm called PageRank that ranked all web pages based on the number and quality of links to that page. Magic!

The founders' letter in the S1 declared that the company strove to provide users "with great commercial information." The financial win here was that a significant percentage of searches on Google (perhaps a third) did have commercial intent—for example, how can I find the cheapest flights to Houston, where can I buy a baseball catcher's mitt, how can I hire a good medical malpractice lawyer. And there were many marketers who were keen to pay to advertise directly against those searches.

There are two key points that help explain why Google has always faced such an enormous TAM—and premium revenue growth—opportunity.

First, Google dramatically eased people's access to information. Google made it relatively easy to find almost anything on the Internet. And since the whole wide world was moving onto the Internet, Google made it relatively easy to find almost anything in the whole wide world . . . quickly . . . and for free. Just think how often you "Google it." Over time, Google has turned fact-memorization into a quaint, antique activity. Why memorize anything when you can just Google it? And Google, along with its video sidekick YouTube, has become one of the greatest teaching tools of our generations.

Second, Google also created one of the greatest advertising and marketing vehicles of all time. Really. You see, with Google search you only pay when someone clicks on your ad and comes to your website. No marketing dollars are wasted on "impressions." Did they really see and pay attention to my billboard while walking through Times Square? Who knows? Now, someone may click on your search ad, come to your website, and then not buy the product or service you are hawking, but at least you know where your marketing money is going. You know that it generates leads for your business. Which means you can calculate exactly what the ROI (return on investment) on your Google search spend is. Better yet, you can generate practically any ROI you want with your Google search spend.

The search math goes something like this. Say you own a boutique hotel in Sonoma, California, and you want to drum up business, that is, put some heads on those fluffy pillows. You bid on the search term "boutique hotels in Sonoma" and decide to pay $3 each time someone clicks on your paid search link on Google. And your search ad only shows up when someone explicitly types in "boutique hotels in Sonoma." Then say the percentage of times someone comes to your website and actually books a room is 10%—a 10% conversion rate. The average stay is two days, and the average price per room night is $150. So for an effective cost of $30, you generate $300 in revenue, or $270 if you deduct the marketing expense. That's a 9-to-1 ROI on that marketing spend.

Two things are really neato about this example. First, with Google search you can actually calculate your ROI. At least, with a lot less guessing than with any impression-based ad model—did they see my ad or not? Second, you can dial up or down your ROI. Want to get more heads on those fluffy pillows? You can increase your bid for the "boutique hotels in Sonoma" search phrase and increase your positioning among the search results, boosting the number of clicks you will get. At $6 a click with the same conversion rate and price per room, you will generate $240 in contribution profit, or a 4-to-1 ROI. Or you can decide to generate a higher ROI by bidding only $2 per click, which would generate a 14-to-1 ROI. You will almost certainly generate fewer leads, as your positioning among search results will be lower. But your ROI is (largely) in your own hands. And that is the secret sauce of Google. A sauce so tasty that marketers have decided to make Google the single largest marketing channel in the world. True. Today, approximately 15 percent of all global marketing spend goes to one company—Google. Arguably, no company has ever had this strong a position before.

One industry expert who figured out early on how disruptive Google was going to be was Mel Karmazin, the former CEO of both CBS and Sirius Radio. Author Ken Auletta, in his great book *Googled: The End of the World as We Know It,* reveals the story of an early Karmazin visit to Google HQ. It was then, after hearing Google execs explain their business model, that Karmazin reportedly uttered the "famous" expression—"You're f&@#ing with the magic." Google was offering a superior marketing channel to all advertisers—better measurement, better analytics, more control, better results.

Put another way, there's a famous quote attributed to retail executive John Wanamaker: "Half the money I spend on advertising is wasted; the trouble is, I don't know which half." What Google did was allow you to see exactly what your ad dollars were delivering—how many leads and how many sales—and what exact percentage of your ad spend was being wasted. Magical indeed.

This background provides a sense of how disruptive Google was and how it could potentially tap into almost all global marketing dollars. Which, if you add those up, is likely somewhere near a trillion-dollar TAM. It's rare you come across companies with T TAMS (trillion-dollar TAMS). But when you do, they warrant extra study as an investment option. That's a major lesson from Google.

Google's Stock Performance

Google (GOOG, then later GOOGL) IPO'd on August 19, 2004, at $85 ($42.50 post the company's March 2014 two-for-one stock split), implying a market cap of approximately $24 billion. After a somewhat controversial IPO process, including possibly selective disclosure in the pages of *Playboy* magazine, the company entered the public market realm and never looked back. By the end of 2004, its share price had more than doubled to $96 (split-adjusted), and by the end of 2005, its share price had reached $207, implying a market cap of over $90 billion (Figure 6.1). If you had bought Google at the IPO, you would have almost tripled your money in 18 months!

FIGURE 6.1 GOOGL: What a 34-Bagger Looks Like

I'm not sure investors realize just how much of a monster stock GOOGL has been over the almost 17 years it has been in the public markets. It's not just that the stock has risen over 4,000% since its IPO, 17x better than the S&P 500 over the same time. GOOGL has consistently outperformed the market over a very long stretch of time.

Stock performance can be measured many different ways. Selective entry and exit points can be used to support almost any claim. But let me try a couple of straightforward approaches. Over the 16 full calendar years that GOOGL has been a public stock, it has outperformed the S&P 500 for 10 of those years. In the three 5-year blocks (2005–2010, 2010–2015, and 2015–2020), GOOGL has outperformed the S&P 500 each time—by 43x in 2005–2010, by 2x in 2010–2015, and by 3x in 2015–2020. (See Table 6.1.)

Beating the marketing by 43x is a lot more impressive than by 2x and 3x, I agree. But beating the market is still beating the market. And if you want to focus on simple absolute returns, which at the end of the day is what we all care about the most, GOOGL traded

TABLE 6.1 Consistent Outperformance by GOOGL

Multiperiod Return	GOOGL	S&P 500	Outperformance Factor
IPO–2020	4,024%	224%	16x
2005–2010	201%	5%	43x
2010–2015	148%	80%	2x
2015–2020	229%	83%	3x

up 201% from 2005 to 2010, 148% from 2010 to 2015, and 229% from 2015 to 2020.

As two last takes, you can compare every three-year period from 2005 to 2020 (so 2005–2007, 2006–2008, and so on) and see that GOOGL outperformed the S&P 500 in 12 of those 14 periods, with the only period of material underperformance being 2010–2012. You can also compare every two-year period and see that GOOGL outperformed the S&P 500 in 14 of those 15 periods, only underperforming in the 2010–2011 period (Table 6.2). The simple takeaway is that GOOGL has been a consistent and substantial outperformer for investors for many years.

Why has GOOGL been such a consistent and substantial stock outperformer for so many years? Because Google has been such a consistent and substantial fundamentals outperformer for so many years. I think the most powerful evidence of this is Google's revenue growth track record over the last decade. For the entire period 2010–2019, Google's revenue growth averaged 23%. That is 40 straight quarters. And we're starting that streak when Google's revenue base was approximately $25 billion, which today—a decade later—only a fifth of the S&P 500 are above. And just so we're airtight on those 40 quarters and that 23% average, the median for those 40 quarters was also 23%, which is a simple way of saying that Google's revenue growth over that decade was consistently close to 23%, with only six quarters below 20% (three at 19%, two at 18%, and one at 17%).

TABLE 6.2 **Search Yourself: How Impressive GOOGL's Performance Has Been**

3-YEAR RETURN	GOOGL	S&P500	OUTPERFORMANCE
2005–2007	250%	22%	228%
2006–2008	–27%	–29%	2%
2007–2009	33%	–21%	54%
2008–2010	–14%	–13%	–1%
2009–2011	109%	35%	74%
2010–2012	13%	26%	–13%
2011–2013	88%	45%	43%
2012–2014	62%	61%	1%
2013–2015	116%	40%	76%
2014–2016	42%	22%	20%
2015–2017	98%	30%	68%
2016–2018	37%	25%	13%
2017–2019	67%	43%	24%
2018–2020	66%	39%	27%

2-YEAR RETURN	GOOGL	S&P500	OUTPERFORMANCE
2005–2006	133%	18%	115%
2006–2007	64%	16%	48%
2007–2008	–34%	–36%	2%
2008–2009	–11%	–23%	12%
2009–2010	92%	35%	57%
2010–2011	3%	11%	–8%
2011–2012	19%	12%	6%
2012–2013	72%	45%	27%
2013–2014	47%	41%	7%
2014–2015	39%	12%	28%
2015–2016	49%	9%	40%
2016–2017	38%	33%	5%
2017–2018	31%	11%	19%
2018–2019	27%	20%	7%
2019–2020	71%	50%	21%

Very few companies have ever generated premium revenue growth this consistently at a scale like this. Actually, only two: Apple and Amazon. Certainly not Microsoft, which averaged 11% revenue growth for the 10 years after it achieved a $25 billion revenue run rate in 2001. Not Intel, which averaged 5% revenue growth for the 10 years after it achieved a $25 billion revenue run rate in 1997. Salesforce.com hasn't even reached a $25 billion run rate yet. Apple averaged 27% revenue growth for the 10 years after it hit the $25 billion level in 2007. Amazon averaged 28% revenue growth for the 10 years after it hit the $25 billion level in 2009. (See Table 6.3.)

TABLE 6.3 Who Has "Pulled a Google"?

TICKER	YEAR REACHED $25B REVENUE	10-YR AVG GROWTH POST
AMZN	2009	28%
AAPL	2007	27%
GOOGL	2009	23%
MSFT	2001	11%
INTC	1997	5%

This financial feat is so rare, I call it "pulling a Google"—a decade of 20%+ growth from a $25 billion revenue level. While that bar may be too high since only three companies have ever achieved it in recorded financial history, I've come to use that term to discuss companies that can generate premium revenue growth (20%+) for multiple years from a position of scale (a revenue base in the billions).

Google's TAM

This kind of financial success has lots of fathers and mothers. First, Google was a highly innovative company. A half dozen or more search engines existed before Google—AltaVista, Excite,

LookSmart, WebCrawler, Lycos, Yahoo! Search, to name a few—and many more came out after: Overture, Ask Jeeves, Inktomi, MSN Search, DuckDuckGo. But the best mousetrap belonged to Google, as measured by that most objective of measures—the number of users. Google's share of global search has always been exceptionally high—70% or higher with a 90%+ share in many markets. Second, Google has throughout its history remained an intensely innovative company; its current investment spend levels (including R&D and capital expenditures) are close to $50 billion a year. Few companies have the capacity and the culture to invest at such high levels. Third, Google has generally executed well, both organically and in terms of some of its key acquisitions—especially YouTube and DoubleClick, two acquisitions that materially expanded its reach among advertisers.

But I believe TAM was also essential in helping Google maintain that premium revenue growth. If Yahoo! had been as innovative and effective as Google, it too could have delivered that extraordinary growth rate for so long. It too could have "pulled a Google." And the other company in the Internet advertising sector that has arguably been as innovative and effective as Google—Facebook—may possibly be able to replicate Google's revenue growth record—start with a $25 billion revenue base and grow revenue at a 20% CAGR for 10 years. Because the TAM these companies are targeting is *so* large—approximately $1 trillion.

That $1 trillion is a huge number and a somewhat soft number. I referenced earlier the $826 billion global advertising estimate in the Pinterest 2019 S1. When I attempted to size the global advertising and marketing market in research reports, I included brand advertising (approximately $450 billion), direct marketing (approximately $300 billion), and promotional spend (approximately $300 billion). That's how I got to $1 trillion. My estimates could have been high, but they could also have been low. And even being in the cheap seats in the $1 trillion ballpark is a massive market.

As an investor, you definitely want to look for large TAMs, which usually requires a company to have a successful global presence, because few markets are of this scale in the United States alone. As a soft rule of thumb, I always prefer companies with substantial international presences, because that implies access to a larger TAM. Google's advantage from the beginning was that it was extraordinarily successful in almost all international markets, with the most glaring exception being China. Since its IPO, Google has always generated at least 40% of its total revenue from international markets.

I also believe that Google was able to expand the TAM it faced by removing friction. Almost by definition, the Internet expanded the size of markets, by allowing business and service providers to cost-effectively expand their target markets. Or to better focus their local sales and marketing efforts. On top of that, Google introduced more powerful self-service tools, making it easier for any individual, organization, and business to run a marketing campaign on the Internet. There's no way that Google could have reached a base of close to the 10 million advertisers it has today if it hadn't made buying ads and running campaigns super simple.

And then there were major innovations like smartphones and voice-activated devices that allowed a broader, more frequent, and more convenient range of Google searches. In hindsight, it's surprising how much of a debate the proliferation of smartphones posed to the Google investment thesis. The Bearish concern for several years around 2010 was that Google wouldn't be able to monetize mobile search queries as well as desktop search queries, because the screens were smaller and the searches were more casual in nature or more location specific. But the overriding logic should always have been that the proliferation of smartphones simply removed friction. It made it easier for consumers to do more searches anytime and anywhere they wanted. And more searches meant more potential leads for marketers and advertisers, i.e., more TAM.

More TAM for Google meant more revenue growth potential, which, along with a profitable business model from the get-go, helped created a great performing long-term stock. So focus on TAMs.

My GOOGL Call

So did I call GOOGL correctly as a stock? The answer is a Big No and a Big Yes. I authored the very first formal Wall Street research report on Google. It was called, "A Conventional Look at an Unconventional IPO," and I wrote it the night that the Google S-1 dropped (April 29, 2004). At the time I was working at American Technology Research as its Internet analyst. Then I formally initiated coverage of Google the day after its IPO with a $110 price target (pre-split) and a Hold rating. I predicted that Google would be the "Beta King of 'Net Stocks.'" What I meant was that Google shares would be highly volatile, even by the standards of a volatile Internet sector. Turns out I was right, though only in the sense that GOOGL shares were volatile *up* over the next three years . . . volatile up like a rocket ship.

Then, in perhaps the single greatest mistake of my analyst career, I downgraded Google to a Sell prior to its first EPS report. I thought the 50% rise in the shares of GOOG prior to that print was excessive, and I believed Yahoo! to be the better fundamental asset. In hindsight, my mistake was threefold. I overly fixated on a near-term price move (I tried to play the quarter), I became too wedded to a stock (I preferred YHOO because I knew the asset better), and I underappreciated the disruptive potential and market opportunity of Google.

I predicted that Google wouldn't meet the lofty expectations of its first public quarter. Instead, on October 21, 2004, Google beat Street revenue estimates by more than 10% and Street EPS estimates by more than 20%. And GOOGL jumped 15% the next day, and kept rising for the balance of the year and well into 2005. In the meantime, I faced the wrath of *Kudlow & Cramer*, the most influential financial news TV show at the time. Because the night of Google's first earnings report—about an hour after the Google EPS results had been released and the stock was soaring in the aftermarket—that show featured two guests, the GOOGL Bull (an analyst named Jordan Rohan) and the GOOGL Bear (me).

Larry Kudlow first introduced Rohan as his "old buddy, old pal" and asked him to explain how he had so brilliantly gotten the Buy GOOG call so right. Then Jim Cramer turned to me with the following intro: "So, Mark, as the analyst with the three-egg omelet on your face, what do you have to say for yourself?" That may not be verbatim, but it is pretty close. One doesn't tend to forget moments like that. And what did I do? I had already mulled over what my response would be to a line of questioning I knew was coming. I knew I had to fess up. So I did. My words were to the effect, "Well, it's clear this guy [me] needs to go the Analyst Woodshed . . ." The rest of the interview was something of a blur. But I somehow escaped with a small shred of dignity. After I got off the air, Cramer complimented me for having the chutzpah to show up and acknowledge my mistake. Boy, what a mistake.

So that was the Big No in terms of how well I called GOOGL as a stock. The Big Yes is that I upgraded GOOGL shares to a Buy a few months later and consistently kept with that call for the next 16 years, with the exception of a small window around the Eric Schmidt–to–Larry Page CEO transition in 2011, when I temporarily switched to a Hold rating. A company with Google's TAM, Google's premium revenue growth track record, Google's extremely high level of innovation, and Google's profitability—you stick with that.

UBER AND DASH—DAMs, SAMs, AND TAMs

Here are two recently public companies that provide good examples of large TAMs—two companies that based solely on their TAMs should warrant at least a brief study by tech and growth investors.

I'll first cover Uber (UBER), the stock that was my top pick in 2020. I actually encouraged tech investors in early 2020 to add U to the FANG acronym out of respect for what I viewed as UBER's very Bullish prospects. I pitched FANGU! Then I watched that stock crater a truly gut-wrenching 63% from February 18 to March 18 in the teeth of the Covid-19 crisis, before recovering to end the year up over 65%, handily beating the market.

Uber filed its S1 with the SEC on April 11, 2020. It was overwhelming. As in the information and the data in that document were overwhelming. TMI. Figure 6.2 shows the key exhibit in the Market Opportunity section of the S1. It details Uber's global TAM, then its SAM (serviceable addressable market, i.e., the part of the global TAM that Uber was currently competing to win). Then it breaks that SAM into the Current SAM (the 57 countries Uber was currently competing in) and the Near-Term SAM (adding in six more countries that the company was planning to enter soon). The only thing missing was the DAM (direct addressable market),

FIGURE 6.2 Quantifying UBER's TAM, SAM, and DAM

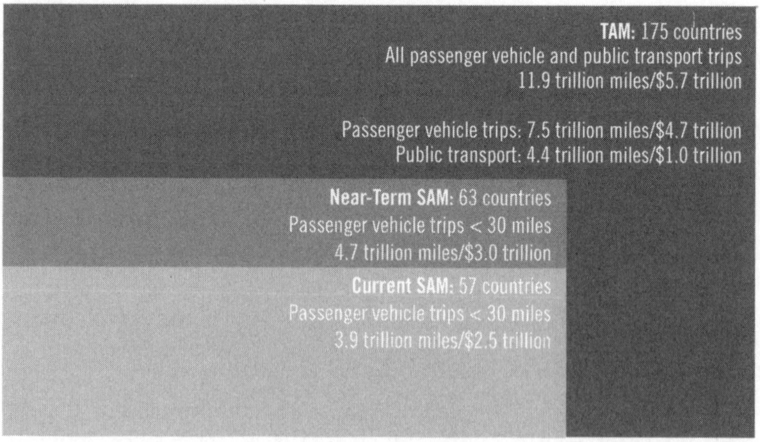

TAM: 175 countries
All passenger vehicle and public transport trips
11.9 trillion miles/$5.7 trillion

Passenger vehicle trips: 7.5 trillion miles/$4.7 trillion
Public transport: 4.4 trillion miles/$1.0 trillion

Near-Term SAM: 63 countries
Passenger vehicle trips < 30 miles
4.7 trillion miles/$3.0 trillion

Current SAM: 57 countries
Passenger vehicle trips < 30 miles
3.9 trillion miles/$2.5 trillion

Source: UBER S-1, US Federal Highway Administration, International Road Federation, OECD's International Transport Forum Outlook.

a concept I came up with out of frustration with the overwhelming amount of detail in the Market Opportunity section.

Sizing it all up, Uber claimed to face a $5.7 trillion global TAM. That is a uniquely massive TAM. The way the company got there was to estimate the total number of vehicle miles and public transportation miles in each country, based on government and industry data, and then multiply those by the cost per mile of vehicle ownership (approximately $0.65) and cost per mile spent on public transportation (approximately $0.25), also based on government and industry data. There was a heck of a lot of math behind these numbers, but only addition and multiplication were required to gut-check those numbers. The real unknown was the quality of the inputs, though the sources seemed legit.

There was also a simple implication behind this TAM. Uber was looking to offer itself as an alternative to *all* transportation needs. *That* is why the TAM was *so* huge. Was this a realistic way to present Uber's market opportunity? In 2014, Uber's bookings in cities like San Francisco were already multiples higher than the local markets for taxi and limousine services, suggesting that the service was becoming an alternative for a lot of transportation needs. So perhaps.

But what most investors really needed to focus on were five things. First, almost any way you cut it, Uber faced a massive TAM. Even if all the estimates were 5x overstated, you still faced a T TAM—a $1 trillion TAM. Second, this was the TAM in the company's core Mobility segment. It also faced large TAMs with its Uber Eats segment (perhaps $2.8 trillion global TAM) and its Uber Freight segment (perhaps $1 trillion+ TAM). Third, what the two prior points meant was that Uber was a platform company with multiple revenue streams, the value of which would come shining through when Covid-19 hit, decimating Uber's Mobility business but mega-boosting the Uber Eats business. Fourth, Uber was already a global platform, with operations in 60 countries and international markets already accounting for at least 40% of its total revenue. Fifth, by removing friction and expanding its use cases, Uber had been steadily expanding its TAM for many years.

This last point was highlighted in a public debate over Uber's valuation in 2014 between Aswath Damodaran, a business school professor at NYU and the author of one of the definitive books on valuation, and Bill Gurley, an early investor in Uber and one of the most experienced venture capital investors in tech. At the time, Damodaran attempted to value Uber as an urban car service and concluded that it was worth no more than $6 billion. Gurley responded that Damodaran's analysis may have underestimated Uber's market opportunity by 25x, because it failed to consider potential use cases like suburban usage, rental car alternative, mass transit alternative, and even car-ownership alternative. To his credit, Damodaran publicly thanked the tech investor for taking him to task for having too narrow a view of Uber's market opportunity.

Seven years later, what's now interesting about Uber is that Gurley's analysis may have underestimated Uber's market opportunity by 25x. OK, perhaps not by *that* much. But Gurley's analysis didn't contemplate Uber Eats or Uber Freight, and those two segments combined could be equal in size to Uber's Mobility business. And Gurley's analysis didn't contemplate these segments because Uber's management and board may not have even considered those opportunities or use cases until several years after 2014. But this is the wonderful thing about platform companies. They build out these businesses with large user bases, and then over time more segments and revenue streams can potentially be layered on. No criticism at all is implied here of Gurley's work. He's smarter, more experienced, and taller than almost every other investor (he's six feet, nine inches tall). And at least he used Uber as a service before trying to value it, unlike Damodaran, who (in)famously valued/analyzed Uber without ever having used the app. (Investors—please use a company's app before making any investment decision about a company's stock.)

Covid-19 pandemic crushed Uber's financials. With mobility shut down globally for much of 2020, Uber Mobility's revenue crashed 40% for the full year, and the company's total revenue declined 10% to around $13 billion. It will take a pretty full Covid-19 recovery and some time, but it's quite possible that Uber will get to that $25 billion revenue level by 2022, and given the size of its TAMs, it's also quite possible that Uber will be able to sustain premium revenue growth for many years after that point. Uber may just be able to "pull a Google," which may well make it a core holding for tech and growth investors.

The second example here is DoorDash (DASH), which IPO'd in December 2000 and promptly rose 86% on its first day. DoorDash generated enormous investor interest because it was already something of a household name when it went public (with over 18 million customers in the United States at the time of the IPO), it was perceived as a Covid-19 winner (one of the companies that saw a surge in demand due to shelter-in-place restrictions), and it was generating extraordinary growth rates (over 200% year-to-year revenue growth).

What was also important about DoorDash for long-term investors was how it described itself. The first sentence in the mission statement in the DASH S1 reads: "Our mission is to grow and empower local economies." To almost all consumers, DoorDash is known only as a food order delivery company. DoorDash delivers Chipotle, Little Caesars, Wing Stop, etc. Growing and empowering local economies sounds a lot broader than food order delivery. And it is meant to be.

Make no mistake, the core food order delivery market is large. The numbers go something like this. In 2019, Americans spent around $1.5 trillion on food and beverages, of which around $600 billion was spent in restaurants, with close to 50 percent of that consumed off-premises. So that's about a $300 billion to-go and food order delivery market. And Covid-19 quarantining has taught a lot of people that work from home also means eat from home, thanks to the increasing speed, selection, and convenience offered by companies like DoorDash, Uber Eats, and Grubhub. So that 50 percent may well be permanently higher in the future. The DASH S1 included a study from the National Restaurant Association that showed that 58 percent of US adults and 70 percent of all millennials were more likely to have restaurant food delivered than they were two years ago, and this study was conducted before Covid-19.

So DASH's food order delivery market is substantial. Whether the company will ever be able to claim a T TAM will depend on two things. First, whether DoorDash can successfully expand into international markets with its food order delivery business. At the time of the IPO, DASH claimed a presence only in Australia and Canada. So this is an unknown and would be key for future potential investors in DASH. That Uber already has a substantial global presence makes it easier to see consistent premium revenue growth at scale from that company than from DoorDash. So successful international expansion will be one key stock unlock factor for DASH going forward.

The second thing will be evidence that DoorDash really does begin to "grow and empower local economies." And by that the company means expanding from restaurants to grocery, convenience, and potentially other specialty retail verticals, such as pet supply stores. Consumers themselves will decide and determine this. The action question for whether food order delivery would work as an industry—that is, would there be sufficient consumer demand—was: Would enough consumers be willing to pay somewhere between \$5 and \$10 for the convenience of having meals delivered to their location within approximately 30 minutes? Given the size of the food order delivery business to date, the answer seems to be an emphatic *yes*! But the answer to that action question for other verticals (groceries, convenience store items, etc.) is less clear. And that is key to determining the real TAM for a company like DASH. Success in those newer categories would almost certainly expand DASH's end market (just in the United States alone) over the $1 trillion threshold.

Professional investors will run extensive consumer surveys and analyze credit card data to try to answer that question. Regular investors won't have that luxury. They'll just have to rely on their own logic, intuition, and experiences, as I did when I noticed the increasing number of 7 Now deliveries (powered by DoorDash) being picked up in the local 7-11 in my small suburban town . . . and when I noticed the occasional order my then 13-year-old son was placing on that app.

Whether the use case really does materially expand to groceries and convenience stores for DoorDash and other companies like Uber and Lyft will be important to try to monitor because it will help determine whether a company like a DASH faces a T TAM with substantial premium revenue growth opportunities or not. The bigger the TAM, the stronger the revenue growth outlook, the greater the stock potential.

Another simple lesson from my DASH experience was: Read the fine (mission statement) print. It often suggests how big a company's TAM might be.

SPOTIFY—WHEN CREATIVITY AND INSIGHT ARE NEEDED TO UNDERSTAND TAMS

Spotify's S1 provided two key datapoints to help investors size up its TAM. First, citing one industry source, Spotify pointed to global recorded music industry revenue in 2016 of $16 billion. Second, citing another industry source, Spotify pointed to global radio advertising revenue of $28 billion. So that maths out to a $44 billion global TAM.

A $44 billion global TAM is solid, but it's not dramatically large. It was accurate for Spotify in that the company generates both subscription and advertising revenue and Spotify has always had a global presence, with the United States accounting for a minority of its overall revenue. But it was problematic in two ways. First, when Spotify went public, its initial guidance implied about $6 billion in revenue in 2018, meaning that Spotify already accounted for over 10% of its TAM. Second, it implied that Spotify would never be able to "pull a Google" in the fullest sense. Were it to reach $25 billion in revenue, it would already account for over 50% of its TAM. And growing 20% per year after that would have it gobble up its entire TAM within four years. All of this clearly implied that Spotify would soon hit a growth wall—that is, it would soon experience a dramatic deceleration in its growth rate.

Now, few companies will be able to "pull a Google" in the fullest sense. (Again, only three have ever done it, as far as I can tell.) Not many companies will actually face a T TAM. And that's fine. Smaller TAMs can enable premium revenue growth for multiple years, just not from dramatic scale levels. I've often wondered whether the right investing lesson is simply to focus on companies with a low-single-digit percentage share of their TAM. But what you really want to find are companies that can scale to large revenue bases, because there are inherent advantages to scale. So the ideal combo is a company with a low-single-digit percentage share of a large TAM. Following that in the pecking order is a company with a chunky double-digit percentage share of a large TAM. Then in order comes the company with a low-single-digit percentage share of a small TAM. There are lots of variations on this depending on the actual percentage share and the actual TAM size, but this rule of thumb can help.

I refer back to Priceline for this point. Here's a company that sustained super premium (30%+) revenue growth (in this case Bookings growth) for essentially a decade up through 2014, in part because it consistently comprised a single-digit percentage of a $1 trillion+ TAM—global travel. It wasn't quite able to "pull a full Google," generating 20%+ growth for "only" five years after it hit the $25 billion Bookings level in 2012. So Priceline "pulled a half Google"! But that small market share and that large TAM combo dramatically boosted its revenue growth opportunity. PCLN arguably didn't reach a double-digit market share until perhaps 2019. So again, look for that delightful combo of single-digit market share and large TAMs.

At the time I was looking to initiate on Spotify, I believed a more creative way to look at the company's TAM was required than just looking at global recorded music industry revenue and global radio advertising revenue. Why? Because those were historic, legacy markets. Legacy markets? Yes. Global recorded music industry revenue included a category called physical sales revenue—CDs, LPs, cassettes—and the digital sales revenue category included permanent downloads. As those categories had faded over the years, something had come in to supplant them. Or that something was what caused those categories to fade in the first place. And that something was smartphones.

I and professional investors ran plenty of surveys over the following years to track this, but the real trick to discovering Spotify's true TAM was to realize that music had become one of the leading apps on *all* smartphones. The mental exercise I asked clients to consider was this: If you were to look at the front screens of 1,000 random smartphones pulled from around the world, what percentage do you think would have a music app on that front screen? I didn't know what the actual answer was, but my strong inclination was that it would be 90%+.

You could do a simple Google search of "top app downloads" and see that Spotify usually ranked as a top 20 download in many countries. Or you could have realized that almost all smartphones come preloaded with some sort of music app. But clearly, this global music market was vastly different from that of pre-smartphone 8-track tape days. It was time to come up with a better TAM construct, and to recognize that smartphones had dramatically reduced friction for the music entertainment industry by allowing users to gain access to all music 24-7 via the device they tended to have at their side 24-7.

My team and I came up with a better TAM construct. Multiple sources suggested that there would be more than 3 billion smartphone users worldwide (excluding China) within a few years. Assuming that half of these could be customers of free, ad-supported services and half would be paid subscribers, we created the analysis in Table 6.4.

TABLE 6.4 Getting Smart About Spotify's TAM

Addressable Market	Monthly ARPU	Smartphone Users	TAM Value (B)
Ad-Supported	$1.00	1.5B	$18
Premium Subscription	$6.00	1.5B	$108
Total TAM			$126

The assumptions were simple. Maybe overly simple. But I think they were much more appropriate than using legacy industry estimates and much more reflective of the actual use case that Spotify and other streaming music services were offering. Spotify and Pandora (another music streaming service) each disclosed their ad-supported ARPU (annual revenue per user) that generally averaged around $1.00. Spotify's paid subscription service was generating close to a $6.00 ARPU at the time of the IPO. Spotify's S1 filing showed that roughly half of its users were paid subscribers and half were ad-supported free users. So we split the 3 billion smartphones into an equally sized group of paid subscribers and ad-supported free users, used those ARPUs, and voilà—a $126 billion TAM. Almost 3x what traditional industry sources would have suggested.

Was our TAM conclusion more accurate? It certainly was more logical, if you think about the consumer use case for music streaming. Given that Spotify has sustained 20%+ growth for the last three years, there is an indication that Spotify's real TAM was bigger than initially considered. There's also another key point. This construct suggests that Spotify may be able to generate premium key customer metric growth for numerous years. At the end of 2020, Spotify reported approximately 350 million total users. If the 3 billion smartphone base is really the right way to think about Spotify's market opportunity, then the idea that its customer base can double, triple, or even quadruple over a 10-year period could be considered a plausible outcome. Which would imply a lot of potential growth for Spotify over the long term.

The takeaway here is that while TAMs are crucial to consider, sometimes one needs to be creative in determining what they are, especially if they involve a company that is disrupting a traditional industry.

This smartphone TAM exercise can be helpful when thinking about a variety of apps or services that are used primarily or significantly via smartphones. Especially ones with legacy markets. Take Netflix and video streaming, for example. There are currently over 200 million accounts around the world that pay Netflix around $11 per month. Assuming two or three users per account, there are arguably around 500 million Netflix users around the world. Sounds like an extremely high number, one that likely wouldn't double or triple over a decade. But when you realize that there are 3 billion smartphone users and counting worldwide, that Netflix was one of the top 10 most downloaded apps worldwide in 2020 according to Apptopia, and that young people these days appear to use their smartphones as their primary screen, you might be open to the idea of consistently high growth for Netflix for the foreseeable future. (See Table 6.5.)

It's all a matter about being creative and logical with the TAM.

TABLE 6.5 The 10 Most Downloaded Apps Worldwide in 2020

1	TikTok	6	Messenger
2	WhatsApp	7	Snapchat
3	Facebook	8	Telegram
4	Instagram	9	Google Meet
5	Zoom	10	Netflix

Source: Apptopia.

WHAT ARE THE BENEFITS OF SCALE?

A couple of times in this lesson, I've mentioned the benefits of scale. Big TAMs lead to potentially lots of revenue growth, which leads to scale, which has benefits. But what are those benefits?

Following are four to keep in mind. Full-blown economists will have better, deeper explanations of these, but these come from my quarter century of observing companies that clearly achieved scale and those that didn't.

First, scale can provide benefits in the form of experience curves. Per Wikipedia, learning or experience curve effects express the relationship between experience producing a good and the efficiency of that production. I'll simplify that as follows—the more one does of something, the better one gets at it. I recall attending an industry trade show on search advertising in 2012 and coming across several employees from Expedia who were there explicitly to learn how and why industry leader Priceline was so effective at search advertising. The answer was that Priceline had been spending materially more on search advertising than Expedia. Priceline had done it longer and stronger than Expedia and had learned through that greater experience how to run a search marketing campaign more effectively, which was the single most important growth channel for online travel companies.

Second, scale provides unit economics advantages. Economics textbooks talk about fixed and variable costs. Fixed costs are those that stay constant regardless of the volume of production. Variable costs are those that rise or fall in proportion to the volume of production. In practice, I found the expression *step-fixed costs* to be more accurate than *fixed costs*. As companies like Amazon, Facebook, and Google grew over time, even their most "fixed" costs—G&A, headquarters overhead, legal expenses—rose to support their rising revenue bases. But the rise was much slower than the revenue growth and more step-like than variable. So these companies were able to show leverage—to reduce some of their operating costs as a percentage of their revenue. Growth—or scale—does drive margin expansion, sometimes dramatically and sometimes glacially, but it does drive it. You want a glacial example? Amazon's G&A went from $3.2 billion or 1.8% of revenue in 2017 to $5.6 billion or 1.6% in 2020, despite its revenue practically doubling. But as every professional investor knows, every little bip helps.

Third, scale can create *competitive moats* around businesses. Sometimes size is hard to compete with. And expensive. Netflix is a good example. Say you decided back in 2016 that this video streaming thing was real and you wanted to compete with Netflix. That year, Netflix spent about $7 billion on content and about $1 billion on marketing. So the cost of fully taking on Netflix would have been somewhere in the $8 billion a year range. Had you decided to wait and see how this streaming thing played out, you could have delayed your launch by three or four years. But by 2020, Netflix was spending over $2 billion on marketing and over $12 billion on content. So the "Netflix take-out" cost was more like $14 billion. Few companies can afford that level of spend. Scale was also creating flywheel effects for Netflix that made it harder to fully compete against it over time. The more global subscribers Netflix gained, the more revenue it generated, which allowed it to buy more content, which attracted more subscribers, which generated more revenue, and so on. Which is exactly why, I believe, Reed Hastings and the Netflix management team so aggressively sought to build out their streaming business, even looking to dissuade customers from their DVD business through a significant price hike. They realized these flywheel effects and competitive moat advantages that scale would bring.

Fourth, scale can help a company tap into *network effects*. A network effect is the phenomenon by which the value or utility a user derives from a good or service depends on the number of users of compatible products. Kind of like "the more the merrier." This concept is widely used in tech investment pitches. But frankly, I think it's one of the least powerful benefits of scale. I learned this the hard way as a Bull who way overstayed my welcome on EBAY shares, even when the company slipped below premium revenue growth levels beginning in 2006. I assumed that its network effects advantages would carry it through to years and years of premium growth. After all, more buyers on eBay created a bigger market for sellers, which attracted more sellers, which created a bigger market for buyers, which attracted more buyers, and so on. But a superior value proposition and better execution by Amazon blew up those network effects advantages. Facebook as a social network should be a superb beneficiary of network effects, but somehow Instagram rose up to compete with it (leading Facebook to acquire it), and so did Snap, and so did TikTok, and so will another company. Still, although their impact has often been exaggerated, there definitely is something to network effects, with a company like Uber being a good example. In any one geographic area, the more drivers there are for Uber, the greater the value of the service is for riders (e.g., shorter wait times), which begets more riders, which makes the service compelling for more drivers (e.g., shorter wait times).

The simple wrap-up point is that bigger TAMs do create more opportunities for companies to benefit from significant scale. This is why TAMs matter.

TAM matters. The bigger the total addressable market, the greater the opportunity for premium revenue growth, which is a major driver of tech and growth stocks. A lot of other factors are important—the level of product innovation, the strength of the product's or service's value proposition to customers, and the quality of the management team—but a large TAM creates the opportunity for substantial growth. A T TAM ($1 trillion TAM like Google faces with the global advertising market) creates the opportunity for substantial growth from scale. T TAMs are very rare, but look for companies that have the potential to "pull a Google"—to generate premium revenue growth from scale. As a rule of thumb, a company with a single-digit percentage share of a large TAM might be an ideal candidate for tech investors to consider.

TAMs can be expanded. By removing friction and by adding new use cases, TAMs can be made larger. That's essentially what Lyft and Uber did over the years. By lowering prices, increasing the number of drivers on its platform, reducing wait times, and making payments and eventually tipping seamless, Uber expanded the use cases for and the appeal of ridesharing. By removing friction, they both expanded the use cases and thus the addressable market for ridesharing. There are also two specific steps that companies can take to expand their TAMs—expand into new geographic markets and generate new revenue streams. As of early 2021, DoorDash is in the process of doing both of these things. Its long-term success in doing so will have a major impact on its perceived TAM, on its growth rate potential, and thus on its stock market success.

Sometimes TAMs are hard to ascertain, especially when a traditional industry is being disrupted. And creative new approaches are required. This was the case with Spotify, which was attacking two well-known markets (the recorded music industry and radio advertising), but was doing it in a way that potentially meant it was facing a much bigger market than appeared at first listen. The proliferation of smartphones (3 billion and counting) has likely upended all media markets, potentially expanding the TAM for all media models. Friction has been removed. Media can now be easily consumed practically 24-7. The market opportunity and the growth opportunity may well be greater for the best media offerings.

Large TAMs can help drive growth that can lead to scale, which has intrinsic benefits. There are four specific benefits: experience curves, unit economics advantages, competitive moats, and network effects. With scale come the learning opportunities to operate better/smarter, with scale come the opportunities to operate more cost effectively, with scale comes the opportunity to increase the entry costs for new competition, and with scale comes the opportunity to feed off network effects. These are all different, but they are all benefits from scale. Scale doesn't just matter. Scale wins. Large TAMs increase the opportunities for companies to tap into these scale benefits.

LESSON 7

Follow the Value Prop, Not the Money

Companies with compelling customer value propositions beat companies with great business models, in terms of both market share and market cap. Or . . . customer-centric companies beat investor-centric ones.

In the summer of 2011, while I was the lead Internet analyst at Citi, I hosted an investor bus tour of some of the leading Internet companies in Silicon Valley. I hosted these two to three times a year, with 20 to 30 of the leading public market tech investors. On this particular tour, we met with eBay and its then CEO, John Donahoe. Donahoe is now the CEO of Nike.

Donahoe was gracious with his time and provided detailed, thoughtful responses to the questions investors threw at him. At one point during that hour-long session, while Donahoe was fielding a question from an investor about eBay's merchant logistics, he stopped midsentence, turned to the group, and said, "You know Amazon is moving toward same-day delivery. It's inevitable."

About five years prior to that meeting, Amazon had announced Amazon Prime, its "all you can eat express shipping" program, which offered two-day guaranteed delivery on millions of in-stock items. About five years after that Donahoe meeting, Amazon did indeed announce same-day delivery in several of its largest US markets, eventually expanding it over the ensuing years.

So Donahoe was right. He foresaw Amazon's future. My strong guess is that he also realized how dramatically expensive the investments required to offer same-day delivery would be. It would require building out a massive network of distribution centers across the country. What I don't know is whether Donahoe realized how much of a tremendous competitive advantage these investments would give Amazon long term. And how much AMZN shareholders would benefit from those investments, despite the material pressure they put on AMZN's earnings and cash flow.

But what has played out in the Amazon versus eBay story is also something that has occurred in several other key verticals, including online food delivery, online car sales, and online real estate. The company with the ugly business model (low margins, lots of capital requirements) but the more compelling consumer value proposition beats the company with the attractive business model (high margins, minimal capital requirements) but the less compelling value prop.

Let's go through some stories.

WHY AMAZON BEAT EBAY—THE PRIME BATTLE

In early 2021, AMZN's market cap was 40x that of EBAY. Amazon generated over 30x more revenue in 2020 than eBay and over 10x more free cash flow. Most investors have a clear feel for how much bigger Amazon is today than eBay. Few investors have an appreciation for how different this story was 10, 15, and 20 years ago.

Just look at Figure 7.1, with the circle indicating when AMZN finally started to carry a larger market cap than eBay. This is one of the most dramatic switcheroos we have seen in tech over the last two decades. And I think it offers some important lessons for investors today.

FIGURE 7.1 The AMZN Versus EBAY Switcheroo

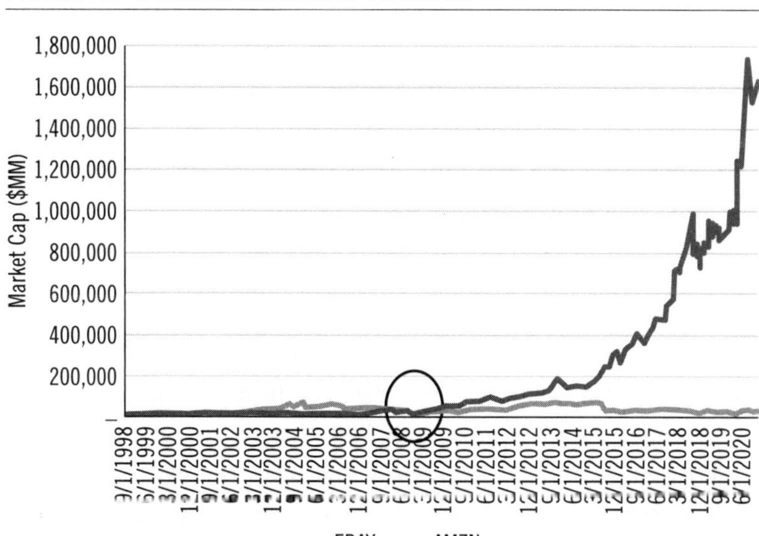

Make no doubt about it, for the "first Internet decade" eBay was the clear winner. Not Amazon. eBay was the king of online retail. Not Amazon. At least up until 2008. And measured three ways.

First, up until 2008, eBay had the bigger market cap (Figure 7.2). Although Amazon had the bigger market cap during the dot-com boom (1998 to March 2000), AMZN's valuation was almost never more than 2x that of EBAY. For example, when AMZN's market cap peaked in November 1999 at $29 billion (and didn't recover for seven full years!), EBAY's market cap was $21 billion. Then starting in mid-2000 and for the next eight years, EBAY always sported the larger market cap, by a factor of 6x in late 2001 ($13 billion versus

FIGURE 7.2 EBAY: The King of Online Retail During the First Internet Decade

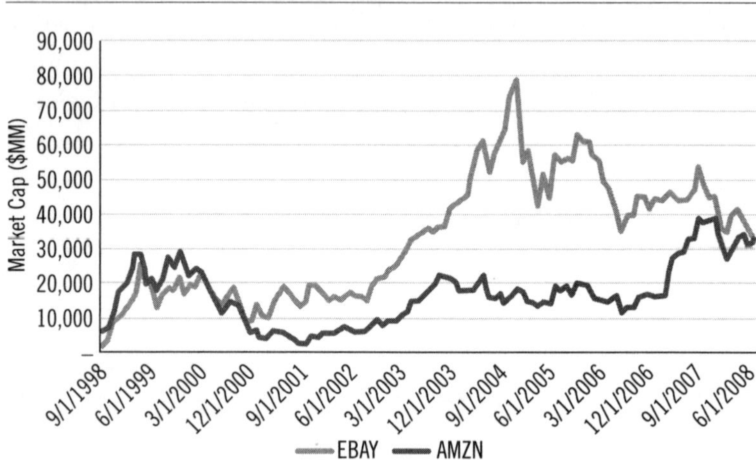

$2 billion), 5x in late 2004 ($65 billion versus $14 billion), 4x in early 2006 ($55 billion versus $15 billion), and 3x in early 2007 ($44 billion versus $16 billion). eBay was the king of online retail!

Second, eBay was consistently and at times dramatically bigger in terms of customers and total online retail volume until at least 2008 (Figure 7.3). At the end of 2003, for example, Amazon reported 39 million customers, while eBay had 41 million customers (5% more). At the end of 2005, Amazon reported 55 million customers, while eBay had 72 million customers (31% more). And at the end of 2007, Amazon reported 76 million customers, while eBay had 85 million customers (12% more). It was only at the end of 2008 that their customer bases began to match up (at 88 million), before Amazon began to consistently surpass eBay in terms of customers. In terms of total online retail volume, eBay disclosed GMV (gross merchandise volume), while Amazon didn't. But there was enough disclosure from Amazon to reasonably guesstimate its GMV, and even in 2008, eBay was almost twice the size of Amazon in terms of its total online retail volume (roughly $60 billion versus $30 billion). Arguably, Amazon didn't surpass eBay in this metric until after 2011,

FIGURE 7.3 All Hail the King of Online Retail—EBAY!

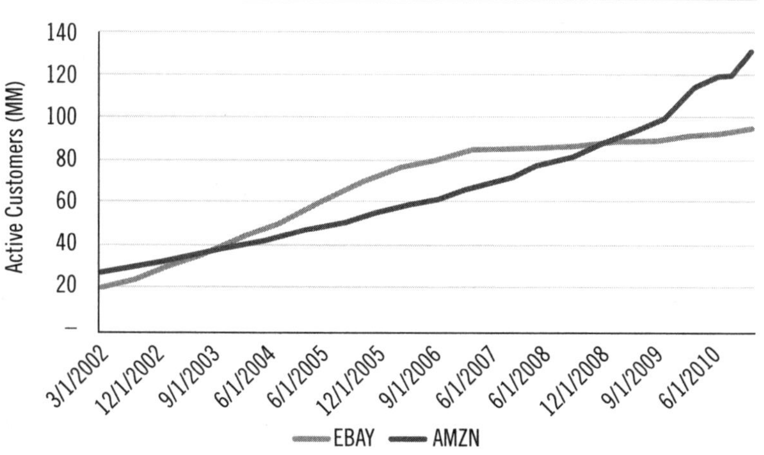

when both companies generated around $70 billion in GMV. Again, eBay was the king of online retail for many, many years.

The third way that eBay was the clear online retail winner for the first Internet decade was in terms of investor sentiment. The market cap comparison captures this. But another way to do this is to follow the relevant articles in *Barron's*, the weekly financial magazine owned by Dow Jones. *Barron's* has long been influential across the stock market, but it became highly influential in the Internet sector when it famously published the "Burning Up" cover story on March 20, 2000, which correctly forecast the popping of the dot-com bubble based on an analysis of the sector's cash burn levels. The article's first two sentences summed it all up: "When will the Internet Bubble burst? For scores of 'Net upstarts, that unpleasant popping sound is likely to be heard before the end of this year." The fact that this cover story occurred one week after the NASDAQ peak and right near the beginning of its dramatic 78% correction gave *Barron's* Street cred among tech investors for years to come.

Barron's had already reached its AMZN conclusion a year previously when it famously published its "Amazon.bomb" cover story in May 1999. Its conclusion was harsh: "Unfortunately for Bezos, Amazon is now entering a stage in which investors will be less willing to rely on his charisma and more demanding of answers to tough questions like, when will this company actually turn a profit?" And: "Increasingly, Amazon's strategy is looking like the dim-bulb businessman who loses money on every sale but tries to make it up by making more sales." Ouch. And *Barron's* stayed cautious/negative on AMZN for years, noting in its "Burning Up" cover story that Amazon had only 10 months of cash left.

eBay, meanwhile, received a different kind of cover story from *Barron's*. In June 2005, *Barron's* featured a cover story on eBay titled "Hit That Bid," which asserted that eBay "has become the world's most important ecommerce company." The article noted that EBAY shares had corrected 35% that year, argued that the company still had a robust growth outlook, and recommended buying the stock, concluding: "The stock looks as cheap as anything you'll find on eBay." What the *Barron's* article also touched on was how attractive eBay's core marketplace business model was, with high gross and operating margins and nowhere near the physical infrastructure demands of Amazon's business. This had been the investment appeal of EBAY from the IPO beginning—a play on online retail, just like Amazon, but with a dramatically better financial model.

Why Amazon Prevailed

I know what narrative fallacy is. I know there is risk in trying to force an explanation on a sequence of facts and then trying to draw lessons from that. But there are some clear facts here. For many years, eBay was fundamentally a bigger online retail platform than Amazon. For many years, eBay was the much bigger company in terms of market cap. That changed dramatically. Again, one of the most dramatic switcheroos we have seen in tech over the last two decades. So with all the caveats, here's my explanation for why Amazon beat eBay, both fundamentally and valuationally. It's based on almost a quarter century of covering these two companies, analyzing every single quarterly EPS release issued by them—that would be close to 200 releases between the two of them—and writing more than 500 reports focused on one or both of these companies.

First, Amazon was better at product innovation than eBay. I could just mention AWS, one of the three most important technology innovations of the last 20 years (along with the iPhone and Tesla cars) and be done with it. AWS by itself is likely worth 20x what eBay is today. But Amazon has also been extraordinarily innovative in other areas—Kindles, Alexa devices, the Prime shipping program, state-of-the-art logistics, cashier-less stores, to name a few. Investors reward highly innovative companies, and Amazon has been highly innovative.

Second, Amazon consistently maintained a longer-term investment horizon than eBay. Amazon's long-term investment style has been well documented. It helps when the founder specifically shouts it out in his first public shareholder letter (1997): "We will continue to make investment decisions in light of long-term market leadership considerations rather than short-term profitability considerations or short-term Wall Street reactions." The first key callout in that first shareholder letter was: "It's All About the Long Term." eBay's management team also thought long term, but it didn't do it as successfully or as consistently as Amazon, I believe. As one tell, while Amazon's executive compensation was tied to annual evaluations, eBay's was tied to quarterly performance up until 2008. It's hard to prove, but my interactions with both management teams over the years consistently left me with the impression that Amazon was much more willing to ignore short-term expectations than eBay was. eBay sought to manage numbers and expectations, much more so than Amazon.

Third, while management comparisons are hard to make, they are important to make. Amazon has arguably had the better management team. It has certainly had the more consistent management team. Per a February 2020 *Seattle Times* article, the average Amazon tenure of the Amazon S Team (its 20 or so most senior executives) was 16 years. That is unusual for any major company and extremely unusual in the tech corporate universe. Also, Amazon has had only one CEO since its IPO until 2021, while eBay has had four.

Fourth, Amazon had the larger TAM. Although eBay did make some efforts to compete in in-season retail, it almost always prioritized the tail ends of those markets—hard-to-find early product cycle items (e.g., Beanie Babies, Cabbage Patch Dolls, the first Xbox consoles, the first iPods, velour tracksuits) and hard-to-find end of product cycle items (e.g., vintage clothing, collectible baseball cards, used car parts). Which meant that Amazon always faced a much bigger TAM than eBay—global retail is a $20 trillion+ TAM, while eBay's target market was a fraction of that, arguably well under $1 trillion. So Amazon could maintain premium revenue growth in its retail segment for more than a decade after eBay could. Amazon had the longer growth runway.

Fifth, Amazon has from the beginning had a more consumer-centric orientation. While the first key callout from that first AMZN shareholder letter had to do with the long term, the second was: "Obsess Over Customers." There are websites devoted to Amazon and Jeff Bezos's customer-centric principles. The line I heard management use most often was: "We start with what the customer needs and work backwards." eBay's challenge was that it was aggressively focused on seller success. Over the years the company shifted its focus from small sellers to large sellers and then back again. For eBay, the customer was oftentimes the seller. For Amazon, the customer was the consumer (at least in the retail business). And that made a huge difference in its long-term success.

Amazon Prime

The event that best captures most of the reasons behind Amazon's success (why it beat eBay and why it beat other retailers) was the

February 2, 2005, launch of Amazon Prime. That afternoon, after the close of the market, Amazon was scheduled to announce its December 2004 quarter EPS results. Earlier in the day, on the front page of the Amazon website, there was a letter from Jeff Bezos. In that letter, Bezos excitedly announced Amazon Prime, its $79 a year express shipping membership program. He expressed his hope that Prime would allow Amazon to earn even more of its customers' business but warned that he expected Prime to be "expensive for Amazon.com in the short term."

As the Internet analyst at American Technology Research, I saw this letter and concluded that Amazon would likely give cautious forward earnings guidance when it reported that night. When a CEO announces a new initiative and states that it will be "expensive in the short term," that's usually a pretty good indicator that EPS estimates are going down. I talked with Cory Johnson, the CNBC reporter who was going to cover the AMZN earnings release, and gave him my prediction. And that's exactly what happened.

Amazon provided operating income outlooks for the March quarter and for 2005 that were well below Street estimates. And the company called for an approximate doubling in its capital expenditures for 2005. Prime shipping *was* expensive for Amazon to offer. The key backdrop here is that Amazon's operating margins had been rising steadily since 2001. And 2004 was on track to be a record year for Amazon in terms of its operating margins. This came to pass. They reached 6.4% in 2004. (What also came to pass was that Amazon's operating margins have *never ever* been this high again. True, as of early 2021.) Prime was going to derail the Amazon profitability train, and investors weren't going to like it.

AMZN shares immediately tanked 15% in the aftermarket that afternoon and proceeded to remain under pressure for the next several months. And Cory introduced his CNBC segment that afternoon with the statement: "Mark Mahaney nailed it!" I nailed it all right, but only in terms of the near-term trade. At the time I was cautious on AMZN shares, with a Hold rating.

I continue to believe that AMZN didn't really prove to be a core Long until sometime around 2008, when it was able to show consistent premium revenue growth in its retail business while demonstrating the ability to successfully launch completely new businesses (e.g., AWS and Kindle). But with the launch of Prime, Amazon proved that it was willing to invest behind long-term initiatives that were clearly consumer beneficial, despite being near-term investor detrimental. For the average Amazon customer ordering twice a month, Prime generated savings within roughly three months. For the average AMZN investor, Prime caused a 15% hit to the investor's portfolio within minutes of the EPS announcement.

And did Prime work? You betcha. I'd argue that Prime has been the single best customer loyalty program in Internet history, maybe in all history. The program reached over 100 million subscribers by 2018 and 150 million by early 2020. Based on extensive survey work I ran for almost a decade, Amazon Prime customers became the most engaged, the most frequent, the most loyal, and the biggest-spending customers that Amazon or any other online retailer had. Prime was one of the major unlocks behind Amazon's premium revenue growth. And survey work showed Amazon's shipping speed to be one of its most attractive features.

The launch and success of Prime checked a lot of the Amazon success story boxes. It was a highly innovative offering—no other major Internet retailer offered a shipping subscription program at that time. It was long-term oriented—near-term expensive but long-term profitable in terms of dramatically deepening customer loyalty. And it was consumer-centric—Prime customers saved hundreds of dollars in shipping costs over time. Investors reacted negatively to it and took the share price down. But consumers reacted positively to it, allowing Amazon to consistently outgrow eBay and other online retail for the next decade. (In March 2017, eBay launched Guaranteed Delivery, which offered three-day or less delivery on 20 million eligible products. Better late than never.)

The key takeaway from the Amazon versus eBay story is that the company that was more willing to aggressively innovate on behalf of consumers—even at the cost of dashing near-term investor expectations—ended up as the bigger long-term winner. There were lots of factors behind Amazon's success, but this customer-centricity—rather than investor-centricity—was a key one.

WHY DOORDASH BEAT GRUBHUB— THE "PROMISCUITY LETTER"

Grubhub (GRUB) has been a remarkable stock (Figure 7.4). After trading up 31% on its first day, GRUB essentially traded flat for three years. It closed April 4, 2014, at $34 and closed April 4, 2017, at $33. It then skyrocketed 320% over the next 18 months to reach $146 in September 2018. It then corrected 77% and went right back to $34 by the end of October 2019.

FIGURE 7.4 The Rise and Fall of GRUB

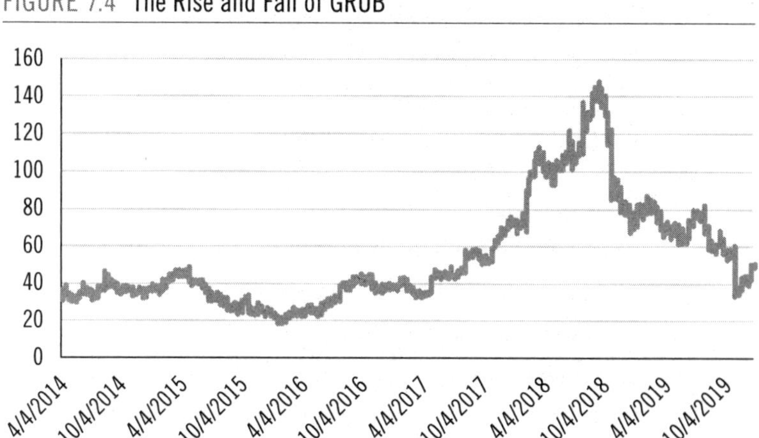

There's gotta be some stock-picking lessons in here somewhere. There are. A great place to start is GRUB's October 28, 2019, shareholder letter, which I like to call the "promiscuity letter."

In that letter, GRUB management disclosed that it had recently seen order growth trend "noticeably lower than our expectations," with softness in customer retention rates and in order frequency rates. GRUB management blamed this overall weakness on industry maturation and on online diners becoming "more promiscuous," that is, ordering from competing services versus exclusively from Grubhub. It then proceeded to materially reduce its guidance for the following quarter. GRUB shares plunged 57% in next day's trading, taking the stock back to that $34 level.

Throughout the "promiscuity letter," the company highlighted the attractiveness and the sustainability of its business model. It referred to "the powerful underlying economics of our business model." It added, "Through our disciplined investment approach and differentiated business model, we've proven to be one of the two companies in the world, and the only one in the United States, that has generated profits at scale in the online food industry." It described its competitors as "continuing to spend aggressively, swallowing steep losses in the process."

Who were those competitors, and what has happened to them? Well, the biggest one was DoorDash (DASH), which ended up going public in December 2020, surging 86% on its first day of trading. Its market cap in early 2021 was approximately $50 billion. At its peak, GRUB's market cap was roughly $15 billion. So DASH now carries a market cap that is 3x that of GRUB at its peak. Stock prices change all the time. So do market caps. DASH's market could get cut in half. Stranger things have happened. But even then it would have a market cap materially greater than that of GRUB at its peak.

One of the biggest reasons DASH carried a much larger market cap than GRUB is seen in Figure 7.5, which was included in DoorDash's S1. It shows that DASH's share of the US online food

FIGURE 7.5 How DoorDash Won the Food Fight

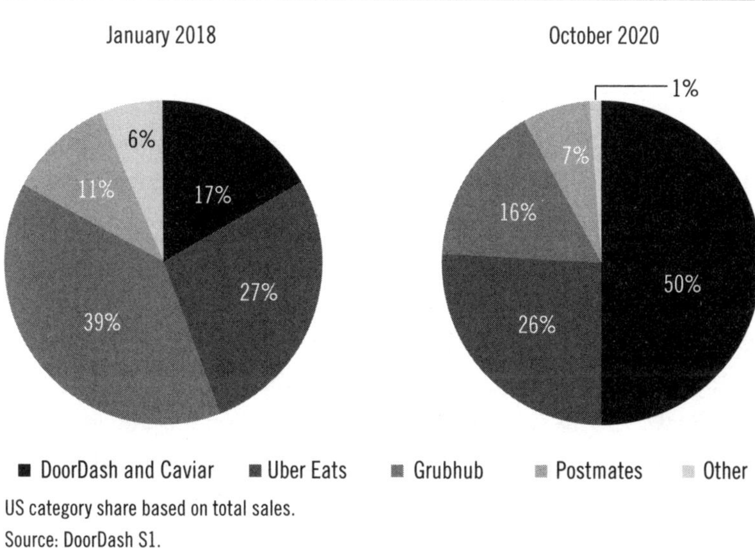

US category share based on total sales.
Source: DoorDash S1.

industry went from 17% in early 2018 to 50% in October 2020, while GRUB's share declined from 39% to 16%.

At the time of the "promiscuity letter," Grubhub claimed to have the "strongest and deepest restaurant-diner marketplace in the United States." That clearly changed. Why? There are several reasons, but one core one is that DoorDash was more consumer-centric, while Grubhub was more investor-centric, in ways that weren't too dissimilar to what transpired between Amazon and eBay.

It's *all* in the "promiscuity letter." GRUB management stated: "We know from experience the single biggest determinant of diners usage on marketplaces is whether it has the restaurants that the diner wants." For a substantial period of time, Grubhub only allowed onto its restaurant network establishments that did their own delivery. Grubhub was essentially an online marketing partner (and not much else) for its restaurant partners, which created a "highly lucrative relationship for both parties," per the letter. Great for investors, but not so great for consumers.

DoorDash and others (Postmates and Uber Eats) also realized that restaurant selection was one of the most important determinants of which online food delivery service consumers would use. So they each dramatically expanded the restaurant supply in their core markets by providing delivery logistics to *all* restaurants in their core markets. This was expensive. It required spending large sums on awareness campaigns and on incentives for diners, drivers, and restaurants. It required building out costly and complicated local logistics networks. DoorDash ended up raising $2 billion in capital to attack the US online food delivery market. Its net loss in 2018 was $200 million. In 2019, it was almost $700 million. But DoorDash's focus on what consumers most wanted allowed it to gain dramatic market share versus Grubhub. And eventually, market cap versus Grubhub. (Key update to story: Grubhub was sold to Just Eat Takeaway in June 2020 for $7.3 billion.)

How about this. You know what promiscuous consumers are? They are consumers. And they are consumers who aren't completely satisfied with your service. That's why they are trying out other services. And if they find one that is more consumer-focused than yours—say, by offering better restaurant selection and providing faster and more reliable delivery—they will switch to that service.

There are several reasons why DoorDash beat Grubhub. DoorDash focused heavily on suburban markets, which had some logistics advantages versus urban markets. DoorDash executed exceptionally well in terms of building out its restaurant supply and in terms of providing consistent and rapid delivery times, another factor that was important to consumers. And DoorDash's immediate post-IPO market cap did carry some expectations that the company could successfully expand its logistics into other verticals, like groceries and specialty retail. But one of the core reasons why DoorDash beat Grubhub was that DoorDash was more consumer-centric than Grubhub.

Companies that are willing and able to invest aggressively to create great consumer experiences can become better long-term investments than companies that seek to merely defend attractive business models. That's overstating it, but it's still one of the big lessons I've learned from tracking these stocks. Both the Amazon versus eBay and the DoorDash versus Grubhub stories suggest that consumer-centric—not investor-centric—companies win in the long term, both in terms of fundamentals and in terms of stock prices.

One relatively popular Silicon Valley take on the whole food fight business is that DoorDash benefited from being a private company, able to "swallow steep losses" that companies in the public market can't do. That may or may not be true. The key lesson about investing in consumer-centric—or avoiding investor-centric—businesses still holds. But there is an intriguing example of a well-known public tech company that dramatically changed its business model—leaving behind a pure high-margin investor-friendly model in exchange for a consumer-centric but highly uncertain business model—and lived to tell the tale. Let me introduce you to Zillow.

THE ZILLOW PIVOT—HOMES FOR SALE, STOCKS FOR SALE

Zillow has become a household brand. In November 2020, the *New York Times* featured an article with the title: "Zillow Surfing Is the Escape We All Need Right Now." Millions of consumers go to Zillow to explore residential real estate listings and daydream about different homes they would want to live in. Kind of like house porn.

Actually, it *is* house porn, as *SNL* pointed out in a brilliant comedic skit aired in February 2021. That skit was based on a mock commercial for Zillow as "the one website to satisfy your sexiest desires"—viewing other peoples' homes. (Hilarious! It's on

YouTube.) And by the way, there may be a great stock-picking lesson in here. *SNL*'s caricature of Netflix's Qwikster fiasco back in 2011 turned out to create a great entry point for NFLX shareholders. Might *SNL*'s caricature of Zillow do the same?!

Zillow had firmly established itself in the American psyche over the prior decade as the central depository of US residential real estate prices. Gosh, that sounds overly formal. How about . . . Zillow provides Zestimates on practically every home in the country, including your friends', your work colleagues', your boss's, and any celebrity's for which you can find a street address. Over time, Zillow has become a key part of every residential real estate transaction. Few deals close in the United States without one or both parties at least checking the Zestimate for the property.

Zillow was founded in 2006 by several key executives, including Rich Barton, Lloyd Fink, and Spencer Rascoff. All three individuals had substantial tech industry experience prior to Zillow, especially Barton, who founded online travel agency Expedia. Zillow IPO'd in July 2011 at $20, enjoyed an 80% pop on its first trading day, and then soared to as high as $160 in late July 2014, giving the company a market cap of over $30 billion. For a variety of reasons, including regulatory issues and a major legal challenge, Zillow shares then plunged almost 90% back to its IPO price over the next year, then traded roughly sideways for the next five years, until a risky, expensive business model change brought it back to its peak 2014 stock price in early 2021. I referred to it at the time as one of the riskiest bets I had seen a tech company take. I called it the "Zillow Pivot." (It was more of an expansion than a pivot, but "Zillow Pivot" sounds . . . well . . . sexier than "Zillow Expansion.")

Prior to that time, Zillow's business model was primarily based around providing marketing solutions to real estate agents. Kind of like Grubhub. Restaurants paid Grubhub for leads—people looking to order from a restaurant. Real estate agents paid Zillow for leads—people looking to buy or sell their home. It was a good model with a good TAM.

By "good model," I mean that online real estate advertising was a high 80%+ gross margin business for Zillow, without the need for substantial capital commitments. And by "good TAM," I mean that the online real estate advertising TAM was somewhere in the $10 billion to $20 billion range. Certainly no T TAM, but a solid market opportunity.

Then, on April 12, 2018, Zillow announced that it would be entering the direct home-buying/-selling market. Instead of simply competing in the high-margin real estate advertising market, where it was the clear leader, it would expand into the market of directly buying and selling homes, sometimes called the iBuyer market, or what I like to call the homeflipping.com market.

As key background, the pitch behind the direct home market is that it dramatically reduces friction in the home-selling/-buying process. Sellers submit a request online for an offer for their home. Companies like Opendoor, Redfin, Offerpad, and Zillow will make a cash offer within 48 hours of the submission, factoring in likely renovations, and then look to resell the home within 90 days. Although the commission to the seller is higher than via the traditional agent listing model, the speed and simplicity of the transaction is potentially dramatically better for the seller, making it easier for sellers to then purchase a new home. To date, in the regional markets where the iBuyer model has gained traction, 10 percent or more of homes are sold via this process.

For Zillow, this was a *major* pivot, and it was risky in many ways.

First, it was dramatically more capital intensive than Zillow's advertising business, requiring well over a billion dollars in debt or equity financing. Second, it involved a lot of asset and economic cycle risk—the company only made a profit if it sold the house for more than it bought it for, but that was not a given. Third, it required a real estate competency that Zillow, a company built on providing marketing tools, didn't necessarily have. Fourth, it carried the risk of disrupting Zillow's core agent advertising model. If the iBuyer market really took off, it carried the risk of gutting real estate industry agent commissions, which were what paid for all that advertising revenue in the first place. (Not too dissimilar to how Netflix's launch of streaming potentially and actually disrupted its core DVD rental business.) Fifth, the iBuyer market was already competitively crowded, with the leading private company (Opendoor) already being aggressively financed by one of the same large funds that had backed DoorDash in its assault on Grubhub.

Risky, indeed! And exactly as Zillow's founders had feared, this was also the market's take—Zillow shares sold off 5% in the aftermarket the night of the Direct Buy announcement. It traded off 42% through the balance of the year, dramatically underperforming the market, as profitability estimates were materially reduced, in part due to the investments required to get the home-buying business off the ground. At the time, I wrote that the pivot was "likely the right move for the company," but that it "materially increased execution risk" for the company. By the "right move," I meant that it clearly seemed to offer a compelling new value proposition for home sellers and that, if successful, it could substantially increase Zillow's TAM. By "execution risk," I meant the five ways described above. As it turned out, I downgraded the stock from Buy to Hold a month later, largely due to that risk.

This story is far from played out. Evidence that the "Zillow Pivot" is succeeding will take a few years, just as it did for the Amazon Prime investment and the Netflix switch to streaming. Tentative evidence in Zillow's fundamentals indicates the pivot is working—the Direct Buy segment, now called Homes, appears in early 2021 to be on the cusp of achieving sustainable profitability. And industry iBuying demand appears to have hit an inflection point. And more importantly in terms of stock-picking lessons, Zillow shares have recovered as of early 2021 to all-time highs. (See Figure 7.6.)

FIGURE 7.6 The "Zillow Pivot"

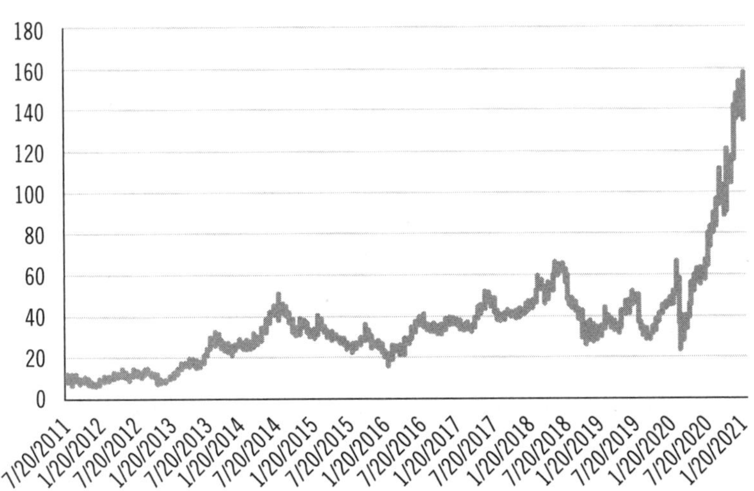

So Zillow will offer a real-time test for the next several years of whether a shift to a more customer-centric approach—but one with much greater near-term investor risk—can actually work and whether investors will be rewarded for this shift. My bias is yes to both questions. My strong guess is that the prior experiences of Zillow board members Rich Barton (on the board of Netflix) and Lloyd Fink (on the board of Grubhub) enabled Zillow to make this pivot. The people at Zillow had already seen what happened when companies embraced (Netflix) and didn't embrace (Grubhub) more compelling value propositions. Also having the three major founders—Barton, Fink, and Rascoff—fully supportive of this pivot helped. Actually, it was crucial.

Perhaps in 5 to 10 years we'll use the expression "to pull a Zillow" as a way of praising companies that successfully pivot away from an investor-centric to a customer-centric strategy. And possibly, we'll wonder what would have happened if eBay or Grubhub had "pulled a Zillow."

WHEN COMPELLING CONSUMER VALUE PROPOSITIONS GENERATE BUSINESS MODEL BENEFITS—THE PRICING POWER FLYWHEEL

2014 was an important year in Internet history. It could also be considered an important year in business history. It was the first time that leading Internet companies were able to successfully raise prices on consumers. That year, Amazon implemented its first-ever price increase for Amazon Prime. And Netflix imposed its first-ever price increase for streaming. Both price increases were successful. And both examples highlight the business model advantage of building consumer-centric businesses—the pricing power flywheel.

Here are the deets.

In March 2014, Amazon announced that it was raising the price of Amazon Prime by $20 from $79 to $99, a whopping 25% increase. It was the first price increase since the program was launched back in 2005. That's nine years at the same price. Amazon's CFO then was Tom Szkutak, a meticulous, low-key, understated financial wiz. Perfect CFO material. On the company's prior EPS call, he had surprised the market by announcing that the company was considering a $20 to $40 price increase, largely in response to rising fuel and transportation costs. A 25% to 50% price hike? By Amazon, the low-price leader! Had Szkutak lost his marbles?

When the announcement with the $20 price increase became official a month later, the letter on the Amazon home page highlighted how much more valuable Prime had become since 2005. The number of items eligible for unlimited free two-day shipping had grown from 1 million to over 20 million. And Prime now included free unlimited access to more than 40,000 movies and TV episodes and more than 500,000 Kindle books.

So Amazon was defending its price increase. But there was no doubt it was a steep one (25%). This was a risky step.

Nine months later, in January 2015, Amazon disclosed that its Prime memberships had grown by 53 percent worldwide in 2014, despite that price increase. Although Amazon didn't reveal the total number of Prime subs, this disclosure strongly suggested that Amazon experienced an acceleration in its Prime sub adds despite the price increase. When you raise prices and your customer base grows at an accelerated pace, *that's* an impressive accomplishment. It certainly indicated Prime was perceived very positively by consumers. Bezos referred to Prime as "the best bargain in the history of shopping." Maybe, maybe not. But consumers clearly viewed it as a great bargain.

In May 2018, Amazon raised the price of Prime again, this time to $119. So it did eventually get the 50% price increase Szkutak had hinted at in early 2014. Again, this seemed to have no negative impact on the popularity of Amazon or of Amazon Prime. My survey tracking of Amazon Prime usage from 2013 to 2020 showed Prime adoption rising almost every single year, reaching almost 70% of all US Internet users by mid-2020 (Figure 7.7). Despite the 50% price increase.

FIGURE 7.7 Prime Adoption Rising Despite Price Increases

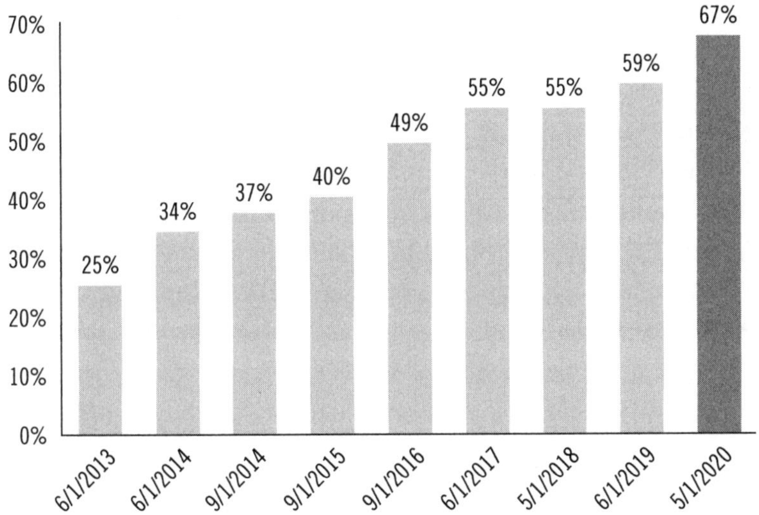

Source: SurveyMonkey survey; percentage of respondents who use Amazon that subscribe to Prime.

On a current base of over 150 million Amazon Prime subscribers, that $40 price increase amounted to a substantial amount. More than $6 billion. Which was the entire net income that Amazon generated between 2014 and 2017. Price increases are wonderful that way. If successful, they are all margin. They flow right down to the bottom line, which is absolutely *not* what Amazon did. Instead, it used that extra revenue to offset those rising fuel and transportation costs as well as to boost the value of Prime—faster delivery (now close to one-day guaranteed delivery), more movies, more music, more e-books, etc. That increases the overall consumer value proposition of Prime, which enables future price increases, which are used to boost the value of Prime, and so on. A pricing power flywheel.

Consumer-centric companies that consistently and aggressively innovate on behalf of their customers can, if they execute well, tap into this flywheel. Amazon did. And so, even more clearly, did Netflix.

In May 2014, Netflix increased the price of its standard streaming service by $1 from $7.99 to $8.99. It was the first time Netflix had done this since rolling out the service in 2007. In a manner similar to what Amazon did, CEO Reed Hastings had suggested a month earlier on an earnings call with analysts that the company was considering a $1 or $2 increase in its standard monthly subscription plan. A 13% to 25% price increase. It settled on the 13% increase. Hasting's justification: "If we want to continue to expand, to do more great original content . . . we have to eventually increase prices a little bit." But Netflix made sure to be extra cautious with the price increase, allowing existing users to maintain their $7.99 standard plan for up to two years before the price impact would affect them. It even introduced a new basic plan at $7.99—standard-definition quality video limited to one screen at a time versus high-def and two screens for the $8.99 standard plan. In other words, this was about as cautious a price increase as you could get.

And it worked. Similar to Amazon, Netflix reported accelerating subscriber adds in 2014, despite the price increase. It added 11 million streaming subs in 2013 and then 13 million in 2014. A year and a half later, it repeated the trick, raising the price of its standard plan by another $1 to $9.99. Two years later, that standard plan went to $10.99. And a year after that, the standard plan went to $12.99, and for the first time Netflix increased its basic plan price to $8.99. And in late 2020, Netflix's standard plan rose to $13.99.

And throughout this time, Netflix has reported accelerating subscriber adds every single year, with the exception of a modest reduction in the number of new adds in 2019 (Figure 7.8). Netflix added 16 million new subs in 2015, 18 million in 2016, 21 million in 2017, 29 million in 2018, 28 million in 2019, and a whopping 37 million in 2020. There are a lot of factors here, including a huge boost in 2020 due to the Covid-19 crisis. But the basic fact that Netflix was able to accelerate its subscriber adds despite price increases suggests just how strong its consumer value proposition has been and still is: $7.99 to $13.99 is a $6 a month increase. That "little bit" that Hastings mentioned in 2014 turned into a 75% price increase over six years! On a base of 200 million subscribers, that's $14 billion in annual all-margin revenue. Of course, Netflix didn't flow that all

FIGURE 7.8 A Pricing Power Flywheel: Netflix Style

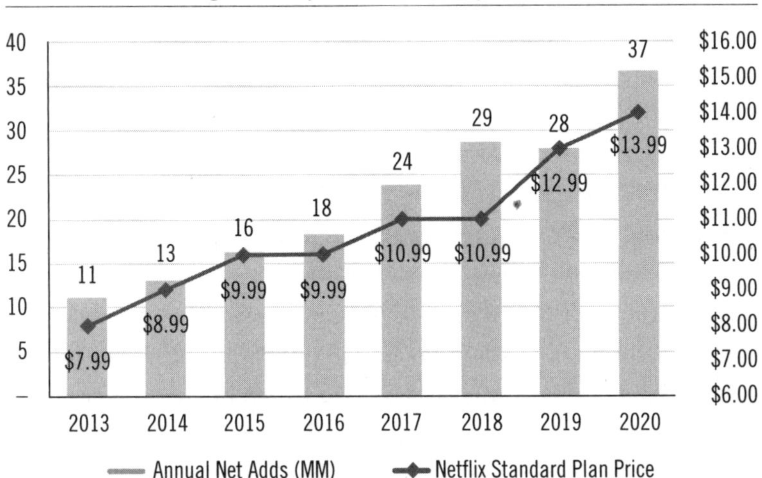

down to the bottom line. It used a lot of that to buy and create more content. Flywheel time. More content creates a better service, which enables more price increases, which helps fund more content, which creates a better service.

Let's bring this all back to stock-picking lessons. Amazon and Netflix have been phenomenal stocks over the last 1, 5, and 10 years in large part because they have been able to consistently generate premium revenue growth. With Netflix, the revenue math has been straightforward. Revenue equals subscribers multiplied by revenue per subscriber. Most of the Netflix revenue growth has been driven by subscriber growth. But a solid quarter to a third of revenue has been driven by growth in revenue per sub. That in turn has been significantly boosted by successful price increases. Companies with pricing power are rare, and they enjoy an extra revenue growth lever.

Both Amazon and Netflix have benefited from this extra revenue growth lever because they have consistently innovated on and improved their consumer value propositions, which also boosted their customer growth. Both have invested aggressively to make Prime and streaming among the best bargains in shopping and in entertainment: $119 a year for expedited shipping and access to a ton of media (video, music, books), $13.99 a month for access to an almost limitless amount of high-quality video content available on any device at any time. Great bargains and ones that are expensive to maintain.

But by building and constantly improving these great bargains on behalf of consumers, Amazon and Netflix were able to tap into the pricing power flywheel, which ended up generating positive business model effects long term. The success of these price increases was far from a sure thing. Analysts like me were unsure whether Amazon and Netflix would be able to pull these off successfully. I certainly didn't predict that Netflix had the ability to raise prices by 75% over six years and still accelerate sub adds in almost every year. Neither did Netflix, or else it wouldn't have been so cautious with its first price increase. By focusing on compelling value propositions—by being consumer-centric—Amazon and Netflix both gave themselves a shot at tapping into the flywheel, and their fundamentals and their stock prices surged.

Another company that appears to be on the verge of tapping into this flywheel? Spotify. Which has built a truly compelling consumer value proposition in the music/audio sector over many years and as of early 2021 is just starting to raise pricing on its subscription service. But we'll see. Or hear.

In the meantime, the investor lesson is to focus on companies that focus on compelling consumer value propositions above all else.

LESSON WRAP-UP

Follow the consumer value proposition. Some of the best performing stocks of the past decade belong to companies that prioritized customer satisfaction *way over* near-term investor concerns. Amazon may well be the poster child here. The company consistently demonstrated a willingness to invest aggressively to offer a more compelling value proposition, even at the sacrifice of near-term profits. Its launch of Prime in early 2005 is a classic example. Margins came down, and capex more than doubled. What came out of that was arguably the single best customer loyalty program in Internet history. And maybe the "best bargain in the history of shopping." Regardless, the company in online retail that developed and aggressively invested to maintain the industry's leading consumer value proposition won, both in terms of fundamentals and in terms of stock price performance.

Investor-centric companies can make lousy investments. I see both eBay and Grubhub as examples of companies that didn't focus enough on innovating to meet consumer needs, in part, I believe, out of a strong desire to preserve highly profitable business models. Because of this, both companies ended up providing mixed results for long-term investors. In all fairness, GRUB was a spectacular Long from early 2016 to late 2018, and eBay performed spectacularly well for the five years post its IPO and selectively well over the past five years. With both companies, however, I am most struck by how much they left on the table, given the truly dramatic market share and market cap gains of their biggest competitors—Amazon and DoorDash—both of which prioritized consumer needs. I don't believe it's game over for either company (though GRUB has been acquired) or for any company that is investor-centric. While pivots toward consumer-centric companies can be expensive and daunting—and will likely be first punished in the public markets—they can be successful, as Zillow may well be proving with its Direct Buy pivot.

Even though compelling consumer value propositions can be expensive to build and maintain, they can eventually carry positive business model effects. Some of this is straightforward in terms of deep customer loyalty, greater customer retention, and lower churn. All of which are long-term beneficial to the business model. But compelling value propositions can also enable pricing power flywheels, which is what both Amazon and, especially, Netflix have benefited from. Pricing power among consumer-facing companies is rare. Who wants to pay more for a good or a service? When that good or service is compelling, then consumers will accept price increases, which enable companies to invest in further improving the good or the service, pushing the flywheel. Which means that consumer-centric companies can generate good returns for long-term investors.

LESSON 8

M Is for Management

In the long term, stocks are driven by fundamentals, and fundamentals are largely driven by management teams. Get the management team right, and you'll likely get the stock right. Look for founder-led companies that have deep technology backgrounds and benches, long-term orientation, great industry vision, a deep focus on product innovation, and a maniacal focus on customer satisfaction.

The Securities and Exchange Commission requires investment funds to warn investors that a fund's past performance is not indicative of future results. Any TV, radio, or print commercial for an investment fund will contain words to this effect. It's a wise and useful warning label. But it doesn't apply to management teams.

As an investor, when you come across management teams with successful track records, you stick with them. And by a successful track record, I don't mean consistently beating Street quarterly earnings estimates or having a fab-looking stock chart. I mean generating consistent premium revenue growth, successfully introducing new products and feature improvements, and winning greater and greater customer satisfaction and loyalty. These fundamentals and their core drivers will likely deliver good-looking long-term stock charts, and the management team is most responsible for those fundamentals and those core drivers.

Over almost a quarter century of covering tech stocks, I have yet to come across great long-term stock outperformance that wasn't driven by great long-term fundamentals. AAPL, AMZN, BABA, FB, GOOGL, MSFT, NFLX, PCLN, SHOP, TCEHY, and TSLA have proved themselves as long-term stock winners because they have been proved as long-term fundamentals winners. They all have benefited from extraordinarily effective management teams but not throughout their entire corporate histories. Even some of the best management teams make egregious mistakes or mis-execute from time to time—Netflix and Qwikster, Amazon and the Fire Phone, Google and Google Glass, and Microsoft initially missing the Internet shift. But practically all of the best performing tech stocks have benefited from extraordinarily effective management teams.

The key point is that stocks are driven by fundamentals, and fundamentals are driven by management teams. Getting the right TAMs helps, but the two other key fundamentals drivers—relentless product innovation and compelling value propositions—are driven by management teams. If you get the management team right, you'll likely get the fundamentals right, and thus the stock right.

Are those 11 stocks I listed above the only great management teams I've come across? No, though I do think it takes multiple years and challenges to really test the mettle of a management team. A caveat here is that as a public market analyst, I've only been able to closely track management teams once they go public. They may have already proved—or disproved—their management skills in the years while the companies were privately owned and run. That's OK. I can only judge what I can track, quarter in and quarter out, year in and year out. Same for the individual investor. So I've generally preferred to wait for three to five years of public market performance before reaching a "final" conclusion on a management team.

Some of the more promising management teams I have tracked in the Internet sector over the last several years have been those of Chewy (CHWY), Etsy (ETSY), Pinterest (PINS), Roku (ROKU), The Trade Desk (TTD), Stitch Fix (SFIX), Snap (SNAP), Spotify (SPOT), Lending Tree (TREE), Wix (WIX), and Zillow (ZG). In fairness, TTD, TREE, WIX, and ZG have also all generated long enough track records to merit the best-in-class management label, in my book.

But let's go into the characteristics that I believe make great management teams. These are what you are looking for as an individual investor. The quick hit list of characteristics includes:

- Founder-led companies
- Long-term orientation
- Great industry vision
- A maniacal focus on customer satisfaction
- Deep technology backgrounds and benches
- A deep focus on product innovation
- The ability to recruit top talent
- The confidence to be forthright with employees and investors about mistakes and challenges

You will rarely get all of these. And you don't need to have all of these. But you'll want to find most of these to be able to believe in the quality of the management team.

THE IMPORTANCE OF FOUNDER-LED COMPANIES

What do Alibaba, Amazon, Apple, Facebook, Google, Microsoft, Netflix, Shopify, Tencent, and Tesla all have in common? They carry some of the largest caps in the world. And they are all currently led—or for a long time were led—by their founders. Ma at Alibaba, Bezos at Amazon, Jobs at Apple, Zuckerberg at Facebook, Brin and Page at Google, Gates at Microsoft, Hastings at Netflix, Lütke at Shopify, Ma at Tencent, and Musk at Tesla (Table 8.1).

TABLE 8.1 Founders and Their Companies

Company	Year Founded	Location	Founder(s)	Founder Tenure (Years)	Market Cap ($B)
Alibaba	1999	Hangzhou, China	Jack Ma and others	20	713.14
Amazon	1994	Seattle, WA	Jeff Bezos	27	1,664.28
Apple	1976	Cupertino, CA	Steve Jobs and others	23	2,283.35
Facebook	2004	Menlo Park, CA	Mark Zuckerberg and others	17	767.31
Google	1998	Mountain View, CA	Larry Page and Sergey Brin	23	1,401.76
Micosoft	1975	Redmond, WA	Bill Gates and Paul Allen	45	1,838.57
Netflix	1997	Los Gatos, CA	Reed Hastings and Marc Randolph	24	247.61
Shopify	2004	Ottawa, Canada	Tobias Lütke and others	17	174.70
Tencent	1998	Shenzhen, China	Ma Huateng and others	23	1,103.22
Tesla	2003	Palo Alto, CA	Elon Musk and others	17	815.36

Steve Jobs's tenure excludes the period when Jobs left Apple in 1985 and rejoined in 1997;
Elon Musk as cofounder per 2009 settlement.
Market cap as of Febuary 9, 2021.

Check out the average tenure of these founders: 24 years! That's more than two times the Malcolm Gladwell 10,000 hours/10 years rule for excellence he offered in *Outliers*. And that's weighed down by the fact that Zuckerberg didn't think to start Facebook until 2004 (when he was 19, two years below the minimum legal drinking age), Lütke didn't help conceive of Shopify until 2004 (when he was 25), and Musk was busy with PayPal before he thought to help launch Tesla in 2003 (at the advanced age of 32). These founders started, built, and helped run these companies over long periods of time. And their lengthy direct involvement with these companies was a key part of the companies' fundamental and market cap success.

At the core, I believe the advantage that founder-led companies have is a greater ability and willingness to stick to a course and a vision in the face of controversy, criticism, and even contempt—this and their ability to think long term and to largely ignore short-term pressures.

These are the examples that come to mind:

- **Example A.** Bezos launching Amazon Prime in 2005 despite the heavy cost associated with it and despite the practical certainty that Wall Street would punish his stock until there was reasonable proof that the program would succeed (which took almost a year). I think it takes an owner's/founder's mentality to make that kind of call, and Bezos had that. One of the often cited quotes from Bezos goes: "If you're going to do anything new or innovative, you have to be willing to be misunderstood." Owners/founders have proved to me to be more willing to be misunderstood than professional managers. If you're running a public company, one of the ways you can be misunderstood is via dramatic stock price moves. AMZN suffered one of those in mid-2000 as the dot-com bubble was imploding. In reaction to the company's share price being cut in half that summer, Bezos wrote: "I am not my stock price" on the whiteboard in his office, encouraging his employees to remain positive and focused. (This story comes from Brad Stone's definitive book on Amazon and Jeff Bezos, *The Everything Store*.) Again, I think it takes an owner/founder to have that perspective.

- **Example B.** Facebook investing super aggressively in platform security and product development in mid-2018. Again, what Zuckerberg and Facebook management did on that June 2018 EPS call was to dramatically slash Street forward estimates, with the near certainty that this would trash FB shares. The only question was for how long. (The answer was about a year.) Estimates did go down 30%, and the stock cratered 40%. Zuckerberg's exact words on that EPS call were: "In light of increased investment in security, we could choose to decrease our investment in new product areas, but we're not going to—because that wouldn't be the right way to serve our community and because *we run this company for the long term, not for the next quarter*" (emphasis added). That's founder talk for you. That's founder attitude for you. And that super aggressive investment led to a fundamentally stronger Facebook, which helped create a great long-term stock.
- **Example C.** In mid-2011, Netflix unsuccessfully attempted to both jack up prices and spin off its DVD-by-mail business. In what became known as the Qwikster fiasco, Netflix separated its DVD and streaming businesses, requiring subscribers who used both services to set up two separate accounts and to pay $16 per month, up from $10. This ended up being the "New Coke" moment of the Internet era—a horrifically botched product decision. The result was subscriber outrage, the loss of 800,000 customers during the September 2011 quarter, and damage to the brand that took over a year to repair. When the company announced that 800,000 sub loss on October 24, 2011, the stock tanked

35% in one day from $17 to $11. *Saturday Night Live* did a wonderful satire of this, cementing this fiasco into the tech history books.

A few months after the Qwikster fiasco, I had dinner with one of the Netflix board members. I asked him how the board could have signed off on what seemed like—with 20/20 hindsight—such a terrible idea. His response illustrated the power of founders. He said that the board did have qualms about the move, but the board endorsed it out of respect for Hastings. The board member's words were: "When Michael Jordan says: 'Give me the ball; I'm going to drive to the hole,' you give Michael Jordan the ball." This is the power of founders.

The real mistake behind the Qwikster fiasco was the attempt by Hastings to force the market. His vision and belief was that the home video market was going to streaming, and there would be significant advantages to being the largest in the market. So he tried to use pricing and product options to accelerate the shift to streaming. He tried to force the market, and it backfired on him. Right vision, wrong strategy. Netflix did eventually recover, and Hastings learned from the fiasco.

What isn't as well remembered is that in the teeth of the Qwikster storm, Netflix announced market launches into the United Kingdom and Ireland, adding to recent international launches in Latin America. Netflix also announced that this international expansion would cause the company to tip from profitability in 2011 back to loss mode in 2012. Essentially, NFLX shares were on fire (as in burning up), and Netflix management was pouring *more* gas on the fire. NFLX shares went as low as $7.70 over the next 12 months, before finally recovering to Qwikster levels ($23) by the end of 2012, then doubling in 2013, as evidence of Netflix's international success started to show up. What kind of company doubles down like that, knowing that its stock is going to get hammered? A founder-led company, that's what kind. And that aggressive international bet, even in the wake of a self-imposed debacle, paid off in spades for Reed Hastings and Netflix and long-term NFLX shareholders.

- **Example D.** In August 2015, Google announced that it was reorganizing the company into a new structure called Alphabet, with all the key Google assets (Search, YouTube, etc.) placed in a core Google segment and the rest being placed in a segment called Other Bets. Larry Page's letter describing Other Bets referred to "smaller bets in areas that might seem very speculative or even strange when compared to our current businesses." These words were actually lifted from the founders' letter included in the S1 filed 11 years earlier. And those "smaller bets" included Life Sciences (which was developing glucose-sensing contact lenses), Calico (focused on longevity . . . as in human longevity . . . as in curing death), Wing (a drone delivery service), and Waymo (Google's autonomous vehicle unit). It all sounded wonderful, until the market realized that those "smaller bets" were generating almost $4 billion in operating losses in 2015. Loss levels that were anything but "small" and were going to continue at that level for at least five years with de minimis revenue to show for it. And you know what kind of companies can insist on making these "smaller bets"? Founder-led companies. It helps that the founders (Brin and Page) owned 51% of the GOOGL voting shares, giving them effective control over the company.

Whether the Other Bets will ever pay off for GOOGL and its public shareholders is uncertain. They have been referred to widely as "moonshots." Given the magnitude of the end markets they address—autonomous driving, human longevity—I think "galaxy shots" might be the more appropriate term. But the key point is that it is its founders' vision and chutzpah that allows Google to run massive losses for years in support of "smaller bets." As Page wrote in his Alphabet letter: "Sergey and I are seriously in the business of starting new things." I don't believe a non-founder would be able to make that kind of statement and act on it. My guess is that GOOGL long-term shareholders will continue to benefit from this approach.

- **Example E.** A lot of management discussion and debate went into the Zillow April 2018 decision to enter the direct home-buying/-selling market. Executives and the board had a reasonably good understanding of the share price risk of this "pivot" into a less desirable, uncertain business model. And that risk certainly came to pass, with ZG shares trading off over 40% post the announcement. But Zillow went ahead with the pivot, precisely because its three key founders (Barton, Frink, and Rascoff) were all determined to go ahead with the move, regardless of any negative reaction by Wall Street. As one of them told me later, they were willing to say, "F off" to Wall Street (at least near term) if the market didn't like or understand the pivot. It helped that Barton and Frink controlled a large chunk of the company's shareholder vote, but as founders, the three individuals had the ability and the credibility to take on this type of risky decision. I am skeptical that a non-founder executive could have pulled off this type of pivot, which has turned out to be enormously beneficial to ZG shareholders.

So those are the main examples of the long-term stock benefits of founder-led companies. One other quick example comes to mind—Tesla and Elon Musk. As an analyst, I never covered TSLA. But as a regular market participant, it was impossible to not notice the audacity, vision, and drive of that company's founder. It's hard to see how Musk hasn't been a key part of that company's and that stock's success.

Now just because almost every single one of the most successful tech stocks has belonged to founder-led companies doesn't mean that all founder-led companies make great stocks. Grubhub was a founder-led company. Pandora (the music streaming company, not the jewelry company) was a founder-led company. Both were acquired at market valuations dramatically below what their biggest competitors (DoorDash and Spotify) currently trade at.

And there's the example of Priceline, which was a monster stock for a decade and extremely well run by an operator CEO (Jeff Boyd) who was not one of the company's founders.

But the stock track records do tend to reflect positively on founder-led companies. So this should likely be a lean-in factor when looking at companies and stocks.

LONG-TERM ORIENTATION

Think long term, win long term. So trite, so true. But I do really believe that this long-term orientation has been a clear characteristic of some of the best management teams that I have tracked in tech. There's one in particular that has done long-term shareholders a great service by maintaining a long-term orientation. I'm not talking Amazon or Google or Netflix. I'm talking Facebook.

Perhaps none of the top tech founders highlighted at the beginning of this lesson has been more surrounded by controversy than Facebook cofounder Mark Zuckerberg. Bezos, Jobs, Gates, Page, Brin—none of them had a sensational Hollywood movie (*The Social Network*) released about them and their company while they were still running a private company. Their IPO roadshow attire didn't stir investor debate in the way that Zuckerberg's hoodie did—"Hoodiegate!" And none of them was accused of undermining democracy and civil society to the extent that Zuckerberg has been, especially in the wake of the 2016 US presidential election.

You could blame this controversy on Zuckerberg himself, possibly on his personality. But I don't believe his personality is dramatically different from that of those other tech founders. Zuckerberg has always struck me as obsessed with the growth and success of his company, but that same charge could be leveled against any of the other major tech founders. And this obsession with growth is pretty much exactly what investors should be looking for in a company leader. Zuckerberg has also struck me, frankly, as at least as concerned with how to promote a healthy civil society as most of the other major tech executives. I'm not sure if that's a high or a low bar, but it's a bar. You may disagree with Zuckerberg on whether and how to defend free speech and regulate hate speech and propaganda, but I give him credit for publicly expressing his free speech views in detail, as he did in a Georgetown University speech in 2019.

I think the controversy around Zuckerberg has largely to do with the incredible influence of the Facebook platform, with its almost 3 billion users. Which means it pretty much represents humankind (except for the 1.4 billion people who live in China). Which means what's expressed on Facebook's platform is good, bad, beautiful, and ugly. It's us. Enabling and then moderating that global human interaction may well be an impossible task. Impossible in that there is guaranteed to be someone who doesn't like how you are doing it. Hence, the controversy around Facebook and Zuckerberg. But enough of that.

What as an analyst I have consistently seen and heard from FB management is a long-term orientation. Frankly, I believe this characteristic of Zuckerberg's company is underappreciated. And for public investors, it was there at the very beginning. Here's Zuckerberg on the company's first public earnings call: *"Hopefully, you'll come away from today's call with a clear sense of the investments we're making to create value over the long term* by making Facebook even more useful for all of the people who use our services worldwide" (emphasis added).

Here's Zuckerberg two calls later: "One of the questions I frequently get asked are *what are the big changes we want to make in the world over the next 5 or 12 years?* Now that we've connected 1 billion people, what is the next big ambition? There are three main goals I would like us to achieve. Connect everyone, understand the world, and help build the knowledge economy" (emphasis added). How many public company CEOs talk about 5- and 12-year plans on their earnings calls? From my experience, very few. But this is exactly what you, as a long-term shareholder, would want a CEO to be talking about. A distinct positive for many earnings calls after that has been Zuckerberg spending time on each call updating investors on the company's progress against those three goals.

Long-term investors want executives to do more than just talk about long-term goals. While talking the talk matters, walking the talk—like when Facebook announced its aggressive investments and slashed forward Street estimates on its June quarter 2018 EPS call—really matters. When you come across management teams that do both of these things, it's a promising sign.

GREAT INDUSTRY VISION

Type "Who invented streaming?" into Google, and you'll learn that George O. Squier did back in the 1920s, when he was awarded patents for a system for the transmission and distribution of signals over electrical lines. You'll also learn that this was the technical basis for what later became Muzak.

So Netflix didn't invent streaming. Nor did it invent Muzak. Lose some, win some. But it did essentially invent the video streaming category that we know today, when it announced its limited streaming service in January 2007. That's industry vision, another characteristic of great management teams.

When Hastings announced the Netflix streaming offering 15 years ago, he made the following two comments to the *New York Times*: "Because DVD is not a hundred-year format, people wonder what will Netflix's second act be." And: "We have seen so many Silicon Valley companies follow a single generation of computing. Investors are rightfully scared of single-model companies." Seems clear early on that Hastings and Netflix knew that the company would have to be much more than a DVD rental company. Heck, a streaming future was already implied in the very name of the company, and it was founded a decade before consumer broadband adoption was advanced enough to make streaming commercially viable. *That's* vision.

Current NFLX investors will smile at one of the other comments Hastings made on the day of the streaming launch back in 2007. In response to a question about competition, Hastings told *Forbes*: "I worry mostly about the competition for time—user-generated videos, online games." More than a decade later, in his December 2018 shareholder letter, Hastings argued: "We compete with (and lose to) Fortnite more than HBO." That Fortnite comment elicited a fair amount of debate among the financial crew, but at least Hastings has been consistent about Netflix's competitive risk from day one. That said, he may have gone a bit over the top when he declared in 2017 that "we actually compete with sleep." Thankfully, he didn't declare that Netflix competes with the other "s" word that people do in their beds.

There was one other comment on that 2007 launch day that proved profoundly prophetic. In comments reported by *Forbes*, Hastings predicted that Netflix streaming would eventually include "a user model, an economic model and a membership model, growing film selection and screen selection. . . . We'd love to have this on cellphone screens, computer screens and televisions connected to the Internet." Keep in mind that this forecast was made before the launch of the iPhone (about two weeks before). I mean, wow! Hastings and Netflix had execution challenges over the following decade, but their vision was *spot on*! That's extraordinarily impressive.

Will Hastings and Netflix's vision of entertainment remain as impressive going forward? Who knows? But the fact that they correctly predicted the mass appeal of both DVD-by-mail and streaming has to give one confidence that they can. This is exactly the kind of successful industry vision you want to find in a management team.

MANIACAL FOCUS ON CUSTOMER SATISFACTION

Warren Buffett has published a shareholder letter every year for over 50 years. These letters are influential among investment professionals and individual investors. They contain invaluable lessons on investing and on managing businesses. You can buy a book with the unedited versions of the first 50 shareholder letters for $274.99 (yikes!) on Amazon.com.

You can also go to the Amazon investor relations site and find all the annual shareholder letters Jeff Bezos has written since 1997. Bezos writes these himself. I have several times published a report basely solely on the release of the annual letter. Some of the most important letters, in my opinion, have been:

1. The 1997 letter, "the original letter," where Bezos introduces the company's long-term mindset and its obsession with satisfying customers.
2. The 2000 letter, where Bezos acknowledged the dramatic decline in AMZN shares, reminded holders that the market is a weighing machine in the long term, and acknowledged errors in investing in Pets.com and living.com.

3. The 2005 letter, where Bezos describes the math-based decision process by which Amazon is managed.
4. The 2007 letter, "the Kindle letter," where Bezos describes the recent successful launch of the Kindle.
5. The 2013 letter, "the Everything letter," where Bezos provides a progress report on nine of the company's segments/initiatives, including AWS, Prime, Fire TV, and Fresh Grocery.
6. The 2014 letter, "the Fourth Pillar letter," where Bezos describes Marketplace, Prime, and AWS as Amazon's three pillars and pledges to find a fourth.
7. The 2016 letter, where Bezos discusses how the company can remain innovative despite its massive size and continue to act like it's Day 1. And . . .
8. The 2019 letter (published in spring 2020), where Bezos describes how Amazon performed during the Covid-19 crisis.

These letters offer invaluable lessons and thoughts from one of the most successful entrepreneurs and executives of the last 25 years. (They're also substantially cheaper than $274.99.)

At the end of each annual letter, Bezos always affixes his original 1997 letter to show, I believe, the consistency of the company, at least in terms of its long-term investment horizon and customer satisfaction obsession.

Of all the tech companies I have followed over the past quarter century, I don't believe there is one that has more consistently, relentlessly, and successfully focused on customer satisfaction than Amazon. Over the long term, that focus and that obsession have generated truly amazing returns for long-term investors. So investors—and executives—would do well to follow the Amazon customer satisfaction blueprint.

How exactly to do that in practice is hard to know, but starting out with the goals and objectives surely helps. In Table 8.2, I pick out from each of the 23 shareholder letters that Bezos has written the comment or the passage that best captures Amazon's obsession with customer satisfaction. At a minimum, look for these sentiments in the comments of any management team you are considering investing behind.

TABLE 8.2 Amazon Founder's Letters to Shareholders: Customer Obsession Nuggets

Year	Quote
1997	"Amazon.com uses the Internet to create real value for its customers and, by doing so, hopes to create an enduring franchise, even in established and large markets."
1998	"I constantly remind our employees to be afraid. . . . Not of our competition, but of our customers. Our customers have made our business what it is, they are the ones with whom we have a relationship, and they are the ones to whom we owe a great obligation."
1999	"Our vision is to use this platform to build Earth's most customer-centric company, a place where customers can come to find and discover anything and everything they might want to buy online."
2000	"Industry growth and new customer adoption will be driven over the coming years by relentless improvements in the customer experience of online shopping."
2001	"Our consumer franchise is our most valuable asset, and we will nourish it with innovation and hard work. . . . To that end, we are committed to extending our leadership in e-commerce in a way that benefits customers and therefore, inherently, investors—you can't do one without the other."
2002	"In short, what's good for customers is good for shareholders."
2003	"We have a strong team of hard-working, innovative folks building Amazon.com. They are focused on the customer and focused on the long term. On that time scale, the interests of shareowners and customers are aligned."
2004	"We work to increase operating profit by focusing on improving all aspects of the customer experience."
2005	"Relentlessly returning efficiency improvements and scale economies to customers in the form of lower prices creates a virtuous cycle that leads over the long term to a much larger dollar amount of free cash flow, and thereby to a much more valuable Amazon.com."
2006	"As we continue to grow, we'll work to maintain a culture that embraces new businesses. We will do so in a disciplined way, with an eye on returns, potential size, and the ability to create differentiation that customers care about."
2007	"Your team of missionaries here is fervent about driving free cash flow per share and returns on capital. We know we can do that by putting customers first."

2008	"In this turbulent global economy, our fundamental approach remains the same. Stay heads down, focused on the long term and obsessed over customers. . . . Our pricing objective is to earn customer trust, not to optimize short-term profit dollars."
2009	"Taken as a whole, the set of goals is indicative of our fundamental approach. Start with customers, and work backwards."
2010	"We have unshakeable conviction that the long-term interests of shareowners are perfectly aligned with the interests of customers."
2011	"Amazonians are leaning into the future, with radical and transformational innovations that create value for thousands of authors, entrepreneurs, and developers."
2012	"Our energy at Amazon comes from the desire to impress customers. . . . We do work to pay attention to competitors and be inspired by them, but it is a fact that the customer-centric way is at this point a defining element of our culture."
2013	"Failure comes part and parcel with invention. . . . We believe in failing early and iterating until we get it right . . . and when we hit on something that is really working for customers, we double-down on it with hopes to turn it into an even bigger success."
2014	"Marketplace, Prime, and Amazon Web Services are three big ideas. We're lucky to have them, and we're determined to improve and nurture them—make them even better for customers. You can also count on us to work hard to find a fourth. . . . With the opportunities unfolding in front of us to serve customers better through invention, we assure you we won't stop trying."
2015	"Amazon and AWS . . . They share a distinctive organizational culture that cares deeply about and acts with conviction on a small number of principles. I'm talking about customer obsession rather than competitor obsession."
2016	"There are many advantages to a customer-centric approach, but here's the big one: customers are always beautifully, wonderfully dissatisfied, even when they report being happy and business is great. Even when they don't yet know it, customers want something better, and your desire to delight customers will drive you to invent on their behalf."
2017	"I sense that the same customer empowerment phenomenon is happening broadly across everything we do at Amazon and most other industries as well. You cannot rest on your laurels in this world. Customers won't have it."
2018	"It's critical to ask customers what they want, listen carefully to their answers, and figure out a plan to provide it thoughtfully and quickly (speed matters in business!). No business could thrive without that kind of customer obsession."
2019	"One thing we've learned from the COVID-19 crisis is how important Amazon has become to our customers. We want you to know we take this responsibility seriously, and we're proud of the work our teams are doing to help customers through this difficult time."

OTHER KEY MANAGEMENT CHARACTERISTICS

Several other key characteristics and factors showed up among the most successful companies and stocks that I have analyzed: founders and CEOs with substantial technology backgrounds, management teams with deep benches and lots of operating experience, a deep commitment to product and service innovation, management teams that are adept at hiring and retaining top talent, and the ability to be forthright with employees and investors about mistakes and challenges.

There is a clear pattern among the most successful founders and CEOs across the tech sector. Almost all of the top tech executives I have tracked have had a background in computer science or engineering. If you're going to run a tech company, it probably does help to have a tech background.

Jack Ma at Alibaba is a big exception to the above rule among the major tech companies. At a conference in 2010, he disclosed that he didn't acquire a computer until he was 33 years old and had never actually written a line of code. I met him several times both before and after the Alibaba IPO. He always struck me as extraordinarily humble. His personal history also implies extraordinary grit. He applied to Harvard Business School 10 times and got rejected every time. He failed the entrance exam for the Hangzhou Teachers College twice. Perhaps his most disheartening setback may have been when he applied for a job with KFC when it opened in Hangzhou. Of the 24 applicants, only he was rejected. These are funny events, but they also suggest an extraordinary amount of tenacity. This is a guy who biked 17 miles a day for nine years to give guided tours to tourists to improve his English. Arguably, Ma's is the grittiest and most impressive story among the Tech Titans. Oh, and he and Alibaba decisively beat both eBay and Amazon in China. Decisively.

In terms of deep management benches and lots of operating experience, Amazon and Google both provide great examples. I believe one of the key success factors for Google over the years was the presence and input of Eric Schmidt, who was considered to have brought "mature supervision" to early-stage Google. After running Novell as its chairman and CEO, he joined Google in early 2001 and became its CEO later that year, three years prior to its IPO. Schmidt certainly increased the credibility of the company with public investors, but he also brought greater focus and discipline to a company that badly needed it. It's been reported that Page and Brin hired Schmidt for three reasons. They recognized that they lacked the operating experience to scale up Google, and they believed Schmidt had that. They respected Schmidt's technical knowledge. Finally, they were impressed by the fact that Schmidt was the only CEO applicant who had actually been to Burning Man, the annual communal event in the Nevada desert geared around "creation, revelry, inclusion, and endurance."

Maybe, in fact, attendance at Burning Man should be considered a key criterion for management excellence. Table 8.3 recalls Table 8.1, suggesting a loose correlation between tech company success and CEO Burning Man attendance. Perhaps the right question for investors to ask any tech CEO is: "Have you been to Burning Man?"

As for the ability to be forthright about mistakes and challenges, three quick examples come to mind. First, the October 19, 2011, public video apology by Reed Hastings ("Netflix CEO Reed Hastings Apologizes for Mishandling the Change to Qwikster") is a rare public mea culpa in the annals of corporate America. Hastings took a lot of flak for that—including for wearing a teal, partly buttoned shirt during the video—but his directness and willingness to accept responsibility did give him and the company long-term credibility in the eyes of some investors. Second, the 2000 Amazon founder's letter, in which Bezos acknowledges his mistake in investing in Pets.com and living.com. All executives make mistakes, but not too many publicly acknowledge them and then explain what they got wrong. Bezos devoted part of the letter that year to

TABLE 8.3 Correlation Between Burning Man Attendance and Tech CEO Excellence

Company	Year Founded	Location	Founder(s)	Founder Tenure (Years)	Burning Man Attendance	Market Cap ($B)
Alibaba	1999	Hangzhou, China	Jack Ma and others	20	No	713.14
Amazon	1994	Seattle, WA	Jeff Bezos	27	Yes	1,664.28
Apple	1976	Cupertino, CA	Steve Jobs and others	23	Yes	2,283.35
Facebook	2004	Menlo Park, CA	Mark Zuckerberg and others	17	Yes	767.31
Google	1998	Mountain View, CA	Larry Page and Sergey Brin	23	Yes	1,401.76
Micosoft	1975	Redmond, WA	Bill Gates and Paul Allen	45	?	1,838.57
Netflix	1997	Los Gatos, CA	Reed Hastings and Marc Randolph	24	?	247.61
Shopify	2004	Ottawa, Canada	Tobia Lütke and others	17	No	174.70
Tencent	1998	Shenzen, China	Ma Huateng and others	23	?	1,103.22
Tesla	2003	Palo Alto, CA	Elon Musk and others	17	Yes	815.36

Steve Jobs's tenure excludes the period when Jobs left Apple in 1985 and rejoined in 1997; it's unclear whether Jobs went to Burning Man, but his image was in the musical *Burning Man*.
Market cap as of Febuary 9, 2021.

explaining this mistake—again, creating long-term credibility in the eyes of some investors.

The third example is a personal favorite. During the depths of the 2007–2008 financial crisis, public Internet executives on EPS calls were constantly asked how the financial meltdown was impacting their business. I know. I was one of the analysts asking that question. Although reported growth rates were clearly slowing, none of the executives were willing to acknowledge on their earnings calls how negative their operating environment was. The Internet sector, including at that time the mighty Google, Amazon, eBay, and Yahoo!, was supposed to be bulletproof, powered by super strong secular tailwinds. No way they could be impacted by something as pedestrian as a global recession! But one executive did acknowledge that the global crisis was seriously impacting his business. Dara Khosrowshahi, the then CEO of Expedia. He opened up his earnings call with the statement: "It's a dog's breakfast out there," and then proceeded to detail the headwinds then facing Expedia because of the crisis. I commended him for his candor in my earnings note. And a decade later, when Khosrowshahi was selected to be CEO of Uber, I specifically pointed out that example of candor as one reason why he could be an ideal CEO for Uber. Long-term credibility in the eyes of some investors . . . and analysts.

The ability to be forthright about mistakes and challenges is another characteristic investors should look for in tech CEOs—in all CEOs, for that matter.

Management teams *really* matter. The quality of the management team is possibly the single most important factor in tech investing. Because in the long term, stocks are largely driven by fundamentals, and fundamentals are largely driven by management teams. Get the management team right, and you'll likely get the stock right. TAMs matter too. As do relentlessly pursuing product innovation and getting the value proposition right. But management teams largely control the last two factors. So if you get the management team right, you'll likely get the fundamentals right, and thus the stock right. Perhaps the most important stock ticker is: CEO.

Here's what to look for in a management team. Founder-led companies (practically all the biggest tech stocks have been founder-led), long-term orientation (like Zuckerberg with 1-, 5-, and 10-year goals), great industry vision (Hastings essentially inventing streaming), a maniacal focus on customer satisfaction (read the Amazon shareholder letters), deep technology backgrounds and operating benches, a deep focus on product innovation, the ability to recruit and retain the best talent, and the ability to be forthright with employees and investors about mistakes and challenges. You will rarely get all of these, and you don't need to have all of these. But you'll want to find most of these to believe in the quality of the management team. Finding management teams that pass the Burning Man Test might also be useful. . . .)

Unlike investment funds, with management teams, past performance *is* an indicator of future performance. When you have management teams that have built successful track records, you stick with them. A successful track record doesn't mean consistently beating Street quarterly earnings estimates—that's expectations management, not fundamentals generation. A successful track record doesn't mean having a fab-looking stock chart—lots of factors go into near-term stock movements. A successful track does mean generating consistent premium revenue growth, successfully introducing new products and feature improvements, and winning greater customer satisfaction and loyalty. These fundamentals and their core drivers will likely deliver good-looking long-term stock charts. The management team is most responsible for those fundamentals and those core drivers.

LESSON 9

Valuation Is in the Eye of the Tech Stockholder

Valuation frameworks can be useful in picking tech stocks. But valuation is not a science. And it carries precision traps—precise answers where precision isn't realistic, possible, or justified. Valuation should *not* be the most important factor in the stock-picking decision process. Action questions will vary based on whether the company is generating robust earnings, minimal earnings, or no earnings. But your overriding action question should always be: Does the current valuation look ballpark reasonable?

Warning—what follows is not a how-to-value-tech-stocks lesson. There are plenty of good books on valuing equities. Rather, these are the lessons learned from a practitioner in the arena who ran countless different valuation models over more than two decades in what seemed like sometimes simple and sometimes challenging valuation circumstances, all with the goal of trying to call a stock. And my most important lesson learned was the fourth sentence in that summary paragraph above: Valuation should *not* be the most important factor in the stock-picking decision process.

Uber (UBER) IPO'd on Friday, May 10, 2019, at $45 and traded off 8% on its first day to below $42. Except for a brief period in late June 2019, it remained a broken IPO for 18 months, consistently trading below its IPO price. In mid-March 2020, in the wake of intense Covid-19 pandemic pressures on ridesharing demand and investor concerns about Uber's liquidity, Uber's share price broke below $15, almost 70% below its IPO price.

Lyft (LYFT) IPO'd on Friday, March 29, 2019, at $72 and traded up 9% on its first day to $78. But as of early 2021, it had yet to reach that price level again. And except for two days in April 2019, it has been a broken IPO, trading well below that $72 level. In mid-March 2020, it plummeted all the way down to $16, almost 75% below its IPO price.

In October 2019, as the share prices of both UBER and LYFT were struggling, influential CNBC contributor "Downtown" Josh Brown wrote that Uber's failed IPO changed investor sentiment from "fantasy valuation back to profitability." Brown elaborated:

> I think the bigger takeaway is that everything changed this spring after Uber's failed IPO. . . . This experiment—bringing a company public at a massive valuation that stated in its S-1 filing that there was a chance they'd never earn a profit—produced a mass sentiment shift among savvy investors and retail buyers alike. It was a time's up moment.

Although the Covid-19 crisis did have a materially negative impact on demand for the two leading US ridesharing services, Uber and Lyft shares were under pressure long before the pandemic because of the large losses both companies were running. In 2019, Lyft generated $2.6 billion in net income loss, while Uber generated $8.6 billion in net loss. These loss levels were practically unprecedented. And in the quarters post their IPOs, there was substantial uncertainty whether Uber and Lyft would ever be profitable. That uncertainty was exactly what Brown's comments captured.

It is striking that UBER then traded up almost 70% in 2020. As of early 2021, Uber's share price had skyrocketed 300% since its mid-March 2020 lows, and it is now more than 30% above its IPO price. And yet the profitability outlook for Uber remains uncertain. Most Street models don't have Uber generating meaningfully positive GAAP earnings and FCF until 2023, at the earliest. On a price-sales basis, UBER and LYFT are trading at similar or higher multiples than when they went public. Arguably, we're right back in "fantasy valuation" land.

Welcome to the world of tech stock valuations.

WHY TECH/GROWTH STOCKS ARE OFTEN EXPENSIVE

Quick, what's the first word you think of when you hear the term "tech stocks"? Some of you may respond, "exciting"; some of you may respond, "high flying." But I'd wager that many of you would respond, "expensive." The "expensive" crowd would be right.

The NASDAQ, a good barometer for tech stocks, has traded at an average forward multiple of approximately 20x over the last 20 years, while the S&P 500 has traded at an average forward multiple of 15x. You can cut these numbers a lot of ways, but most ways will clearly show that the NASDAQ (i.e., tech stocks) trades at a premium.

Does this mean tech stocks are expensive? Yes, intrinsically. But not if you adjust for their growth. P/E multiples in a vacuum aren't that useful. It's more useful to know whether a stock is trading at a premium or a discount to the market. It's also more useful to know whether a stock is trading at a premium or a discount to its industry comps. But it's most useful to know how a stock is trading relative to its own growth rate. Valuation that isn't growth-adjusted is almost meaningless.

As a rule of thumb, the higher the growth rate, the higher the multiple will likely be. Companies that are growing earnings and free cash flow faster are more valuable than those that are growing them slower, all else being equal. And all else would include factors like capital/investment intensity, working capital requirements, and so on.

High growth rates can turn "expensive" stocks into reasonable stocks over time. Here's a quick example.

Say you have two stocks. The first is a $20 "tech stock" that is generating $1.00 in EPS and thus trades at a 20x P/E (approximately the median NASDAQ P/E over the last 20 years). The second is a $15 "regular stock" that is also generating $1.00 in EPS and thus trades at a 15x P/E (roughly the median S&P 500 P/E over the last 20 years). So the second stock appears less expensive than the first stock.

But suppose that "tech stock" trades at a 20x P/E multiple because the market believes it's a sustainable 20% EPS grower, while the "regular stock" trades at a 15x P/E multiple because the market believes it's a sustainable 10% EPS grower (which is close to the average S&P 500 EPS growth over the last 20 years). As another rule of thumb, stocks typically trade consistent with their perceived growth rate or at a modest premium to that. I have found that a consistent 10% EPS grower will trade between 15x and 20x, while a 20% EPS grower will trade between 20x and 40x. While lower-growth stocks can often trade at 2x their perceived growth rate (20x for 10% EPS growth), I find it rarer that high-growth stocks do, because the market is inherently suspicious that premium growth rates can be sustained. Clever market.

Getting back to what can cause high growth rates to turn "expensive" stocks into reasonable stocks, see Table 9.1. Again, you have a 20x P/E stock and a 15x P/E stock. The latter is less expensive. However, if the respective share prices don't change (we're in hypothetical land here), and the EPS growth rates stay consistent, the P/E

TABLE 9.1 How Growth Turns "Expensive" Stocks into "Reasonable" Stocks

$20 Tech Stock—20% Growth			$15 Regular Stock—10% Growth		
Year	EPS	P/E	Year	EPS	P/E
1	$1.00	20.0x	1	$1.00	15.0x
2	$1.20	16.7x	2	$1.10	13.6x
3	$1.44	13.9x	3	$1.21	12.4x
4	$1.73	11.6x	4	$1.33	11.3x
5	$2.07	9.6x	5	$1.46	10,2x
6	$2.49	8.0x	6	$1.61	9.3x
7	$2.99	6.7x	7	$1.77	8.5x
8	$3.58	5.6x	8	$1.95	7.7x
9	$4.30	4.7x	9	$2.14	7.0x
10	$5.16	3.9x	10	$2.36	6.4x

multiples will converge in four years, and the more expensive "tech stock" will be less expensive than the "regular stock" in five years.

No, don't rush out and buy tech stocks. But at least appreciate the importance of growth-adjusting valuation multiples.

Here's another way to look at it. *If* tech stocks can hold their premium multiple, then any premium growth they generate can translate into premium stock performance. Take that $20 tech stock currently trading with a 20x P/E and generating 20% EPS growth. *If* that stock can hold its multiple and its growth rate, in the third year, it will be looking at $1.44 in EPS and a $28.80 stock price, for a return of 44%. Meanwhile that "regular" stock, if it can hold its 15x P/E multiple and its 10% EPS growth, will be looking at $1.21 in EPS in its third year and a stock price of $18.15, for a return of 21%. Take this analysis out five years, and the relative returns are 107% for the tech stock and 46% for the "regular" stock. (See Table 9.2.)

TABLE 9.2 How Premium EPS Growth Translates into Premium Value

$20 Tech Stock—20% Growth					$15 Regular Stock—10% Growth				
Year	EPS	P/E	Price	Return Versus Year 1	Year	EPS	P/E	Price	Return Versus Year 1
1	$1.00	20.0x	$20.00	—	1	$1.00	15.0x	$15.00	—
2	$1.20	20.0x	$24.00	20%	2	$1.10	15.0x	$16.50	10%
3	$1.44	20.0x	$28.80	44%	3	$1.21	15.0x	$18.15	21%
4	$1.73	20.0x	$34.56	73%	4	$1.33	15.0x	$19.97	33%
5	$2.07	20.0x	$41.47	107%	5	$1.46	15.0x	$21.96	46%
6	$2.49	20.0x	$49.77	149%	6	$1.61	15.0x	$24.16	61%
7	$2.99	20.0x	$59.72	199%	7	$1.77	15.0x	$26.57	77%
8	$3.58	20.0x	$71.66	258%	8	$1.95	15.0x	$29.23	95%
9	$4.30	20.0x	$86.00	330%	9	$2.14	15.0x	$32.15	114%
10	$5.16	20.0x	$103.20	416%	10	$2.36	15.0x	$35.37	136%

Again, don't rush out and buy tech stocks. But appreciate the importance of growth-adjusting valuation multiples. Actually, it's not just important. It's critical.

To make this point more realistic, let's look at the example of Facebook over the last several years. Over the five-year period 2016–2020, FB shares traded in a forward P/E multiple range of 17x to 25x, although it did for brief moments break above and below that range. For a company like Facebook, I believed this multiple range to be at times attractive. Yes, it was a premium to the market for almost that entire time, but Facebook proved to be a consistent premium revenue growth company. Over those five years, FB's top line grew 54% (2016), 47% (2017), 37% (2018), 27% (2019), and 22% (2020)—what I called rare-air growth. Remember that only about 2% of the S&P 500 have sustained 20%+ growth for multiple years. And generating 22% revenue growth in 2020 (the year of Covid-19) as an advertising revenue company was a truly impressive, even shocking, feat.

Over those five years, Facebook also maintained premium EPS growth, as detailed in Table 9.3. The one year in which its EPS growth was pedestrian (7% EPS growth, excluding a one-time $5 billion payment to the FTC) was 2019, when it was in heavy investment mode.

TABLE 9.3 Facebook's Fab Fundamental Story

	2016	2017	2018	2019	2020
Revenue ($MM)	**$27,638**	**$40,653**	**$55,838**	**$70,697**	**$85,965**
Revenue Growth	54%	47%	37%	27%	22%
GAAP EPS	**$3.49**	**$5.39**	**$7.65**	**$8.18**	**$10.09**
EPS Growth	171%	54%	42%	7%	23%

And what happened to FB shares over that five-year period? They dramatically outperformed the market. FB shares soared 161%, almost 2x the return of the S&P 500 (up 84%). FB did underperform the market in 2018 and traded roughly in line with the market in 2016, but it materially outperformed in the remaining three years.

To me, this was similar to the outperformance period of PCLN from the period 2003–2018, when its shares rose over 120x. While there was volatility with both stocks, they both provided the long-term investor (somebody investing with a time horizon of more than a year) with excellent returns, because they were premium revenue growth companies *and* because they traded at a discount to their growth rates—that is, their P/E multiples were below their EPS growth rates.

This leads to one clear stock-picking lesson. Stocks that trade at a discount to premium growth rates (e.g., 20x P/E for a 30% EPS grower) can be attractive. These opportunities don't come up too often, but they do come up—PCLN and FB, for example. They should almost always be investigated as potentially great investment opportunities.

So, yes, tech/growth stocks can appear—and can be—expensive, but that's because earnings that are growing faster are intrinsically worth more than earnings that are growing slower. The market almost always applies a higher multiple to higher-growth stocks than to lower-growth stocks. So don't be deterred by a high multiple stock. The key action question should be—is the high multiple stock likely to sustain premium revenue and EPS growth? If so, then the high multiple stock can well be a good investment.

COMPANIES WITH ROBUST EARNINGS—KNOW YOUR P/E'S AND YOUR E'S

Sometimes, valuation can be real simple. A stock trades at $100, trading at a 25x P/E on $4.00 in next-year earnings, which are growing 25% from this year. Where will the stock be in 12 months? If it holds its multiple (25x), and it is expected to continue to grow at 25%, then in 12 months, the stock will be at $125 ($5.00 in EPS multiplied by 25x P/E).

Rarely is it that easy. But here's a nice, simple, accurate, and lucky example: 2017 was a monster year for Facebook shares (Figure 9.1). They rose 53%, from $115 to $176. In early February of that year, I wrote a Bullish FB earnings note covering their strong Q4 EPS results. The title of the note was: "Still So Much to Like." With the stock then at $133, I raised my estimates and my 12-month price target to $175. This means that my 12-month price target actually came in within 0.8% of where the stock ended that year—$176. Trust me, this rarely happens. Like I said, this is a lucky example.

In that early February EPS report, I noted that FB at $133 was then trading at roughly 30x my 2017 EPS estimate of $4.51, which implied about 38% EPS growth. To come up with my price target, I estimated that FB would generate $6.29 in EPS in 2018 (which implied similar EPS growth to what I thought the company could do in 2017), and I assumed that FB's P/E multiple would fade modestly, but still remain very premium, given the consistent EPS

FIGURE 9.1 Anatomy of a (Lucky) Target Price

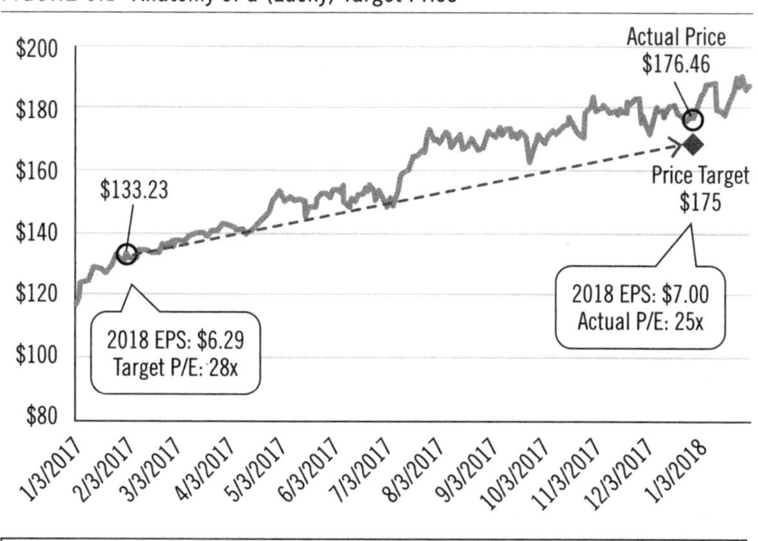

	Stock Price	2018 EPS Estimate	P/E Multiple
Estimate Versus Actual	0.8%	11.3%	–9.4%

growth I was modeling. So I applied a 28x P/E target multiple to that $6.29 in 2018 EPS to come up with a $175 price target.

Was I good, or was I lucky? Well, Facebook's 2017 EPS came in at $5.40 (about 20% higher than I had projected), which meant that FB grew its EPS an extremely strong 54% in 2017. And by the end of 2017, my 2018 EPS estimate had increased to $7.00 (about 11% higher than I had first projected). Which meant that FB ended up 2017 trading at 25x 2018 P/E (a multiple that was around 9% below what I had thought the stock would carry).

So I totally nailed the stock call—FB ended the year within 1% of my target price: A+. But my in-year 2017 EPS estimate was about 20% too low, and my forward-year 2018 EPS estimate forward EPS estimate was about 11% too low: B. And my target multiple was about 9% below where the stock actually traded: B+.

That was a simple (and lucky!) example. But it gets at what you're trying to do with valuation when there are clear and robust earnings and when the stock is trading within ballpark range of the market—call that 10x to 40x P/E. I use 40x P/E as a high-end P/E multiple because that is 2x the historical average of the NASDAQ.

Earlier I described a good stock-picker as being both a good economist (being able to reasonably forecast earnings out a year or two) and a good psychologist (being able to reasonably forecast what multiple the market will apply to those earnings). When companies have clear and robust earnings, their P/E multiples are primarily influenced by three factors: the market multiple, their sector multiples, and their perceived growth rate. If any of these change, the company's P/E multiple will probably change. So in some ways, the job of the psychologist is similar to the job of the economist, except that the economist is trying to estimate the future growth outlook of earnings, and the psychologist is trying to estimate whether there will be a change in that future growth outlook.

So the action question for the company with robust earnings is: Is its earnings growth sustainable? A 30x P/E stock with a perceived 20% EPS growth outlook will likely remain a 30x P/E stock (barring major market or sector multiple changes) as long as its perceived 20% EPS growth outlook remains unchanged (and assuming there aren't any major balance sheet or cash flow dynamics changes).

This also means that if a company's EPS growth and growth outlook slow, its multiple will likely decline or fade. The rate of the fade will depend on how quickly the EPS growth decelerates. How well the stock does will depend on whether its earnings growth remains faster than the rate at which the multiple declines. The worst situation for a stock is when its forward EPS estimates get cut and its forward EPS growth outlook gets trimmed. It's a negative double whammy, because both the E and the P/E are going down. This is exactly what happened with Snap in the year following its IPO, except in this case it was revenue estimates and forward revenue growth rates that were slashed. And that caused a material derating in SNAP shares and significant stock underperformance.

Conversely, if a company's growth and growth outlook accelerate, its multiple will likely rise. And the rate of the rise will depend on how quickly the EPS growth accelerates. This creates the possibility of a positive double whammy—when forward EPS estimates get increased and the forward EPS growth outlook gets raised. And this is exactly what happened with Netflix in early 2018 when it implemented a series of GCIs (growth curve initiatives), including a price increase and an accelerated rollout of new original content. Estimates went up, Netflix's perceived future growth outlook increased, NFLX's multiple re-rated, and NFLX shares materially outperformed.

COMPANIES WITH MINIMAL EARNINGS AND SKY-HIGH P/ES

In the case of companies with minimal earnings, you can often expect to see super high (> 50x) P/E multiples, but these can still be good investments. Both Amazon and Netflix proved this. The key action questions are: Can the company sustain premium revenue growth for a substantial period of time? Are current earnings being materially depressed by major investments? And is there reason to believe the company's long-term operating margins can be dramatically higher than current levels? If the answers to these questions are positive, then those super high P/E multiples may well be justified.

I was a Bull on NFLX shares for pretty much the entire period 2010–2020. One of the hardest parts of being a NFLX Bull during that period was defending its valuation. Yes, the company had impressive revenue and subscriber growth over that time, but for only three of those years (2010, 2011, and 2020) did the company generate positive free cash flow. And the free cash flow losses between 2012 and 2019 actually rose—and rose materially—almost every single year, from $67 million in 2012 to a whopping

$3.2 billion in 2019. Further, for many of those years, Netflix management was insistent that it planned to run the company with negative free cash flow for the foreseeable future. It refused to be pinned down to a date or a year when it would start producing positive free cash flow—not much help for an analyst trying to defend NFLX's valuation.

But what Netflix did have over that decade was consistent GAAP EPS profitability, albeit for most of that period only minimal earnings. This was a bit of an anomaly. Normally, positive EPS goes hand in hand with positive FCF. But Netflix's business model contained some unusual factors, particularly a switch from licensed content, where cash payments are made over the term of the license (usually several years), to original content, where cash payments are almost entirely up front.

Anyway, investors looking at NFLX over the last decade could definitely find a P/E pulse, but it was an extremely rapid pulse. Over the five years 2016–2020, NFLX's average forward P/E multiple was 72x (Figure 9.2). Even in early 2021, Netflix still sported an extremely high P/E multiple—approximately 55x the Street's 2021

FIGURE 9.2 **NFLX: Just Try to Justify This!**

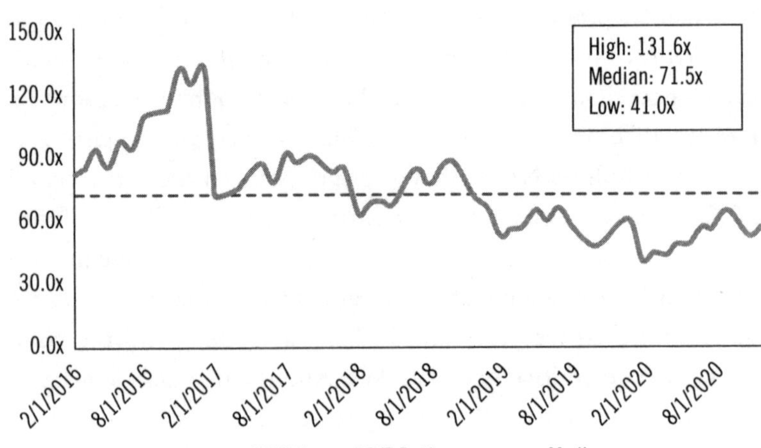

EPS ($550 stock price over $10.00 EPS). How can one possibly argue that NFLX's valuation was ballpark reasonable when it was carrying a 72x P/E multiple?!

The answer comes down to those three key action questions: Are current earnings being materially depressed by major investments? Is there a reason to believe that the company's long-term operating margins can be dramatically higher than current levels? Can the company sustain premium revenue growth for a substantial time?

On the first question, Netflix management was clear throughout 2010–2020 that it was determined to invest aggressively in marketing and, especially, in content to drive its business. International market launches necessitated a lot of marketing spend. Netflix was going into markets where no streaming service had gone before. It required a lot of advertising dollars to build up its brand awareness. The 2010 marketing spend was $300 million. It doubled to $600 million by 2014. It more than doubled to $1.4 billion by 2017. And it almost doubled again to $2.7 billion by 2019. There was always a silver lining in this marketing spend cloud. Successful subscription businesses almost always show leverage in their marketing spend (i.e., it declines as a percentage of revenue), because that marketing spend is largely geared toward acquiring new subscribers. As subscription businesses grow, their existing customer bases grow, and their new customers become a smaller percentage of their total subscriber base. That marketing spend was depressing near-term earnings, but it was an investment that would likely allow margins to rise strongly over time.

The major investment spend, however, belonged to content. During the 2016–2019 period, Netflix's spend on content more than doubled from almost $7 billion to over $14.5 billion. I referred to it as Netflix's Khrushchev strategy, after the former Soviet premier who once promised to "bury the West." Netflix's plan was to spend so much money on content that its offering would be compelling to just about any subscriber, reducing the chances subscribers would sign on with another service. Netflix would bury its competition in content spend. This was also part of Netflix's flywheel strategy—more content draws more subs, which generate more revenue, which funds more content, and so on. Near term, this content spend was depressing earnings, but long term, there was a real opportunity for Netflix to turn content spend into a step-fixed cost and thus enjoy material operating margin expansion.

The first question bleeds into the second question: Can the company's operating margins rise materially from current levels? The answer to the second question for Netflix seemed like a pretty emphatic yes. In part, because there were plenty of media companies (including Disney, Viacom, CBS, and Fox) that were generating operating margins materially higher than the low-to-mid-single-digit percentage levels that Netflix was running at from 2012 to 2016. But also because Netflix publicly committed to expanding its operating margins by 3% annually beginning in 2016. It was an odd commitment. I can't recall another public company laying out operating margin expansion as such a specific financial target. But I appreciated the financial discipline that the target implied. Much more importantly, Netflix actually delivered against those targets, driving margins from 4% in 2016 to 7% in 2017 to 10% in 2018 and to 13% in 2019. And that expansion not only burnished the credibility of Netflix management with Wall Street; it also helped drive powerful EPS growth.

On the third key action question, I believed strongly that Netflix could sustain premium revenue growth for multiple years. It faced a large TAM. It had a good management team. Netflix established and then continued to improve a powerful consumer value proposition, which in turn gave it pricing power, which fed further revenue growth. And Netflix was a subscription business, which meant that there was normally a lot of visibility into future revenue. All of this, along with that operating margin expansion, did in fact drive powerful EPS growth.

The powerful EPS growth details are shown in Table 9.4, but there's also a key insight here into the power of margin expansion. I'll still stick with the point that the highest-quality EPS growth driver is revenue growth. But operating expansion can also be powerful, especially from low levels. It's great to have high operating margins and generate lots of operating income, but in terms of EPS growth, it can be even better to have low operating margins that can significantly expand. Between 2017 and 2020, Netflix grew its EPS between 47% and 194% each year. There's always a lot of noise in EPS results, related to changing tax rates, one-time investment gains, and the like. So I always look at EPS growth in combination with operating income or EBITDA growth. Look at 2018, for example. Netflix's operating income soared 91% that year, driven by a robust 35% revenue growth and by a 42% growth in its operating margin. A 3% point increase in operating margin doesn't sound like much, but on a 7% base, that's almost 50% EPS growth right there. The truly beautiful thing is that revenue growth and operating margin growth compound into operating profit growth and EPS growth.

TABLE 9.4 NFLX EPS Growth—Is This Fast Enough for You?

($ Millions)	2016A	2017A	2018A	2019A	2020A
Revenue Y/Y Growth	**$88,307** 30%	**$116,927** 32%	**$157,943** 35%	**$201,564** 28%	**$249,961** 24%
x					
Operating Margin Y/Y Growth	**4.3%** —	**7.2%** 67%	**10.2%** 42%	**12.9%** 27%	**18.3%** 42%
=					
Operating Income Y/Y Growth	**$3,798** —	**$8,387** 121%	**$16,052** 91%	**$26,043** 62%	**$45,853** 76%
EPS Y/Y Growth	**$0.43** 51%	**$1.25** 194%	**$2.68** 115%	**$4.13** 54%	**$6.08** 47%

So, yes, Netflix sported a crazy-high 72x P/E multiple over 2016–2020, but it also had crazy-high EPS growth. Over that time, its average EPS growth was, in fact, 92%. And this was while its marketing and content investments were depressing earnings, though this was more the case in the first half of the decade.

So this is how I defended NFLX's valuation from 2011 to 2020—by addressing those three action questions. You can use these same questions to try to answer whether or how a sky-high P/E multiple may actually imply ballpark reasonable valuation with other tech stocks.

The stock-picking lessons from Amazon are somewhat similar to those from Netflix. Figure 9.3 shows a stock that also held crazy-high multiples—also a five-year median P/E of 72x. (What is it with these 72x P/E multiple companies?!) The answers to the three action questions were somewhat similar. Amazon has consistently maintained aggressive investments in a wide range of areas that have depressed its near-term EPS results. Amazon could never be seriously accused of overearning. There was certainly reason to believe that Amazon could sustain premium revenue growth given

FIGURE 9.3 AMZN's Crazy-High P/E Multiple

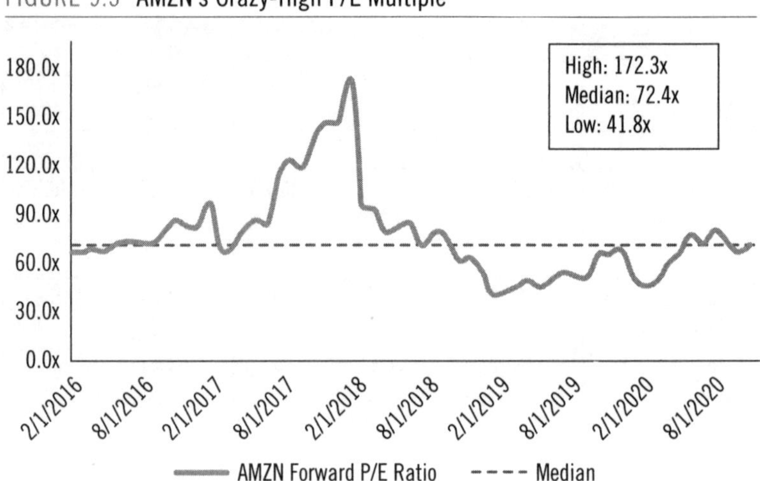

the trillion-dollar sizes of its retail sales and cloud computing TAMs and the quality of its management team. But Amazon never made the clear commitment to operating margin expansion that Netflix did. So it didn't have as consistently high an EPS growth as Netflix did. Yet it carried a similar P/E multiple. How come?

The answer came from two major factors that Amazon had that Netflix didn't have. And these two factors helped me argue that Amazon's valuation—despite its sky-high P/E multiple—was ballpark reasonable. The first factor was that Amazon likely was the best mix-shift story in tech. What I meant by that was that two of its fastest growth segments (AWS and advertising revenue) were growing materially faster than its core online retail segment, and they had much higher operating margins—roughly 25% versus 2–5% for the online retail segment. So these two segments were growing 2x as fast as the online retail segment and had something like 10x the operating margin. This meant that structurally, inexorably, inevitably, Amazon's operating margins were going to climb materially higher over time. Aggressive investments in areas like groceries and logistics could slow down this trend, but the trend itself would eventually reveal. We actually argued in a report in mid-2018 that Amazon's long-term operating margins could expand to as high as 20% because of the "best mix-shift story in tech"—essentially 4x the level that Amazon was running at that year. So, yes, there was reason to believe that Amazon's operating margin could rise materially from current levels.

The second major factor that Amazon had that Netflix didn't have was that it became a platform company. Netflix may one day expand into markets other than video subscription. But to date it hasn't. Amazon has, however, proved its ability to extend into and to succeed in a variety of different, large markets. From online retail to cloud computing to advertising to hardware devices. My guess is that it will also demonstrate success in expanding into business products/supplies, pharmacy, groceries, and logistics. That's a platform company—and a highly successful one at that—which, while it may require EPS-depressing investments near term, can help generate large revenue and profit pools in the future. So this platform reality both provided evidence that investments were masking Amazon's true earnings potential and provided more evidence that Amazon could sustain premium revenue growth for many years, even at massive scale. Amazon could "pull a Google." And at least qualitatively, this helped with the argument that AMZN's valuation was ballpark reasonable.

COMPANIES WITH NO EARNINGS—WHAT TO EXPECT WHEN YOU'RE NOT EXPECTING ANY EPS

Here's the most challenging edge case. How do you determine whether valuation is ballpark reasonable when there aren't any earnings? If there isn't an E, then there can't be a P/E, and you can't then look at growth rates or the quality of earnings to decide whether that P/E is ballpark reasonable.

This case comes up a lot, especially with tech stocks. About a third of NASDAQ companies are currently not profitable. This case comes up a lot with IPOs. Almost all the Internet IPOs I tracked over the last 10 years were of companies that had not yet achieved GAAP EPS profitability when they went public. And many of these didn't achieve GAAP EPS profitability for several years after they went public.

Table 9.5 is a partial list of these profitless IPO companies.

Professional investors use a variety of techniques to assess valuation in these cases. Many still run multiyear DCF models, with the big difference being that more of the total value is generated in the out years when profits are eventually hopefully generated, and perhaps a higher than normal discount rate is used to capture what may be greater execution risk as the company has no material public track record. Another approach is to run a model out several years until

TABLE 9.5 Going Negative? Profitless Companies @ IPO

Ticker	Company	IPO Year	Ticker	Company	IPO Year
ABNA	Airbnb	2020	QUOT	Quotient	2014
APRN	Blue Apron	2017	RDFN	Redfin	2017
BMBL	Bumble	2021	REAL	RealReal	2019
CHWY	Chewy	2019	RMBL	RumbleOn	2016
CVNA	Carvana	2017	ROKU	Roku	2017
DASH	DoorDash	2020	SHOP	Shopify	2015
DKNG	DraftKings	2019	SKLZ	Skillz	2020
EB	EventBrite	2018	SNAP	Snap	2017
ETSY	Etsy	2015	SPOT	Spotify	2018
EVER	EverQuote	2018	SVMK	SurveyMonkey	2018
FTCH	Farfetch	2018	TRUE	TrueCar	2014
FUBO	fuboTV	2013	TRUP	Trupanion	2014
FVRR	Fiverr	2019	TWTR	Twitter	2013
JMIA	Jumia	2019	UPWK	Upwork	2018
LYFT	Lyft	2019	VRM	Vroom	2020
MGNI	Magnite	2014	W	Wayfair	2014
OPEN	Opendoor	2020	WISH	Wish (ContextLogic)	2020
PINS	Pinterest	2019	WIX	Wix	2013
POSH	Poshmark	2021	WTRH	Waitr Holdings	2016
PRCH	Porch Group	2020	YEXT	Yext	2017
PTON	Peloton	2019			

robust earnings are reasonably expected to be generated, then put a growth-adjusted P/E on those earnings, and discount the resulting value back to the present using an appropriately high discount rate.

Still another approach is to look at comparable companies that are publicly traded and then to apply a multiple (e.g., price to sales, price to gross profit, or enterprise value to EBITDA) to the EPS-less company based on that comp set. There is always some "art" here in determining which comps to use. Aggressive Bulls tend to try to include high multiple stocks in the comp set to win a higher multiple for the IPO company. I tend to weigh four factors most heavily in coming up with the best comps for a profitless company: scale (companies with similar-sized revenue bases), growth (companies with similar revenue growth outlooks), gross margin, and long-term operating or EBITDA margin potential. Rarely are there perfect comps, but usually there are enough companies to come up with a reasonable range of multiples that can help determine whether a profitless company's valuation is ballpark reasonable, at least based on comps.

Uber and Lyft

This brings us back to Uber and Lyft and the "fantasy valuation" that we talked about at the start of this lesson. Again, both these companies went public in 2019 in the wake of substantial losses. Neither company was expected to generate a material profit in the near future. The 10-year DCF I published in my UBER initiation report didn't have EBITDA or free cash flow turning positive until 2023. I had a comps table (Table 9.6) in that initiation report that included Lyft, Grubhub, Etsy, and two European online delivery companies (Delivery Hero and Just Eat). The median enterprise value-to-sales multiple of that comp set was 4.0x. UBER at the time of my initiation report was trading at 3.5x, so I could conclude—and I did—that UBER's valuation at the time was ballpark reasonable, if I was willing to make one major assumption: that UBER could achieve the same profitability status as three of those comps (Grubhub, Etsy, and Just Eat), all of which were profitable.

But there were also two action questions I worked hard to address that I thought were particularly important in this case of a profitless company. They are the same two action questions that individual investors should ask in these edge valuation cases.

First, how sustainable is the company's top-line growth? Typically, these profitless companies are profitless because they are early-growth companies that have yet to achieve sufficient scale and/or are in deep investment mode. The key point is that they are early-growth

TABLE 9.6 Looking for the Right Comps for UBER

Company	Price	Market Cap	2020 Revenue	2020 Revenue Growth	2020 EV/ Sales	2019 Gross Margin	2019 EBITDA Margin
Etsy	$62	8,115	974	23%	8.1x	70%	24%
Delivery Hero	$43	7,984	1,649	44%	4.6x	57%	–27%
Just Eat	$8	5,214	1,295	24%	4.0x	67%	18%
Lyft	$58	16,745	4,210	27%	3.7x	46%	–32%
Grubhub	$65	6,054	1,734	27%	3.6x	51%	18%
			Median	27%	4.0x	57%	18%
			High	44%	8.1x	70%	24%
			Low	23%	3.6x	46%	–32%
Uber	$40	74,008	19,079	34%	3.5x	44%	–27%

Note: Price as of 5/31/2019.

companies, which means they are likely reporting premium or super premium growth. (Again, Airbnb was the rare exception—a somewhat early-stage company that was actually reporting year-over-year revenue declines at the time of its IPO, but this was due to the Covid-19 pandemic.) In the case of Lyft, the company reported 103% revenue growth in 2018, the last full year prior to its IPO. And Uber reported 43% revenue growth in 2018, its last full pre-IPO year.

I initiated coverage of both Uber and Lyft with an Outperform rating, in large part because I thought both companies would be able to generate premium revenue growth for long periods of time. And this was because I believed that ridesharing was a massive trillion-dollar TAM segment that was still early in its consumer adoption. Survey work I had run indicated that less than a third of US consumers had ever even used a ridesharing service, and I thought this penetration could more than double over time. I also believed that ridesharing carried compelling value propositions for both consumers and drivers. I declared a preference for UBER over

LYFT because it had a global presence (thus a larger TAM), while Lyft was purely a US service, and because Uber had a much stronger market share position than Lyft in the United States. The founders of Lyft (John Zimmer and Logan Green) were actively involved in running Lyft, which was a distinct positive, but I also had confidence in the management capabilities of Uber CEO Dara "Dog's Breakfast" Khosrowshahi, which I thought somewhat mitigated the fact that Uber's founders were no longer actively involved. Finally, I believed that Uber's diversification into online food delivery was a distinct positive and would help generate premium revenue growth.

Within a year of their respective IPOs, Covid-19 crushed these companies' growth rates. After 68% revenue growth in 2019, Lyft reported a 35% decline in 2020. Uber posted 26% revenue growth in 2019 and then a 15% decline in 2020. So it will take a few years to know whether their TAMs, value propositions, and management teams can deliver premium revenue growth in "normal" market conditions. But the core first question to ask in the case of a profitless company remains: How sustainable is a company's top-line growth? If you believe premium revenue growth is sustainable, it's a good reason to consider investing in the profitless company.

And That Second Question

The second key action question to ask in the case of a profitless company is . . . drumroll, please: Can the company be profitable? Gosh, that sounds brain-dead obvious. Sorry, but it's a key question. And given the number of profitless companies in the tech sector, it's one that all individual investors will likely have to answer at some point or another.

Actually, you don't have to answer this question if you don't want to. There's nothing wrong with waiting until a company has proved that it can be consistently profitable before investing. There are public investment funds with mandates that include the requirement that its portfolio companies be free cash flow positive or have a multiyear positive earnings results. To be included in the S&P

500 index, a company's most recent quarter's earnings and the sum of its trailing four consecutive quarters' earnings must be positive. That's one reason why Tesla wasn't added to the S&P 500 until late 2020, after it posted its fifth straight profitable quarter. And after it had gained a $400 billion market cap. And after its stock had risen approximately 21x or 2,000% since its IPO. That's a *lot* of market cap and stock price appreciation to leave on the table.

Although Netflix has been GAAP EPS profitable for over a decade, it generated negative free cash flow for eight straight years before returning to positive free cash flow status in 2020. Over this past decade, Netflix has been one of the best performing stocks in the S&P 500 and has added over $100 billion in market cap. If you make positive free cash flow an investment requirement, that's a *lot* of market cap and stock price appreciation to leave on the table. But again, nothing wrong with that.

Across the Internet sector that I have followed, there has been an enormous amount of market cap created by companies that are not profitable. Table 9.7 is a quick snapshot of 10 well-known public

TABLE 9.7 **Profits Schmofits—Large Tech Companies Without Profits**

Company	Market Cap*
Airbnb	$123B
Chewy	$45B
DoorDash	$63B
Lyft	$18B
Pinterest	$53B
Snap	$94B
Spotify	$67B
Uber	$111B
Wix	$16B
Zillow	$46B
Total	$636B

*As of 2/17/2021.

tech companies that have created a *lot* of market cap (approximately $636 billion) without generating any consistent GAAP EPS results. So clearly, the public markets are willing to find value where there are no earnings.

Now, it's possible that the financial markets have gone completely insane, and all this profitless market cap will be blown away overnight. I wouldn't assume that all this market cap was or is justified, but I would strongly argue that the markets are willing to bet—on a company-by-company basis—that profitless business models can eventually be profitable. That's why they can generate a lot of stock price returns before profitability is proved. So we're back to the second action question: Can the profitless company become profitable? Or how can it become profitable? Or how profitable can it become? And how can you be sure of any of this? The honest answer is . . . you can't.

The Four Profitability Logic Tests

But there are four logic tests you can run to test the profitability potential of a company. The first logic test is to ask: Are there any public companies with similar business models that are already profitable? This was the key question that allowed public investors to become comfortable investing in Pinterest, Snap, and Twitter at the time of their IPOs, when none of them were profitable. In my May 2019 initiation report on Pinterest, I listed up front one of the key investment risks: Lack of profitability to date. In my March 2017 initiation report on Snap, I listed as a key investment risk: No track record of profitability. In my November 2013 initiation report on Twitter, I highlighted as an investment risk: Uncertain monetization outlook. Not sure, in hindsight, why with Twitter I didn't just state: Lack of profitability. Blame it on youth and naïveté . . .

Anyway, despite being materially unprofitable, all three companies had one major advantage over other profitless companies. Their business model had already been proved. By Facebook. All three were essentially social media companies or UGC (user-generated content) businesses. And social media and UGC companies have *great* business models. Get this: Individual users generate almost all the content consumed on the platform . . . for free! The rest of the content on the platform is advertisements, which are paid for by advertisers. So these are all media platforms, but the platform owners end up paying little for the actual media. What an amazing business model! No wonder traditional media companies have been so jealous—and critical—of social media companies.

I am oversimplifying these businesses, but the business model reality is that these companies all benefit from structurally high gross margins (free, user-generated content means cost of goods sold is low), which certainly helps with the long-term profitability profile. And Facebook—the ultimate social media company—has proved how profitable the business model can be (Table 9.8). When Twitter went public in late 2013, it was unprofitable, but it already had 68% gross margins; and at that time Facebook was generating 36% operating margins and $3 billion in annual free cash flow. When Snap went public in 2017, it was unprofitable, and its gross margin was only 21%, but its incremental gross margin was over 50% and rising rapidly; and at that time Facebook was generating 50% operating margins and $17 billion in annual free cash flow. And when Pinterest went public in 2019, it was unprofitable, but it already had 71% gross margins; and at that time Facebook was generating 41% operating margins (excluding a one-time regulatory fine) and $21 billion in annual free cash flow.

TABLE 9.8 It Helps to Have Friends with Good Business Models

IPO Year	Company	Gross Margin @ IPO	FB Operating Margin	FB FCF
2013	Twitter	68%	36%	$3B
2017	Snap	51%*	50%	$17B
2019	Pinterest	71%	41%	$21B

* Incremental gross margin.

So Pinterest, Snap, and Twitter all passed the first logic test. They had a public company (Facebook) with a similar business model that was already profitable. So there were good reasons to believe these three companies could be nicely profitable at some point.

The second logic test question is: If the company as a whole isn't profitable, are there segments within the business that are? Profitable segments within the business may well show the path to future profitability for the company as a whole. If you are lucky, companies will disclose their profitability cohorts in their SEC filings—their S1s and their 10-Ks. If a company isn't profitable as a whole, but it provides evidence that its oldest markets or its oldest customer bases are profitable, then there is the potential for the whole enterprise to turn profitable as its newer markets and customer bases age up. Unfortunately, few of the profitless tech companies I covered ever provided this level of disclosure; almost none provided it consistently. That said, management teams would often be pressed to discuss their cohort performance on earnings calls, and occasionally clues would pop out. So the second logic test question is usually hard to conclusively answer, but it's the right question, and a positive answer should give an investor greater confidence in the future profitability of the company.

The third logic test question is: Is there a reason why scale can't drive a business to profitability? Scale doesn't solve everything, but it sure solves a lot of things. Given that a significant amount of any company's cost structure is either fixed or step-fixed, significant revenue growth almost always helps drive a business to profitability. The example I think of here is Redfin, the online real estate brokerage company that IPO'd in July 2017. RDFN shares popped 45% on their first day of trading. Asked about the surge, Redfin's CEO Glenn Kelman quipped: "It's better than going down." (Full disclosure—analysts appreciate management teams with dry senses of humor.) At the time, Kelman also referred to Redfin as the "Amazon of real estate." (Full disclosure—analysts are skeptical of companies that refer to themselves as the "Amazon of anything," unless, of course, they are Amazon.)

Anyway, Redfin was one of those profitless IPO companies. But one key future profitability measure could be found in the company's S1, when the company disclosed its gross margin by cohort by year. Table 9.9 summarizes the key S1 factor.

TABLE 9.9 A Nice (and Rare) Cohort Profitability Disclosure by Redfin

		Cohort of Markets Opening in Years		
		2006–2008	2009–2013	2014–2016
Number of Markets		10	19	55
Revenue ($000)				
	2014	$97,801	$23,268	$735
	2015	$136,261	$37,786	$7,399
	2016	$186,922	$55,334	$18,127
Gross Profit ($000)				
	2014	$28,747	$4,168	($731)
	2015	$41,522	$8,981	($579)
	2016	$64,483	$15,967	$3,525
Gross Margin				
	2014	29.4%	17.9%	N.M.
	2015	30.5%	23.8%	–7.8%
	2016	34.5%	28.9%	19.4%

Table 9.9 shows that through scale (revenue growth), each of its segments was becoming more profitable (generating higher gross margins). With the 2006–2008 cohort, as revenue between 2014 and 2016 rose from $98 million to $187 million, gross margin rose from 29.4% to 34.5%. Did this prove that Redfin, which generated a $23 million net loss in 2016, would be a profitable company in the long term? No, but it did indicate that the company could scale its way to profitability. Which meant that RDFN passed the third logic test. This is the kind of evidence an individual investor should be looking for.

The fourth logic test question is: Are there concrete steps that management can take to drive the company to profitability? I'm going to go back to Uber on this one. Mike Isaac, the technology reporter for the *New York Times,* wrote a book about Uber called *Super Pumped: The Battle for Uber*. Isaac does a masterful job detailing the birth, the growth, and the controversy around Uber. One clear takeaway is that Uber under cofounder Travis Kalanick was a company run with a growth-at-all-costs mentality—or a growth-regardless-of-the-costs mentality. I'm not sure Uber could have initially succeeded without that type of mentality, given the entrenched and fiercely competitive interests it was taking on in local cities and in international markets. From a financial perspective, the key insight was that Uber's P&L contained a *lot* of waste, inefficiency, and not-strategic bets, which is exactly the opportunity you match up with a seasoned, energetic executive like Khosrowshahi.

That's one of the key reasons I was Bullish on UBER from its IPO. I thought there were plenty of concrete steps Uber management could take to drive the company to profitability without materially sacrificing growth. There was evidence right there in the S1, where Uber disclosed the revenues and profits/losses of its key segments. Table 9.10 is a quick summary of Uber's financials for 2018 (in the S1), 2019, and 2020. The key takes were:

1. Uber's Rides segment was actually reasonably profitable—17 percent EBITDA margin in 2018.
2. Uber's Other Segments, which contained its Freight business and its Autonomous Vehicle group, were losing a lot of money—$689 million.
3. Uber was spending a shockingly large amount on G&A and what it called Platform R&D—$1.9 billion in 2018.

Through the selling off of underperforming assets like Uber Eats in South Korea and through forced austerity measures in the wake of the Covid-19 pandemic, Uber was able to materially improve its

TABLE 9.10 UBER: Baby, You Can Drive My Car . . . and Cut Costs

	2018	2019	2020
Rides/Mobility			
Revenue	$9,165	$10,622	$6,104
EBITDA	$1,541	$2,071	$1,169
EBITDA Margin	17%	19%	19%
Eats/Delivery			
Revenue	$759	$1,383	$3,903
EBITDA	($601)	($1.372)	($873)
Other Segments			
Revenue	$373	$892	$1,145
EBITDA	($689)	($967)	($694)
G&A and R&D			
	($1,971)	($2,457)	($2,136)

operations over the next two years without materially sacrificing growth. In 2020, Uber Rides was able to generate higher EBITDA margins versus 2018 on one-third less revenue (due to Covid-19 shutting down rideshare demand). Uber Eats revenue rose more than 4x between 2018 and 2020, while its EBITDA loss rose only 50%, suggesting cost efficiencies and scale benefits were kicking in.

No, Uber's profitability hasn't yet been proved. It will likely take several more years for it and Lyft to be able to consistently generate positive GAAP EPS. But there was some evidence in its public filings—and in public documents like Isaac's book—that there were concrete steps management could take to drive the company to profitability.

So does this prove that unprofitable companies can have ballpark reasonable valuations? I still don't think you can "prove" that. But positive responses to these four logic test questions can at least give an investor some confidence that an early-stage company can eventually achieve profitability. At a minimum, it provides some confidence that using price-to-sales multiples in comps tables that include profitable companies is a reasonable shortcut to answering the question of whether a valuation is ballpark reasonable.

One last quick point here has to do with stories and logic. The criticism I hear far too often of unprofitable tech stocks is that they are story stocks. The criticism of a name like Netflix would go something like this: "Because Netflix is generating materially negative free cash flow, it's a story stock. Numbers simply don't support its valuation. Eventually, the story will become less exciting, and people will jump to a sexier story. Investors will focus on the real NFLX numbers, and the stock will implode." I strongly disagree with the assumptions implied in the term "story stock." There are often good reasons for companies to be deep in loss mode, especially if they are aggressively investing against large opportunities. The challenge isn't to decipher "the story." It's to answer the logic test questions to see whether profitability in the future is a distinct probability.

THE PRECISION TRAP

I enjoy the certainty, precision, and elegance of numbers as much as the next person. Perhaps a wee bit more. It's comforting to run a valuation model on a company and come up with *the* answer. But therein lies the problem. Or what I call the *precision trap*.

You can run a full-blown 10-year DCF and come up with an exact value for an equity. But at the very least, the large number of assumptions that go into a 10-year DCF should give one pause in believing that its result is *the* answer. How many assumptions are we talking about? Well, a standard DCF can require inputs for revenue, operating income, depreciation and amortization, stock-based compensation, cash taxes, capex, and working capital. That's 7 inputs. Multiplied by 10 years, that's 70 inputs. And then you have to apply a WACC (weighted average cost of capital) and a future growth rate. So that's 72 inputs. And small changes in just a couple of those, especially the WACC and the future growth rate, can have a dramatic impact on that exact equity value.

I'm not saying don't do that valuation work. Instead, I suggest you avoid the overconfidence that can come from relying on one valuation framework and one result. Remember, valuation is "future science." It's about forecasting revenues, earnings, and cash flows in the future—when company, sector, market, and global conditions can change overnight. How accurate do you believe those DCFs published in January 2020 turned out to be, once Covid-19 changed everyone's world a month later?

The key action question should be: Is the current valuation ballpark reasonable? In my day job, when I need to come up with target prices like that $175 lucky winner on Facebook in 2017, I typically come up with a range of outcomes—Bullish and Bearish to go along with my Base case. For the Bull case, I try to imagine scenarios that would lead to faster revenue growth and greater profitability and apply a higher multiple to that outcome. For the Bear case, I try to imagine scenarios that would lead to lower revenue growth and less profitability and apply a lower multiple to that outcome. The result is less math-driven than logic-driven. And it helps avoid the precision trap.

LESSON WRAP-UP

Valuation should *not* be the most important factor in the stock-picking decision process. Valuation frameworks can be useful in picking tech stocks, but valuation is not a science, and it carries what I call precision traps—precise answers where precision isn't realistic, possible, or justified. Action questions will vary based on whether the company is generating robust earnings, minimal earnings, or no earnings. But your overriding action question should always be: Does the current valuation look ballpark reasonable?

Tech stocks can at times look expensive, but that doesn't make them bad stocks. P/E multiples in a vacuum aren't that useful. It's always important to look at them on a growth-adjusted basis. Higher growth stocks warrant higher P/E multiples, because the earnings stream of a high-growth company is worth more than the earnings stream of a low-growth company (assuming similar capital intensity and cash flow dynamics). High-quality earnings—earnings that are driven first by revenue growth and second by operating margin expansion and earnings that convert strongly into free cash flow—will also warrant higher P/E multiples.

In the case of companies with robust earnings, a P/E multiple in line with or at a modest premium to a company's forward EPS growth is ballpark reasonable. For example, a company with a 20% EPS growth outlook can reasonably trade at a 20x P/E multiple to as high as a 30x or even 40x P/E multiple and still be considered to be ballpark reasonably valued. The key action question: How sustainable is that earnings growth? How much confidence do you have in that 20% growth, which is rare, premium growth. Does the company's TAM, management team, level of product innovation, and customer value proposition support that level of growth?

High-quality stocks that trade at a discount to premium growth rates can make excellent investments for long-term investors. These situations are rare, but they do happen. Both PCLN and FB traded for long stretches of time at discounts to their growth rates, which helped create great Long opportunities with both stocks. The win for investors is that these stocks will be powered by those premium growth rates, with limited risk of P/E multiple declines and the potential for P/E expansion—the double positive whammy outcome!

In the case of companies with minimal earnings, you can often expect to see super high (> 40x) P/E multiples, but these can still be good investments. Both Amazon and Netflix proved this. The key action questions: Are current earnings being materially depressed by major investments? Is there a reason to believe that long-term operating margins for a company can be dramatically higher than current levels? And can the company sustain premium revenue growth for a substantial period of time? If the answers to these questions are positive, then those super high P/E multiples may well be justified.

The case of companies with no earnings provides the toughest valuation challenges, but four logic test questions and valuation comparisons based on factors like revenue (price to sales) can help determine whether a valuation is ballpark reasonable. The four logic test questions for companies that are currently unprofitable:

1. Are there any public companies with similar business models that are already profitable?
2. If the company as a whole isn't profitable, are there segments within the business that are?
3. Is there a reason why scale can't drive a business to profitability?
4. Are there concrete steps that management can take to drive the company to profitability?

LESSON 10

Hunt for DHQs— Dislocated High-Quality Stocks

One of the best ways to make money as an investor in high-growth tech stocks is to identify the highest-quality companies and then to buy them or add to positions when they are dislocated. Investing in high-quality companies—marked by premium revenue growth and driven by large TAMs, relentless product innovation, compelling customer value propositions, and great management—reduces fundamentals risk. Buying companies when they are dislocated—20–30% corrections and/or when stocks are trading at a discount to their growth rates—reduces valuation/multiple risk. My experience has been that every single high-quality company gets dislocated at some point or another, providing patient long-term investors with plenty of opportunities.

The average annual return of the market (the S&P 500) since 1990 has been approximately 10–11%. A popular rule of thumb used to estimate the number of years required to double invested money at any given rate is called the Rule of 72. You divide 72 by the annual rate of return and voilà! With an average annual return of 10%, you can expect your investment to double in approximately seven years (72/10 = 7.2).

That average annual S&P 500 return of 10–11% hasn't occurred in a vacuum. Median annual EPS growth for the S&P 500 since 1990 has been 11–12%. The market has largely followed fundamentals. Over the long term. In the tech sector, especially the Internet sector that I have most focused on, I have found this to be very strongly the case. Stocks have followed and have been driven by fundamentals. Over the long term. The biggest Internet companies in terms of revenue and profits have generally been the biggest Internet companies in terms of market cap.

A quick snapshot (Table 10.1) of the largest US Internet companies in early 2021 hints at this. The four companies with the largest revenue and EBITDA base in 2020 have the largest market cap (AMZN, GOOGL, FB, NFLX). Looking beyond the Big Four, it's clear that the market values size, profitability, and growth. The market is valuing these companies based on their projected future revenue, profits, and cash flows. The market doesn't expect any of these stocks to be as big as Amazon, Facebook, Google, and Netflix in the future. That may be right. That may be wrong. We'll see. And it's a reasonable bet that the market's implied fundamental forecast for all 20 of these stocks won't be accurate.

If consistent 11–12% annual EPS growth can translate into consistent 10–11% share price appreciation, then in theory 20% annual EPS growth should translate into 20% share price appreciation. Per the Rule of 72, that would lead to a stock doubling in about 3½ years. Boy, wouldn't it be great if investing were this simple. If only.

The historical statistical analysis I have run on Internet stocks over the years shows a correlation between share price moves and revenue and EPS growth (and operating income and EBITDA growth). But that correlation is pretty low, especially over one-, two-, and three-year periods. (Remember that the 20% revenue growth rule

TABLE 10.1 The Largest Internet Companies: Fundamentals and Market Caps

Company	Ticker	Market Cap ($B)	Revenue 2020 ($MM)	Revenue Y/Y 2020	EBITDA 2020 ($MM)	EBITDA Y/Y 2020
Amazon.com, Inc.	AMZN	$1,686	$386,064	38%	$56,743	31%
Alphabet Inc.	GOOGL	$1,452	$182,527	13%	$67,783	16%
Facebook, Inc.	FB	$770	$85,965	22%	$46,152	17%
Netflix, Inc.	NFLX	$246	$24,996	24%	$5,116	64%
Shopify, Inc.	SHOP	$181	$2,929	86%	$474	552%
Airbnb, Inc.	ABNB	$134	$3,267	–32%	–$347	–37%
Uber Technologies, Inc.	UBER	$115	$11,139	–21%	–$2,528	7%
Snap, Inc.	SNAP	$108	$2,507	46%	$45	122%
Booking Holdings Inc.	BKNG	$96	$6,764	–55%	$1,036	–82%
DoorDash, Inc.	DASH	$77	$2,853	222%	$188	140%
Spotify Technology SA	SPOT	$71	$9,466	27%	–$25	–123%
Roku, Inc.	ROKU	$66	$1,778	58%	$150	319%
Pinterest, Inc.	PINS	$61	$1,693	48%	$305	1,724%
Twitter, Inc.	TWTR	$61	$3,716	7%	$997	–18%
Zillow Group, Inc.	ZG	$49	$3,340	22%	$343	782%
Peloton Interactive, Inc.	PTON	$49	$1,826	100%	$118	262%
Chewy, Inc.	CHWY	$49	$7,062	46%	$23	129%
Trade Desk, Inc.	TTD	$45	$836	26%	$284	33%
eBay Inc.	EBAY	$44	$10,271	–5%	$3,849	5%
Match Group, Inc.	MTCH	$42	$2,391	17%	$897	15%

Market cap as of 2/21/2021.

was based on five years of growth.) Too many variables—interest rates, GDP growth, regulatory changes—impact stocks in the near and medium terms.

But let's stick with the goal of trying to double an investment in two to three years. That would be handily beating the market in most periods. The best way to do that is to identify high-quality companies that are trading at ballpark reasonable valuations and sticking with them. Based on my experience, investing in high-quality companies that are generating premium revenue growth materially increases an investor's odds of achieving that two-to-three-year double. I'll reference Peter Lynch's credible quip on the topic of investing in high-quality companies: "In the end, superior companies will succeed and mediocre companies will fail, and investors in each will be rewarded accordingly."

In terms of when to buy or add to positions, focus on high-quality stocks that are dislocated. It's the best stock-picking advice I can relay from my experience following tech stocks: Hunt for DHQs—dislocated high-quality stocks.

What do I mean by dislocated? Here are two rules of thumb. First, a stock that has traded off 20–30% is a dislocated stock. Although straightforward, a little judgment is required here. A stock that retraces 20% after shooting up 100% in three months isn't terribly dislocated. And a stock that trades off 20–30% during a major market meltdown—such as March 2020 during the Covid-19 crisis—isn't uniquely dislocated. But a stock that trades off 20–30% when the overall market is rising, holding, or only modestly trading down is a decent dislocation candidate. As is one that does this from a not-elevated position, that is, not after a dramatic run-up. So keep the rule simple—a 20–30% trade-off—but use some judgment.

The second rule of thumb focuses on stocks that trade at a discount to their growth rates. Specifically, when their P/E multiples are lower than their growth rates—such as a 20x P/E (based on next year's EPS, or EPS over the next 12 months) for a company expected to grow EPS 25% next year. Again, the market norm is for companies that generate robust earnings and thus trade on P/E multiples to carry P/E multiples reasonably consistent with their growth rates or at a modest premium. Like with 20–30% corrections, some judgment is required here. Generally, the steeper the discount to the growth rate, the greater the dislocation.

If you are patient, you will likely find dislocation opportunities with high-quality stocks. Why do I think this? Because it has happened in the past.

Looking back at AMZN, FB, GOOGL, and NFLX over 2016–2020, I found that the total number of dislocations (20%+ corrections) among these four stocks was 14, with NFLX experiencing 5 and AMZN, FB, and GOOGL each experiencing 3 (Table 10.2). (These stocks also suffered a handful of mid-to-high-teens percentage sell-offs over these five years.) The key point is that even these high-quality stocks have experienced corrections over the last five years, at a pace of approximately one every other year.

TABLE 10.2 Dislocation, Dislocation, Dislocation: 20%+ Corrections

Start Date	Start Close	End Date	End Close	Correction	Duration (Days)
AMZN					
12/29/2015	$694.0	2/9/2016	$482.1	–31%	42
9/4/2018	$2,039.5	12/24/2018	$1,344.0	–34%	111
2/19/2020	$2,170.2	3/16/2020	$1,689.2	–22%	26
FB					
2/1/2018	$193.1	3/27/2018	$152.2	–21%	54
7/25/2018	$217.5	12/24/2018	$124.1	–43%	152
1/29/2020	$223.2	3/18/2020	$147.0	–34%	49
GOOGL					
7/26/2018	$1,285.5	12/24/2018	$984.7	–23%	151
4/29/2019	$1,296.2	6/3/2019	$1,038.7	–20%	35
2/19/2020	$1,524.9	3/23/2020	$1,054.1	–31%	33
NFLX					
12/4/2015	$130.9	2/5/2016	$82.8	–37%	63
4/15/2016	$111.5	7/19/2016	$85.8	–23%	95
6/20/2018	$416.8	12/24/2018	$233.9	–44%	187
5/3/2019	$385.0	9/24/2019	$254.6	–34%	144
2/18/2020	$387.8	3/16/2020	$298.8	–23%	27

What's also interesting from Table 10.2 is the takeaway that the dislocation periods were generally reasonably short. The median duration of the 14 corrections among these companies was roughly two months. All four of the stocks suffered dislocations that lasted over three months, with FB, GOOGL, and NFLX suffering dislocations that lasted five months and NFLX also suffering a dislocation that lasted six months (187 days). But none of these stocks went through a dislocation that lasted more than six months.

This now begets the question: What are high-quality stocks? From the perspective of a seasoned tech sector analyst, my argument is that the best fundamental tell of a high-quality company is consistent premium revenue growth (20%+).

There are definitely judgment calls here: 20% revenue growth on scale ($1 billion in revenue) is a lot more impressive than 20% on modest revenue bases ($100 million). And 20%+ growth that is paired with material deceleration—where the revenue growth gets cut by a half in one year—is not a good fundamental tell. At the same time, few companies will have the ability to "pull a Google"—20% growth for a decade starting at a $25 billion revenue run rate. Only three companies have been able to do this in history—Amazon, Apple, and Google. These three companies are in a class by themselves. You don't have to be able to "pull a Google" to be in the premium revenue growth club. But five years of consistent 20%+ revenue growth at reasonable scale is a good fundamental tell of a high-quality company.

And what are the key fundamental drivers of premium revenue growth? This book has laid out four that I have observed from my experience as a tech analyst: relentless product innovation, large TAMs, compelling customer value propositions, and great management. (See Table 10.3.)

There are certainly other investing strategies in the tech sector. And plenty of trading strategies. But looking for dislocated high-quality stocks is a compelling investing strategy. First, investing in

TABLE 10.3 What Makes a High-Quality Tech Company?

Fundamental Tell		Factor #1	#2	#3	#4
	5-Year Revenue CAGR	Product Innovation	Large TAM	Customer Value Prop	Great Management
AMZN	29% on $107B revenue base	Amazon Prime, Kindle, AWS, same-day delivery, Alexa, . . .	$5T	Best price, selection, and convenience in online retail, largest scale and leading services with lowest prices in cloud computing	Jeff Bezos
FB	37% on $18B revenue base	The Like button, news feed, Messenger, Marketplace, Instagram Reels, . . .	$1.3T	(Free) Community, connection, entertainment, and information for consumers, massive scale and targeting for marketers	Mark Zuckerberg
GOOGL	20% on $75B revenue base	Worlds's leading search engine, Google Maps, Gmail, Android, Google Assistant, Waymo, . . .	$1.3T	(Free) Connection, entertainment, and information for consumers, massive scale and targeting for marketers	Larry Page and Sergey Brin
NFLX	30% on $7B revenue base	Video streaming, not Muzak, local-language originals, binge-watching, . . .	$150–$400B	An extremely broad selection of high-quality video content for the monthly price of four cups of coffee	Reed Hastings

high-quality companies reduces fundamentals risk. Second, buying these stocks when they are dislocated—down 20–30% and/or trading at a discount to their growth rates—reduces valuation/multiple risk.

Let's look at some examples.

DHQ 2018—FACEBOOK

That Facebook Faceplant in mid-2018, when management dramatically lowered the Street's revenue and EPS growth estimates, is a great example of a DHQ opportunity. From July 25, 2018, to December 24, 2018, Facebook shares corrected a massive 43%, falling from $218 to $124, as a result of the company talking down its forward revenue growth rate and talking up its investment spend plans (Figure 10.1). Remember, this was largely self-inflicted.

FIGURE 10.1 FB: From Faceplant to Facelift

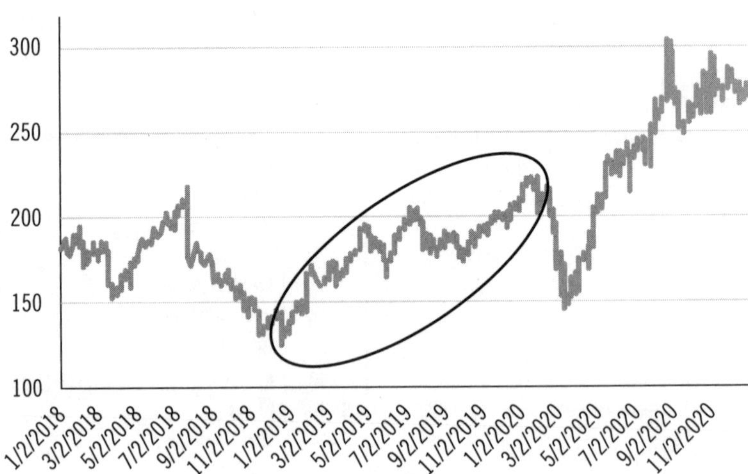

If you had bought FB shares at that $124 trough, you would have experienced a 65% return in 12 months, nicely outperforming the market (which grew 37% over that same time period). Of course, you could say this about almost any stock that suffers a severe correction and then rebounds. Cherry-picking the exact bottom of a temporary stock correction is practically guaranteed to generate great portfolio returns. But you can't do that. No one can consistently pick the exact bottom on any given stock.

With the FB Faceplant, by the way, you could have beaten the market over a 12-month period, even if you hadn't perfectly called the bottom. Say you bought FB after it had declined 30%—to $151 on October 10, 2018, and then held it a year. That falling knife would have continued to cut and would have fallen another 10%+ for another two months after you bought it, but over the next 12 months you would have returned 19% versus the market at 5%, so about 4x better than the market. Even if you had bought it after it declined "only" 20%—$175 on July 27, 2018—you would have made 14% in the next 12 months versus the market at 7%, about 2x better than the market.

It's almost impossible to call the bottom on a stock that's correcting materially, but you can call a 20%, a 30%, and a 40% correction (again, using some judgment). If it's a high-quality company, you may be able to get good returns over time using those material corrections as entry or adding points.

As FB faded over that five-month period in 2018, I was constantly asked when it would bottom out. I told clients $160, based on Facebook's historical trading multiples, and the stock traded below that level. I told clients $140, based on sector trading comps, and the stock traded below that level. Having a major market sell-off in late 2018 due to concerns over escalating trade wars, slowing global GDP growth, and rising interest rates certainly didn't help put a bottom in on FB.

So, no, I didn't "call the bottom" on FB. But I did "call" Facebook a dislocated high-quality stock. I stuck with my Buy rating, and I made FB one of my top Long recommendations, though I had plenty of moments of doubt. I second-guessed myself. I third-guessed myself. It is *not* fun to own or recommend a stock that's correcting 43%. But I did believe valuation was becoming extremely attractive when in late 2018 FB began trading at an 18x P/E level, which I viewed as a material discount to the 20–30% EPS growth that I believed Facebook would recover to.

But was Facebook really a high-quality company? I certainly thought it was. Here's the quick scorecard based on the fundamental tell and the four fundamental factors:

- **Premium revenue growth?** Check. Going into 2018, Facebook had generated average revenue growth over the prior five years of 52%. And it was doing this at scale—$28 billion in revenue in 2016, for example—and it was doing this consistently; in fact, the lowest revenue growth FB saw in those five years was 44% in 2014. A trillion-dollar TAM certainly suggested that Facebook could continue to generate premium revenue growth—some proof of this came a few years later when FB generated 22% revenue growth during the advertising recession that was attributed to Covid-19. And Facebook's own guidance on that June quarter 2018 call suggested that the company could maintain close to 20% annual revenue growth, despite all its near-term challenges.
- **Continuous and successful product innovation?** This one may be debatable and harder perhaps to document, but I'll still give it a check. User interface changes have been constant and substantial with Facebook and Instagram over the years, with a series of new features and apps rolled out, including Facebook Marketplace, Stories, Facebook Watch, News, and Instagram Reels. I also believe Facebook's virtual reality segment (Oculus) is highly innovative.

- **Large TAM?** A trillion-dollar TAM pretty much settles this. And this is based on about $500 billion in global brand marketing, $300 billion in direct marketing, and $300 billion in trade promotion spend.
- **Compelling customer value propositions?** The movie *The Social Network* debuted in 2010. The movie *The Social Dilemma* debuted in 2020. That pretty much sums up the decade of debate over the social, cultural, and political impact of Facebook. But what investors need to focus on is whether or not Facebook has maintained a compelling value proposition for its two most important customers—consumers and advertisers. I may be wrong, but I believe it has. What Facebook and its properties (Instagram, Messenger, and WhatsApp) offer consumers is straightforward, but often overlooked—community, connectivity, information, and entertainment, all for free. Consumer survey work I conducted over a five-year period consistently ranked Facebook and Instagram the two most popular social media properties, with relatively high customer satisfaction levels. What Facebook and its properties offer advertisers is dramatic reach (matched only by Google) and targeting (arguably matched only by Google). Advertiser survey work I conducted also over a five-year period consistently ranked Facebook one of the two best online advertising platforms (along with Google). I would assert that Facebook's customer value proposition was one of the strongest of any tech company I have covered over the last quarter century.
- **Great management team?** In the lesson on management, I highlighted Zuckerberg and Facebook as an example of a management team that consistently maintained a long-term focus. My eventual take on the Facebook Faceplant was to view it as a great example of that dedication to a long-term

> focus. Don't let the risk of a near-term stock correction and a temporary reduction in investor growth expectations cause you to slow down your product development plans. It's also key to remember that the mid-2018 aggressive investments that dinged near-term profitability were largely—though not fully—elective investments made by Facebook to further support future growth initiatives.

So, yes, Facebook was and is a high-quality stock that in mid-2018 suffered a material dislocation. That created an excellent DHQ opportunity. Facebook was *the* DHQ opportunity of 2018. In 2019, it was Netflix.

DHQ 2019—NFLX

Netflix was arguably a dislocated high-quality stock twice in 2019 (Figure 10.2). First, NFLX began the year dislocated, having traded off a whopping 44% from $417 on June 20, 2018, to $234 on December 24, 2018. What caused this sharp correction was a June quarter subs miss against elevated expectations. That subs miss was caused by a combination of World Cup distractions, the lack of a strong new content slate, summer seasonality, and the inherent challenge of forecasting a still young, global, secular growth business. Then Netflix shares crashed again, 34% from $385 on May 3, 2019, to $255 on September 24, 2019. The immediate cause was also a subs miss in both the March and June quarters, with two additional factors—heightened churn due to a somewhat aggressive price increase and the pending launch of the Disney Death Star (aka Disney+).

Both of these corrections—44% and 34%—fit the definition of dislocation, although since the 44% came right in the wake of a six-month doubling of NFLX shares, the second might be considered a more "legitimate" dislocation. It's a judgment call.

FIGURE 10.2 Profiting from NFLX's Double Dislocation

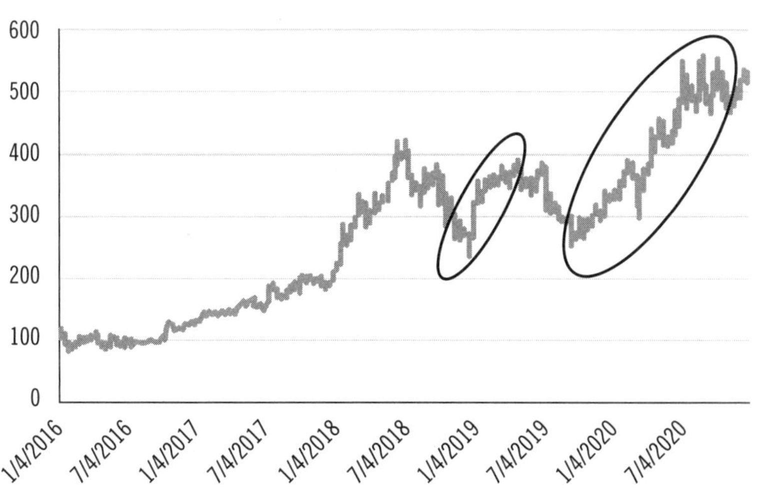

Anyway, time to pick cherries. If you had bought NFLX at the first trough ($234 on December 24, 2018) and held it for a year, you would have enjoyed a return of 42%. Although a very good one-year return, that actually would have only modestly outperformed the S&P 500, which rose 37% over that same period. The problem is that 12 months after that first trough (December 24, 2019), NFLX was working its way through its second major dislocation. You would have had to hold it longer to meaningfully outperform the market. You could tack on a second year and find material outperformance, but that would take you well into the Covid-19 market, which dramatically benefitted a few companies (like Netflix) while punishing most of the market. So that's not really a fair comparison. What is a fair comparison is charting NFLX from that first correction to the peak of the S&P 500 prior to the Covid-19 crash, which would be February 19, 2020. From that first trough to then, NFLX shares gained 65% versus 44% for the S&P 500. Perhaps not dramatic outperformance, and you are cherry-picking a trough entry point, but the result is noteworthy.

However, if you had bought NFLX at the second trough ($255 on September 24, 2019) and held it to February 19, 2020, you would have gained 51%, dramatically outperforming the S&P 500, which rose 14% over that period. Again, we're cherry-picking the trough, but that's a *lot* of outperformance. If you jumped in right at the 20% correction line ($307 on July 23, 2019), you would have only had a 26% return by February 19, 2020, but that would have been 2x the return of the S&P 500 over that period (13%).

The simple takeaway is that Netflix was a highly dislocated stock for much of 2019, but buying NFLX on those dislocations created significant outperformance to the market. I maintained a Buy on NFLX that entire year—as part of practically a decade-long Long recommendation—because I believed the core Buy thesis was fundamentally intact. And with those dislocations, I also made NFLX one of my top picks. I described it as the most dislocated of the high-quality Internet stocks that year. Did I have my moments of doubt and panic? Sure. I was particularly concerned about whether Netflix had pushed too aggressively on the price increase. I worried about Qwikster Part 2. I wondered how long it would take Netflix to recover from this price increase shock, and I was somewhat put off by the arrogant tone of management's responses to challenging questions about that price increase. But I stuck with NFLX.

Is Netflix a high-quality company? You already know my answer, but let's go through the scorecard:

- **Premium revenue growth?** Check. Netflix had been generating 20%+ annual revenue growth since 2013. Its trailing five-year average going into 2018 was 27%. Its five-year average going into 2019 was 29%. And its five-year average going into 2020 was 30%. Yes, its five-year average was getting stronger. Because of accelerating sub adds and its pricing power, Netflix was enjoying overall accelerating revenue growth. Although its free cash flow trends were anything but promising, they were explainable, and operating margins were consistently rising.

- **Continuous and successful product innovation?** Well, Netflix did practically invent video streaming, though not Muzak. But its key innovation over the last few years has been in the form of more original content and especially local-language original content. Netflix has also rolled out other innovations—such as the immediate and full release of video series. This in turn triggered the trend of binge-watching (for better or worse). But this clearly was a relatively novel and pro-consumer innovation.
- **Large TAM?** Check. Per the annual *Theme Report* from the Motion Picture Association (MPA), the global market for theatrical, home, and mobile entertainment topped $100 billion in 2019. That would imply that Netflix has already reached 25% of its TAM, given its $25 billion in revenue in 2020. However, similar to the analysis in the TAM lesson on Spotify, Netflix and streaming video have the ability to materially expand the size of its TAM. Another way to look at this is to view Netflix's current 200 million subs (perhaps 500 million total users) against the 3 billion smartphones worldwide (excluding China), which would imply perhaps mid-teens penetration of its current global potential user base. Yes, a large TAM, and one that Netflix has only modestly penetrated. You could also batch in all entertainment spend, such as video game spend—Netflix does compete in a way with Fortnite—and come up with a $400 billion-ish TAM.
- **Great management team?** Check, check. The lesson on management lists several factors to look for in a management team, and Netflix would seem to check the box on practically all of these factors—a founder-led company, long-term orientation, great industry vision, a deep focus on product innovation, and the ability to be forthright with employees

and investors about mistakes and challenges (while wearing unbuttoned teal-colored shirts).

So, yes, Netflix was and is a high-quality stock that in 2019 suffered two material dislocations. That created excellent DHQ opportunities. Netflix was *the* DHQ opportunity of 2019. In 2020, it was Uber.

DHQ 2020—UBER?

After correcting dramatically in 2018, Facebook was a great stock in 2019, rising almost 60%, reaching a new all-time high in early January 2020. Likewise, after its second 2019 major correction, Netflix rocketed 50% over the next five months and then achieved a new all-time high in April 2020.

So, near the end of 2019, I looked around for the best candidate for DHQ 2020. And I decided to make it Uber. At an investment conference in November 2019, I pitched a new best-in-class tech stock "portfolio"—Facebook, Amazon, Netflix, Google, and Uber. FANGU! As in "FANGU very much," delivered with an Elvis Presley accent. I made UBER my top Long recommendation. This call was controversial both at the time and in hindsight.

Near term, there was at least one thing going for this call. The IPO lockup expiration had passed earlier in November, removing a sizable overhang. But my pitch was based on the idea that UBER was a DHQ stock—a high-quality stock that was currently dislocated.

Was UBER dislocated? Perhaps. In mid-November 2019 at $26, it was off 40%+ from its May IPO. Of course, I didn't realize at the time that the stock was going to become a lot more dislocated a few months later—along with the market—due to the Covid-19 crash. But UBER in late 2019 was plausibly a dislocated stock, one that was still viewed as a failed IPO with "fantasy valuation." Technically, I wouldn't consider a 20–30% correction off an IPO price as a dislocation. IPOs and the six-month period after them can often have wonky supply-demand imbalances that make stock prices less than normally resilient and reliable. But 40% was big, and sentiment on the name was clearly negative.

Was Uber a high-quality company at that time? Not really. At least, the quality of Uber as a company wasn't anywhere near as strong as Facebook, Amazon, Netflix, or Google, though those are high bars. But there was promise. Here's the checklist:

- **Premium revenue growth?** Partial check. Uber generated 42% revenue growth in 2018 and by November 2019 was on track to generate approximately 25% growth for the full year, with my outlook calling for an acceleration to roughly 35% revenue growth in 2020. There was not a history of consistent 20%+ growth—that 2018 growth of 42% marked a sharp deceleration from prior years. Hence, the partial check.
- **Continuous and successful product innovation?** Partial check. This is a hard one to judge convincingly, but Uber in 2019 was rolling out a reasonably new loyalty program for its Uber Rides and Eats customers, and it was investing aggressively in autonomous vehicle technology. The company was also investing aggressively in ways to reduce Rides wait times for both riders and drivers and in batching solutions for its Eats offering.
- **Large TAM?** Check. Per the "TAM, SAM, and DAM" section in the TAM lesson, Uber faced a multitrillion-dollar TAM, given its core ridesharing business and its online food order delivery business, both of which were already operating globally in 2019. Uber was proving to be a platform company, with the ability to expand the range of services it offered its customers, for example, expanding from online food delivery to online grocery and convenience store and general retail delivery.

- **Great management team?** TBD. One of its two cofounders (Travis Kalanick) was no longer involved with the company. And CEO Khosrowshahi had only been with the company for two years. So this call was too early to make, despite my belief that Khosrowshahi was a good selection for Uber.

Anyway, that was the pitch in November 2019 for UBER to be *the* DHQ of 2020. From mid-November to the end of 2019, Uber rallied 14% to close out the year at $29.74. Looking smart. UBER then roared 38% to $41.05 in mid-February in anticipation of and in reaction to strong December quarter financial results that were reported in early February. Looking like a genius. Then Covid-19 hit, causing a 64% one-month correction in UBER shares down to $14.82. Looking like an idiot, I quickly went from the Axe on UBER to the A@# on UBER.

But I did stick with the call. Despite the correction. And that second clear dislocation created what would be the true 2020 DHQ opportunity for the Internet sector, with UBER rallying 244% from mid-March to end the year at $51. And there's not much risk of being accused of cherry-picking here. For the full year, UBER rose 71% and reached record highs, despite the dramatic correction in its fundamentals caused by the Covid-19 pandemic. (See Figure 10.3.)

So, yes, Uber arguably was the DHQ of 2020, with a couple of caveats on that HQ part.

And the process of locating high-quality companies and buying them when they became dislocated did help in the Uber investment process.

FIGURE 10.3 **UBER: Buying the Potholes**

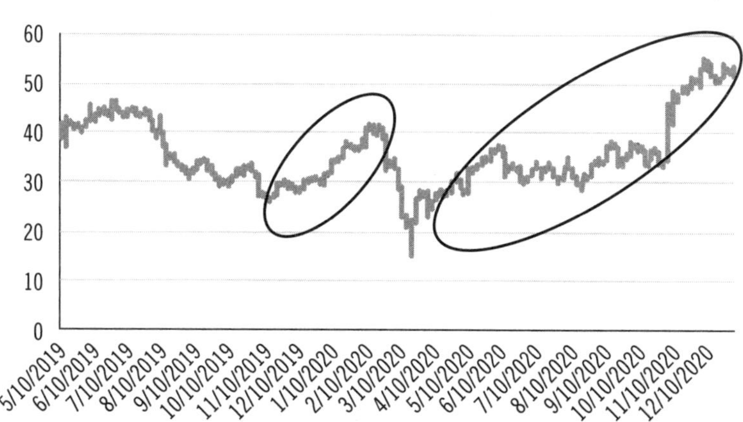

ENOUGH OF THE STORIES . . . WHAT ABOUT SOME DATA?

I don't believe in foolproof solutions. I don't believe in sure things. I have found the stock market to be an odds business, but one where your decisions can materially impact those odds.

Investing in DHQ stocks is no guarantee of beating the market, but it's a strategy that can significantly increase the odds of beating the market. The single biggest factor in tech investing success has been to invest in high-quality companies. Totally echoing Peter Lynch here. The market in early 2021 has deemed the four highest-quality Internet stocks to be Amazon, Facebook, Google, and Netflix. I 100 percent agree and have for many years, even when some of these have been out of favor. Or dislocated. But I'm also fully cognizant that the market can be wrong. I also believe the Internet sector contains several other potential high-quality companies, such as Airbnb, Chewy, Doordash, Etsy, Lending Tree, Roku, Shopify, Snap, Spotify, The Trade Desk, Trupanion, Wix, and Zillow.

The fundamental tell of and the four factors that drive high-quality companies are ones that I have pulled largely—though not entirely—from my experience tracking technology stocks, principally Internet stocks. So their application may be limited to technology stocks, principally Internet stocks. I tested the 20% revenue growth rule against the broader S&P 500 universe and provided the data analysis behind that in Lesson 4, "Revenue Matters More Than Anything." So that rule should have broader application, but the four factors are drawn directly from my experience.

Looking to test the dislocation thesis, I went back and tested whether buying the high-quality FANG names on 20% and 30% corrections would have outperformed the market. Details are in Table 10.4, and the answer is yes. Over 2016–2020, buying the FANG stocks on 20% corrections would have outperformed the S&P 500 78% of the time on a one-year basis and 100% of the time on a two-year basis. And over this period, buying the FANG stocks on 30% corrections would have outperformed the S&P 500 60% of the time on a one-year basis and 100% of the time on a two-year basis. The sample set is small, admittedly, but these are the results.

Likewise, buying the FANG stocks over 2016–2020 when they were trading at a discount to their growth rate—at a PEG (a P/E multiple versus the EPS growth rate) of less than 1—would have led to greater outperformance versus the S&P 500 than buying them when they were trading in line with or at a premium to their growth rates. These results aren't perfect. The analysis on Netflix actually shows the stock outperforming more when it traded at a PEG greater than 1 than less than 1. And for all four stocks, there was outperformance in both scenarios—PEG less than and greater than 1. Amazon, for example, outperformed the market 89% of the time when it was trading at a PEG less than 1, whereas it outperformed the market 74% of the time when it was trading at a PEG greater than 1. (See Table 10.5.)

TABLE 10.4 The Returns from Buying the Dislocations on High-Quality Tech Stocks

AMZN	Date	AMZN Price	S&P Price
Peak	12/29/2015	694.0	2,078.4
20% Correction	2/2/2016	552.1	1,903.0
1 Year from –20%	2/2/2017	840.0	2,280.9
2 Years from –20%	2/2/2018	1,429.9	2,762.1
1-Year Return		**52%**	**20%**
2-Year Return		**159%**	**45%**
30% Correction	2/9/2016	482.1	1,852.2
1 Year from –30%	2/9/2017	821.4	2,307.9
2 Years from –30%	2/9/2018	1,339.6	2,619.6
1-Year Return		**70%**	**25%**
2-Year Return		**178%**	**41%**
Peak	9/4/2018	2,039.5	2,896.7
20% Correction	10/29/2018	1,538.9	2,641.3
1 Year from –20%	10/29/2019	1,762.7	3,036.9
2 Years from –20%	10/29/2020	3,211.0	3,310.1
1-Year Return		**15%**	**15%**
2-Year Return		**109%**	**25%**
30% Correction	12/21/2018	1,377.4	2,416.6
1 Year from –30%	12/20/2019	1,786.5	3,221.2
2 Years from –30%	12/21/2020	3,206.2	3,694.9
1-Year Return		**30%**	**33%**
2-Year Return		**133%**	**53%**

(continued on the next page)

TABLE 10.4 The Returns from Buying the Dislocations on High-Quality Tech Stocks (*continued*)

FB	Date	FB Price	S&P Price
Peak	2/1/2018	193.1	2,822.0
20% Correction	3/27/2018	152.2	2,612.6
1 Year from –20%	3/27/2019	165.9	2,805.4
2 Years from –20%	3/27/2020	156.8	2,541.5
1-Year Return		**9%**	**7%**
2-Year Return		**3%**	**–3%**
Peak	7/25/2018	217.5	2,846.1
20% Correction	7/30/2018	171.1	2,802.6
1 Year from –20%	7/30/2019	197.0	3,013.2
2 Years from –20%	7/30/2020	234.5	3,246.2
1-Year Return		**15%**	**8%**
2-Year Return		**37%**	**16%**
30% Correction	10/10/2018	151.4	2,785.7
1 Year from –30%	10/10/2019	180.0	2,938.1
2 Years from –30%	10/10/2020	264.5	3,477.1
1-Year Return		**19%**	**5%**
2-Year Return		**75%**	**25%**

GOOGL	Date	GOOGL Price	S&P Price
Peak	7/26/2018	1,285.5	2,837.4
20% Correction	11/19/2018	1,027.4	2,690.7
1 Year from –20%	11/19/2019	1,312.6	3,120.2
2 Years from –20%	11/19/2020	1,758.6	3,581.9
1-Year Return		**28%**	**16%**
2-Year Return		**71%**	**33%**
Peak	4/29/2019	1,296.2	2,943.0
20% Correction	6/3/2019	1,038.7	2,744.4
1 Year from –20%	6/3/2020	1,439.3	3,122.9
2 Years from –20%	—	—	—
1-Year Return		**39%**	**14%**
2-Year Return		—	—

TABLE 10.4 The Returns from Buying the Dislocations on High-Quality Tech Stocks (*continued*)

NFLX	Date	NFLX Price	S&P Price
Peak	12/4/2015	130.9	2,091.7
20% Correction	1/15/2016	104.0	1,880.3
1 Year from –20%	1/13/2017	133.7	2,274.6
2 Years from –20%	1/16/2018	221.5	2,776.4
1-Year Return		**29%**	**21%**
2-Year Return		**113%**	**48%**
30% Correction	1/27/2016	482.1	1,882.9
1 Year from –30%	1/27/2017	142.4	2,294.7
2 Years from –30%	1/26/2018	274.6	2,872.9
1-Year Return		**56%**	**22%**
2-Year Return		**201%**	**53%**
Peak	4/15/2016	111.5	2,080.7
20% Correction	5/12/2016	87.7	2,064.1
1 Year from –20%	5/12/2017	160.8	2,390.9
2 Years from –20%	5/11/2018	326.5	2,727.7
1-Year Return		**83%**	**16%**
2-Year Return		**272%**	**32%**
Peak	6/20/2018	416.8	2,767.3
20% Correction	8/15/2018	326.4	2,818.4
1 Year from –20%	8/15/2019	295.8	2,847.6
2 Years from –20%	8/14/2020	482.7	3,372.9
1-Year Return		**–9%**	**1%**
2-Year Return		**48%**	**20%**
30% Correction	11/14/2018	286.7	2,701.6
1 Year from –30%	11/14/2019	289.6	3,096.6
2 Years from –30%	11/13/2020	482.8	3,585.1
1-Year Return		**1%**	**15%**
2-Year Return		**68%**	**33%**

TABLE 10.5 The Advantages of Buying High-Quality Stocks When Their PEGs Are < 1

	1-Year Forward Outperformance Versus S&P		Rate of Outperformance		
	Median	Average	Total Days	Number of OP	Rate of OP
AMZN					
PEG > 1	30%	29%	168	124	74%
PEG < 1	31%	32%	624	557	89%
FB					
PEG > 1	7%	5%	498	339	68%
PEG < 1	17%	16%	294	250	85%
GOOGL					
PEG > 1	7%	7%	744	598	80%
PEG < 1	13%	13%	48	48	100%
NFLX					
PEG > 1	36%	47%	151	136	90%
PEG < 1	40%	38%	641	499	78%

The biggest takeaway from the analysis is simply to buy and hold the highest-quality stocks—they simply consistently outperform if you hold them for a reasonable period of time (one year). But there is some help in here in terms of looking for buying/adding points.

The old maxim is: "Buy low and sell high." My experience analyzing tech stocks alters that as follows: "Buy high-quality stocks, especially when they are dislocated. Be patient, and over the long-term, you will likely outperform the market." If that's too wordy, remember: Look for DHQs.

WHEN SHOULD YOU SELL A STOCK?

When the fundamentals materially change to the negative. That's my answer. To be more specific, when revenue growth decelerates materially (50% deceleration within a year or less) or when revenue growth materially dips below 20%. Of course, there are many great stocks of companies that don't generate consistent 20%+ revenue growth. 98% of the S&P 500 can't be wrong.

But we're focusing on high-growth tech stocks, and if their top-line growth is well under 20%, then they don't qualify as high growth. You also want to be careful about companies that decelerate sharply. As we saw in the Snap and Twitter examples earlier, when revenue growth decelerates, the multiple derates—that is, goes down. Stocks can still work when their multiples derate, but it is much harder for stocks to outperform in those scenarios. What's interesting with both Snap and Twitter is that when their growth rates stabilized, so too did their multiples, and the stocks tended to outperform, especially Snap.

Matching up Snap's revenue growth outlook (i.e., the Street's consensus revenue growth forecast) with its stock price provides a clear picture (Figure 10.4). As that revenue growth outlook faded sharply from 80% at the time of SNAP's IPO in early 2017 down to 30% in early 2019, SNAP's stock cratered. When that revenue growth outlook stabilized at that premium 30% level, the stock began to outperform materially.

FIGURE 10.4 SNAP, Crackle, Pop!

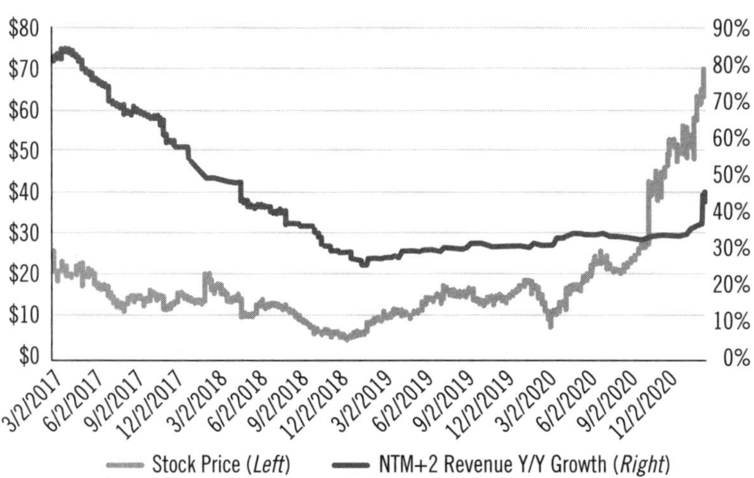

Likewise with Twitter. Matching up Twitter's revenue growth outlook with its stock price also provides a clear picture (Figure 10.5). As that revenue growth outlook faded sharply from 60% at the time of TWTR's IPO in late 2013 down to below 10% in early 2017, TWTR's stock cratered. When that revenue growth outlook stabilized and began to recover back up close to 20%, the stock began to outperform materially. Earlier, I mentioned the TWTR Smile. As of early 2021, that smile was broad and wide.

FIGURE 10.5 The TWTR Stock Smile

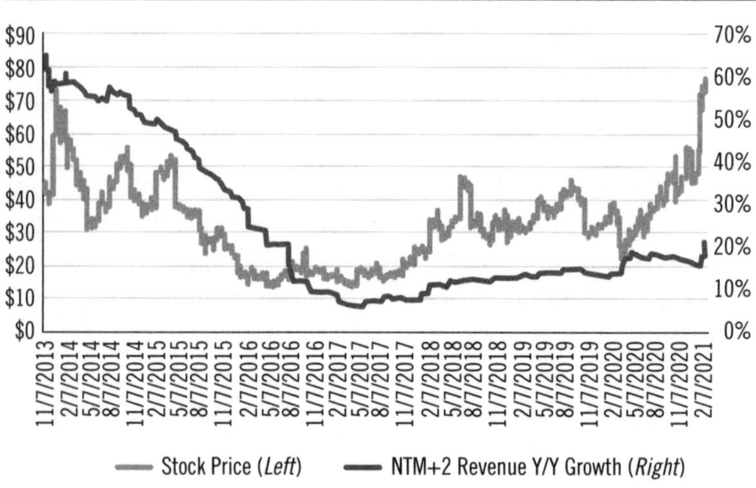

To more fully illustrate the point about avoiding/selling tech stocks with sharply decelerating revenue, let's look at five companies—Tripadvisor, Yelp, TrueCar, Criteo, and Shutterstock. All five of these companies have stocks that materially underperformed the market over a long period of time over the last 5 to 10 years.

Perhaps this is clearest with Tripadvisor (TRIP), the online travel company best known for its user-generated reviews of travel destinations, hotels, restaurants, and local activities. Tripadvisor was spun off from Expedia in late 2011 and soared almost 4x over the next 2½ years, driven by premium revenue growth and relatively high profitability levels. Then TRIP tripped up. The stock experienced a collapse from $110 in mid-2014 to $30 in late 2017, as its growth rate sharply decelerated from over 20% to under 10%. (See Figure 10.6.)

FIGURE 10.6 Tripping over TRIP

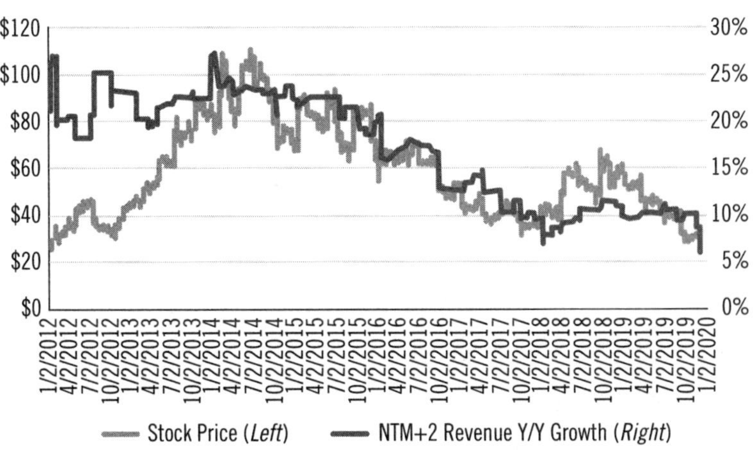

There were a series of factors at play here:

1. Intense competition from Google, which generated its own travel reviews offering.
2. Revenue concentration risk with Priceline/Booking and Expedia at times accounting for 50 percent or more of TRIP's revenue, which became a major issue when those two companies started cutting back on their marketing spend on Tripadvisor.
3. Inadequate product innovation. This last point is a judgment call. Tripadvisor has been effectively run by one of its founders (Stephen Kaufer) since 2000, making it one of the longest-lasting and most durable public Internet companies. Tripadvisor also has almost half a billion monthly users around the world, making it one of the most popular web properties globally. So there is platform potential here.

But the key historical stock-picking insight here is that as the company's growth slowed, especially as it fell below 20%, its stock price suffered.

Another example is Yelp (YELP), the online local business review site. This company and this stock share a lot of commonality with Tripadvisor (Figure 10.7). Yelp IPO'd in early 2012 at $15 and then experienced a 6x increase in its stock price over the next two years, as it produced consistent hypergrowth revenue (between 60% and 70% between 2011 and 2014) and a sharp ramping up of profitability. Then revenue growth began to consistently and materially decelerate, falling to 46% in 2015, 30% in 2016, 19% in 2017, 11% in 2018, and 8% in 2019.

FIGURE 10.7 YELP Needs Some Help

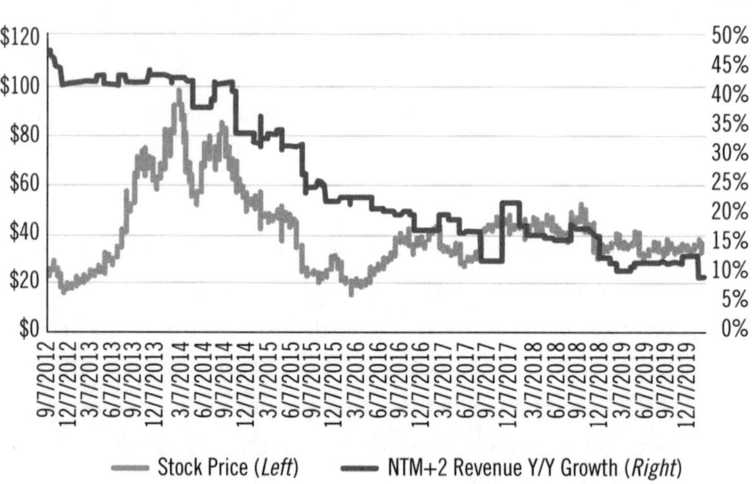

And as with TRIP, with the revenue growth deceleration came a reduction in YELP's multiple and a prolonged decline in its stock price, from close to $100 in early 2014 to $30 in late 2018. There were a series of factors here:

1. Similar to TRIP, there was intense competition from Google and other companies.
2. Several growth initiatives that either failed (international expansion) or took a lot longer than expected to pan out (creating a transactional capability for local service providers like plumbers).
3. Possibly, there was inadequate product innovation.

Yelp remains a sizable business with at least 30 million consumers, over 500,000 paying business customers, and over 200 million cumulative reviews. There is potential here. But the key historical stock-picking insight here is that as the company's growth slowed materially, its stock price suffered.

If I could pick one tech company to work for based purely on its location, I would pick TrueCar, the online car-buying marketplace. Its headquarters location on Broadway in Santa Monica is directly across from the beach and a short distance from the Santa Monica Pier. Amazing location. Amazing views.

Anyway, TrueCar (TRUE) is a company that has had a volatile stock since its 2014 IPO, with most of that volatility being down (Figure 10.8). I participated in that IPO—as I did with YELP—as an analyst. TRUE IPO'd at $9 in May 2014, in the wake of 75% revenue growth in its March 2014 quarter. Twice later in 2014, TRUE shares reached $24, but then began a sharp two-year correction as the company's revenue growth outlook quickly decelerated, going down close to 10%. Under a new CEO, the company's revenue growth outlook stabilized and then improved, causing the stock to spike back up to north of $20. But TRUE's revenue growth outlook began to fade again in 2019 to single-digit percentage levels, and the stock slipped back below its $9 IPO price level in 2019. As of early 2021, it was still there.

The challenges at TrueCar included:

1. A large number of competitors in both the used and new car marketplace segments
2. Arguably, a customer value proposition to dealers and to consumers that wasn't robust enough

FIGURE 10.8 When the Stock Chart Points TRUE South

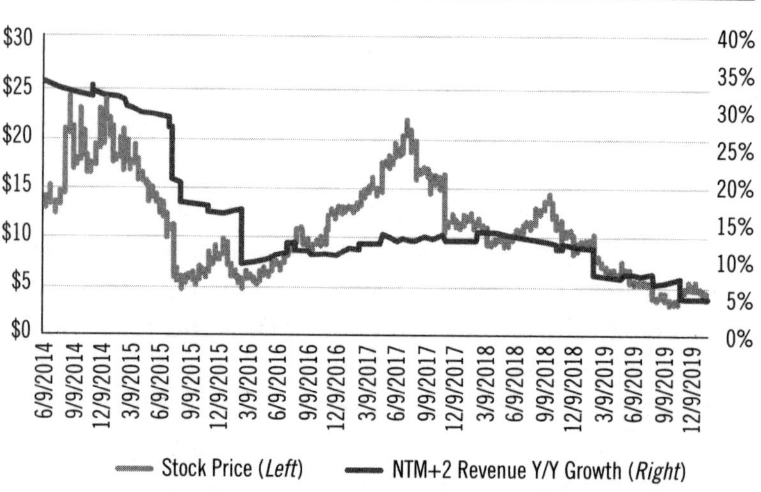

In terms of the stock, as with TRIP and YELP, it followed the rate of revenue growth. And when that revenue growth slowed materially, the stock underperformed.

I'll just briefly refer to two more companies to highlight the stock challenges associated with materially decelerating revenue growth. The first is advertising technology company Criteo (CRTO). "Ad tech" has been a difficult sector for public investors to make money—The Trade Desk (TTD) is one of the very few exceptions. That said, Criteo did bring to market a differentiated and effective personalized retargeting solution. Criteo IPO'd at $31 in October 2013, hitting peaks near $55 several times in 2014, 2015, and 2017. But as its revenue growth outlook decelerated from 30% in 2015 to

20% in 2017 to sub-10% in 2019, its stock price sharply declined to below $20. Criteo's share price did begin to recover nicely in late 2020 and into early 2021, but the lesson about the stock challenge associated with materially decelerating revenue growth holds. (See Figure 10.9.)

FIGURE 10.9 The Criteo Crater

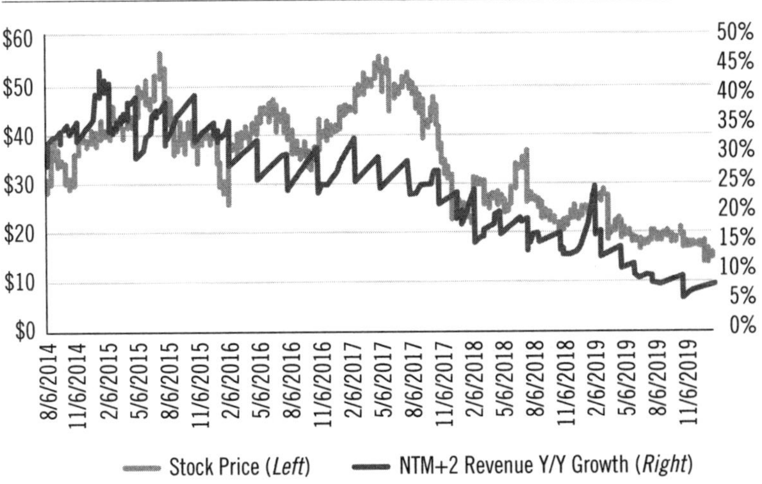

Finally, there's Shutterstock (SSTK), the stock photography company, which largely traded flat to down over 2014–2019 as its expected growth outlook deteriorated from 25% to below 10% (Figure 10.10). SSTK rebounded sharply in 2020 and as of early 2021 was within spitting distance of its all-time high of $99 (from early 2014). But it's hard not to pin that multiyear underperformance to the notable deceleration in the company's top-line growth.

FIGURE 10.10 Don't Close Your Eyes—SSTK

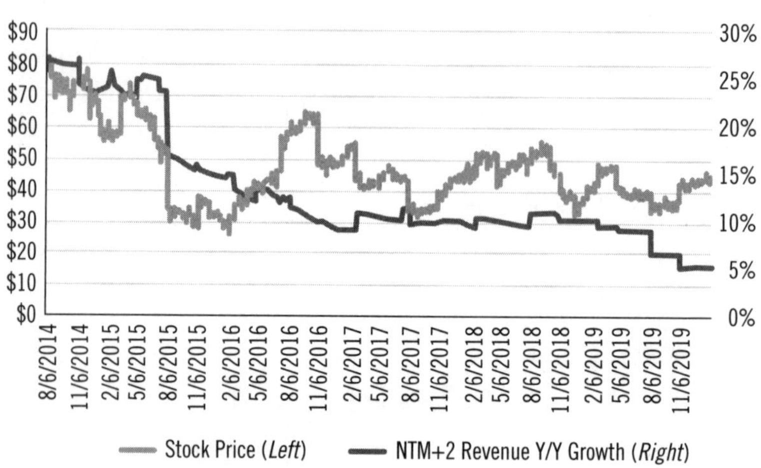

These are just a handful of examples of the situations I tracked where stocks deteriorated when growth outlooks deteriorated. So when do you sell or avoid a stock? When its fundamentals are sharply deteriorating, but with tech stocks especially when the company's revenue growth falls materially below 20% and/or the company's revenue growth decelerates rapidly (roughly by 50% within a year's time frame).

Look for DHQs—dislocated high-quality stocks. One of the best ways to make money as an investor in high-growth tech stocks is to identify the highest-quality companies and then to buy them or add to positions when they are dislocated. Investing in high-quality companies—marked by premium revenue growth and driven by large TAMs, relentless product innovation, compelling customer value propositions, and great management—reduces fundamentals risk. Buying when they are dislocated—20–30% corrections and/or when stocks are trading at a discount to their growth rates—reduces valuation/multiple risk.

How to tell when stocks are dislocated. Two rules of thumb:

- When a stock has traded off 20–30%
- When a stock trades at a discount to its growth rates—that is, when its P/E multiples are lower than its expected forward EPS growth rate or a PEG < 1

Both these rules require some judgment calls. For example, a stock that retraces 20% after shooting up 100% in three months isn't terribly dislocated. But these rules can help identify dislocated stocks. My experience has been that every single high-quality company gets dislocated at some point, providing patient long-term investors with plenty of opportunities. Even the highest-quality stocks I covered over the last five years (Facebook, Amazon, Netflix, and Google) were each dislocated a handful of times over that period.

LESSON WRAP-UP

How to judge a high-quality company. From the perspective of a seasoned tech analyst, my argument is that the best fundamental tell of a high-quality company is consistent premium revenue growth (20%+). And the key fundamental drivers of premium revenue growth are four: relentless product innovation, large TAMs, compelling customer value propositions, and great management. Lots of judgment calls in here, but these are the drivers that I have found most important in determining the long-term fundamental outlook for companies.

When to sell a stock. The key Sell indicator that I have observed has been a material deterioration in the fundamentals of a company. To be more specific, when revenue growth decelerates materially (50% deceleration within a year or less that is not driven by a macro shock like the Covid-19 pandemic) or when revenue growth materially dips below 20%, adjusting for comps and macro shocks. These indicators are specific to high-growth tech stocks, but there is a rather long list now of tech stocks that have gone from outperforming to underperforming for a lengthy period when they have experienced material revenue growth deceleration: Booking, Criteo, eBay, Snap, Shutterstock, Tripadvisor, TrueCar, Twitter, Yahoo!, Yelp, and others. Tech investors should be wary of sharp revenue growth deceleration. Growth thrills. (Substantial) Deceleration kills.

The 10-Lesson Lineup

OK, 10 LESSONS. HERE'S THE CHEAT SHEET VERSION

Lesson 1: There Will Be Blood . . . When You Pick Bad Stocks

If you invest in the stock market, you *will* lose money from time to time. Being a good stock-picker involves being both a good fundamentalist: correctly forecasting revenues and profits, and a good psychologist: correctly guessing what multiples the market will place on those revenues and profits. It's almost impossible to get both of those exactly right most of the time.

There are always market shock events—like the onslaught of the Covid-19 virus in early 2020—that can undermine the best-laid stock-picking plans.

There will also be the bad stocks that you pick.

The odds of batting 1,000% are, well, one in a thousand. Markets change. Competitors compete. Managements make mistakes. And sure things can quickly turn into sore things. If you want to invest in the market, you need to be ready for setbacks.

Lesson 2: There Will Be Blood . . . Even When You Pick the Best Stocks

Even best-in-class stocks aren't immune from company-specific major sell-offs. Facebook, Google, and Netflix—three of the best performing stocks of 2015–2020—all experienced major corrections (from 20% to 40%) at one point. In the case of Netflix, it was twice in a 12-month period. Despite fundamentals that were at times dramatically better than those of other tech stocks—and 95%+ of the S&P 500—these stocks experienced major setbacks, before recovering to continue to materially outperform the market.

And even best-in-class stocks aren't immune from broad market sell-offs. In late 2018, in the wake of a broad market correction tied to trade war concerns, slowing global GDP growth, and rising interest rates, AMZN lost a third of its value, despite no change in its estimates or growth outlook. Have patience.

Lesson 3: Don't Play Quarters

Successfully trading around quarters requires both an accurate read of fundamentals and a correct assessment of near-term expectations, a tricky task for individual (and most professional) investors to pull off. Trades around quarters can also be misleading and can cause investors to miss long-term fundamental and stock trends. Between 2015 and 2018, AMZN rocketed up 386%, with 4 of the 16 quarters during that period generating a material 10%+ one-day pop and 4 quarters generating a material 5%+ one-day slide.

Staying invested throughout would almost certainly have been more profitable than trying to play those quarters.

Invest in names with strong fundamentals, and ignore short-term stock fluctuations, whether around quarters or not.

Lesson 4: Revenue Matters More Than Anything

Over the long term, fundamentals really do move stocks, and for tech stocks, the fundamentals that matter the most are revenue,

revenue, and revenue. Companies that demonstrate an ability to consistently generate 20%+ top-line growth can potentially provide good stock returns, almost regardless of their near-term profitability outlooks. That's the 20% revenue growth rule.

Consistent 20%+ top-line growth is rare (only about 2% of the S&P 500 generate this) and can often reflect large market opportunities, relentless product innovation, compelling value propositions, and top-quality management teams. This is exactly what you want to be looking for in good long-term investing opportunities.

As a start, look for companies that have generated 20%+ growth for five or six quarters in a row.

That said, companies with sharply decelerating revenue growth—such as revenue growth rates that get cut in half over three or four quarters—are likely to work poorly as Longs (except when that cut is due to macro shocks like the Covid-19 crisis), whereas stocks of companies that are successfully executing GCIs (growth curve initiatives) and generating revenue growth acceleration can be very good outperformers.

However, successful tech investing doesn't mean being oblivious to profits. Profitless growth creates no value in the long run.

Lesson 5: It Don't Mean a Thing, If It Ain't Got That Product Swing

Product innovation matters. Relentless product innovation is one of the biggest drivers of fundamentals, especially revenue growth, and that's what drives stocks. Successful product innovation can generate entirely new revenue streams (Amazon with cloud computing), replace existing revenue streams (Netflix with DVDs and streaming), and enhance existing revenue streams and boost key customer metrics (Spotify with podcasting and plausibly Stitch Fix with direct buy functionality).

Product innovation is also spottable. Some of the most interesting product innovation going on today is consumer-driven. You're a consumer. You can try out the services, and if you find one you love, it could be the making of a great stock.

Further, when you see one company's innovations aggressively copied by others (e.g., Snap's new features copied by Facebook), chances are that first company is a legitimate innovator. Finally, product innovation is a repeatable offense. A management team that generates one or two impressive product innovations will likely have the ability to continue to generate more innovations.

Lesson 6: TAMs—The Bigger the Better

TAM matters. The bigger the total addressable market, the greater the opportunity for premium revenue growth. They are rare, but look for companies that have the potential to "pull a Google"—to generate premium revenue growth from scale. As a rule of thumb, a company with a single-digit percentage share of a large TAM might be an ideal candidate for tech investors to consider.

TAMs can be expanded. By removing friction and by adding new use cases, TAMs can be made larger. That's essentially what Uber and Lyft did over the years. By lowering prices, increasing the number of drivers on its platform, reducing wait times, and making payments and tipping seamless, Uber and Lyft expanded the use cases for and the appeal of ridesharing. There are also two specific steps that companies can take to expand their TAMs—expand into new geographic markets and generate new revenue streams.

Sometimes TAMs are hard to ascertain, especially when a traditional industry is being disrupted, and creative new approaches are required. This was the case with Spotify, which was attacking two well-known markets (the recorded music industry and radio advertising) but was doing it in a way that potentially meant it was facing a much bigger market than appeared at first listen.

Large TAMs can help drive growth that can lead to scale, which has intrinsic benefits: experience curves, unit economics advantages, competitive moats, and network effects.

Lesson 7: Follow the Value Prop, Not the Money

Follow the consumer value proposition. Some of the best performing stocks of the past decade belong to companies that prioritized customer satisfaction *way over* near-term investor concerns. Amazon may well be the poster child here. The company consistently demonstrated a willingness to invest aggressively to offer a more compelling value proposition, even at the sacrifice of near-term profits (e.g., Prime).

Investor-centric companies can make subpar investments. eBay and Grubhub are companies that didn't focus enough on innovating to meet consumer needs, in part, I believe, out of a strong desire to preserve highly profitable business models. Because of this, both companies ended up providing mixed results for long-term investors.

Even though compelling consumer value propositions can be expensive to build and maintain, they can eventually carry positive business model effects. Some of this is straightforward in terms of deep customer loyalty. But compelling value propositions can also enable pricing power flywheels, which is what both Amazon and, especially, Netflix have benefited from.

Lesson 8: M Is for Management

Management teams really *matter*. The quality of the management team is arguably the single most important factor in tech investing. In the long term, stocks are largely driven by fundamentals, and fundamentals are largely driven by management teams. Get the management team right, and you'll likely get the stock right.

Know what to look for in a management team. Founder-led companies (practically all the biggest tech stocks have been founder-led), long-term orientation (like Zuckerberg with 1-, 5-, and 10-year goals), great industry vision (Hastings essentially inventing streaming), a maniacal focus on customer satisfaction (read the Amazon shareholder letters), deep technology backgrounds and operating benches, a deep focus on product innovation, and the ability to be forthright with employees and investors about mistakes and challenges.

Unlike investment funds, for management teams, past performance is an indicator of future performance. When you have management teams that have built successful track records, you stick with them.

Lesson 9: Valuation Is in the Eye of the Tech Stockholder

Valuation should *not* be the most important factor in the stock-picking decision process. Your overriding valuation action question should always be: Does the current valuation look ballpark reasonable?

High-growth tech stocks can at times look expensive, but that doesn't make them bad stocks. Look at P/E multiples on a growth-adjusted basis. High-earnings growth stocks and high-earnings quality stocks warrant high P/E multiples.

In the case of companies with robust earnings, a P/E multiple in line with or at a modest premium to a company's forward EPS growth is ballpark reasonable.

High-quality stocks that trade at a discount to premium growth rates can make excellent investments for long-term investors. Both PCLN and FB traded for long stretches at discounts to their growth rates, which helped create great Long opportunities with both stocks.

In the case of companies with minimal earnings, you can expect to see super high (> 40x) P/E multiples, but these can still be good investments. Both Amazon and Netflix proved this. The key action questions: Are current earnings being materially depressed by major investments? Is there a reason to believe that long-term operating margins for the company can be dramatically higher than current levels?

The case of companies with no earnings provides the toughest valuation challenge, but four logic test questions can help determine whether a valuation is ballpark reasonable:

1. Are there any public companies with similar business models that are already profitable?
2. If the company as a whole isn't profitable, are there segments within the business that are?
3. Is there a reason why scale can't drive a business to profitability?
4. Are there concrete steps that management can take to drive the company to profitability?

Lesson 10: Hunt for DHQs—Dislocated High-Quality Stocks

One of the best ways to make money as an investor in high-growth tech stocks is to identify the highest-quality companies and then to buy them or add to positions when they are dislocated. Investing in high-quality companies—marked by premium revenue growth and driven by large TAMs, relentless product innovation, compelling customer value propositions, and great management—reduces fundamentals risk. Buying when they are dislocated—20–30% corrections and/or when stocks are trading at a discount to their growth rates—reduces valuation/multiple risk.

Every single high-quality company gets dislocated at some point or another, providing patient long-term investors with plenty of opportunities. Even the highest-quality stocks I covered over the last five years (Facebook, Amazon, Netflix, and Google) were each dislocated a handful of times over that period.

The key indicator to sell a stock is a material deterioration in the fundamentals of a company. To be specific, when revenue growth decelerates materially (50% deceleration within a year or less, adjusting for comps and macro shocks) or when revenue growth materially dips below 20%, again adjusting for comps and macro shocks.

Extra Credit

I am closing with a few short extracurricular lessons and thoughts that can make your stock-picking better and that address some recent issues that have surfaced regarding technology stocks.

A SUGGESTION FOR THE MEME TRADERS

A funny thing happened while writing this book. Actually, it wasn't funny. It was fascinating. During January 2021, shares of GameStop (GME) skyrocketed $1,900% from $17 to $348, before correcting 90% over the next month back down to $41. This was one of the biggest roller-coaster rides I have ever seen, and I have been to more than my share of amusement parks.

The GME rally was a dramatic short squeeze featuring Bullish options bets that helped popularize the concept of meme stocks—stocks that are popular with millennial-aged retail traders and move more on hype than on underlying fundamentals. Comments on Reddit's WallStreetBets forum suggested a lot of momentum day-trading activity with one popular goal being to go Long the most heavily shorted stocks in the market, of which GME was certainly one. Some of the comments also suggested thoughtful investment themes, with a focus on GME's growing TAM, a potentially changing business model, new management, and the active involvement of Ryan Cohen, the highly successful founder of Chewy, the online pet supplies retailer.

I don't have an investment opinion on GME. But I do have an investment opinion on investing. There's nothing wrong with day trading or pure momentum trading. It can be fun . . . and highly lucrative. But one can also lose a lot of money in a short time. Kind of like Vegas. Nothing wrong with Vegas. I like Vegas as much as the next person. Probably more, actually.

But I would ask the meme traders to consider investing. You can make good returns investing in the public markets. Maybe not overnight. But there's a distinct opportunity to do so over the course of a year. You can do your own research. You can make your own calls. Some of the high-growth tech stocks mentioned in this book are among the most dynamic of my and maybe your generation. Learning about them is fun. Really! Hunting for the next Amazon, the next Apple, the next Netflix, the next Google, the next Tesla is stimulating, and if you get it right, highly rewarding. As an added bonus, some of these executives and entrepreneurs really are going to the moon. If you're patient, you can avoid or ride through most major market shocks and let fundamentals drive and determine your stock performance and not be at the mercy of daily price fluctuations that are too often largely divorced from specific company actions.

Just a suggestion.

COVID-19 COMPS COMMENTS

On a human level, the Covid-19 pandemic was a tragedy. For some high-growth tech stocks, the pandemic provided many benefits. That sounds cold. But there's some truth to it. To be clear, many high-growth tech stocks were materially negatively impacted by

Covid-19. Travel names like Airbnb, Booking, and Expedia suffered horrendous declines in demand—with revenue crashing as much at 80% year-over-year. As Peter Kern, the Expedia CEO, correctly put it, the June quarter of 2020 was "the worst quarter the travel industry has seen in modern history and Expedia was of course not spared." Almost all Internet advertising names experienced drastic slowdowns in the first half of 2020. Google actually printed its first ever revenue decline quarter (down 2% year-over-year) with the June 2020 quarter. And ridesharing companies like Uber and Lyft saw business all but evaporate over a six-to-nine-month period as the desire and need for mobility collapsed. Covid-19 pandemic had a negative impact on a large number of high-growth tech stocks, in some cases robbing them of all their growth.

But there was a basket of high-growth tech stocks that directly benefited from Covid-19 crisis—the work-from-home (WFH) or live-from-home (LFH) basket. These included names like Amazon, Chewy, DoorDash, eBay, Etsy, Netflix, Peloton, Wayfair, Zoom, and others that experienced massive surges in demand for their products and services. With those surges in demand came surges in their fundamentals, especially revenue but also earnings. DoorDash achieved profitability on an EBITDA basis for the first time in the June 2020 quarter, perhaps a full year earlier than it would have without that pandemic demand surge. So there were clearly Covid-19 beneficiaries among tech stocks.

There was another way the Covid-19 crisis benefited high-growth tech stocks, at least those that were able to maintain high growth during the crisis. Their scarcity value became stronger. Growing your top-line 20%+ in a 3% GDP growth world is inherently impressive. Growing your top-line 20%+ in a year when global GDP is declining 3% is incredibly impressive. But some of the leading tech companies—Amazon, Facebook, Netflix, Shopify—were able to sustain 20%+ growth in 2020, and that growth made them even more attractive to investors.

So what do you do with high-growth tech stocks in a Covid-19 recovery world? This book offers stock-picking lessons, not specific stock advice. But two key points from those lessons are directly relevant to thinking about high-growth tech stocks in a Covid-19 recovery and then in a hopefully post-Covid-19 world.

First, comps will be an unusually material issue for almost all tech companies in 2021—either materially challenging for the WFH/LFH companies or materially easy for the companies that suffered severe demand hits during the Covid-19 pandemic. We should expect to see major growth deceleration with the first group, and major acceleration or recovery with the second. Anticipation of that deceleration could well pressure multiples temporarily for the first group, whereas anticipation of that acceleration could well boost multiples temporarily for the second group. It will be critical to look at growth rates versus those comps. Material revenue growth acceleration is great, but it's more impressive if it's faster than the rate at which comps eased in the prior year. Likewise, material revenue growth deceleration is a negative, but it's not that meaningful if it's in line with the rate of acceleration in the prior year.

Second, the scarcity value of high-growth tech stocks will be reduced during the Covid-19 recovery because many companies will experience heightened growth during the recovery. Companies in the restaurant, transportation, travel, live events, and other verticals should see dramatic growth coming out of the crisis. Investors looking for growth will have plenty of options. The relative advantage—the scarcity value—of high-growth tech stocks will be limited temporarily, which will dampen their appeal.

The key word in the above two paragraphs is "temporarily." The market is a discounting mechanism. During the Covid-19 pandemic, it was a discounting mechanism on steroids. In February and March of 2020, the market crashed 34% in just 23 trading days. It then gapped back up 52% to recover to that February high in 103 trading days. The recovery time was longer than the crash time, but three months is still a very short time given a global pandemic and recession. What happened? The market aggressively anticipated and discounted the crisis and then the recovery. The WFH/LFH basket of stocks contained some great outperformers in 2020, but the most dramatic part of the outperformance for most of the stocks occurred in a tight three-to-six-month period.

Making predictions is dangerous, but my strong guess is that the Covid-19 recovery trade will last about as long as the Covid-19 crisis trade did (three to six months). After that, the market will focus on the sustainability of companies' fundamentals into 2022 and beyond. Perhaps the most important action question is: Did the Covid-19 crisis and the Covid-19 recovery cause a company to become structurally stronger or weaker for the long term? That's the key question that investors should focus on.

ADDRESSING THE RELEVANCY CRITICS

So let me get this right. An analyst covering a once-in-a generation secular growth opportunity (the Internet) during a period of unusually low interest rates (2010–2020) decides to try to draw broad stock-picking lessons from a handful of dramatically successful companies (the Big Longs—AMZN, FB, GOOGL, NFLX). Just how relevant could these lessons possibly be? Great question! Let me try to address it.

The Internet has been an amazing secular growth opportunity. The Internet is woven throughout the market caps of the largest companies in the world today—Alibaba, Amazon, Apple, Facebook, Google, Microsoft, and Tencent. As of March 8, 2021, these were seven of the eight largest market cap companies in the world. What's the eighth? The Saudi Arabian Oil Company . . . *not* an Internet company. But what is so obvious today wasn't in 1995, 2000, 2005, or even 2010. Skepticism about Internet market opportunities, business models, and management teams was the reality for a majority of the last 25 years.

I can still vividly recall running into a former boss from my management consulting days at Newark Airport in 2001, well into the dot-com bust. When I told him I was an Internet analyst, his response was: "Well *that* must have been amusing! What are you going to do next?" I also recall attending a Yellow Pages industry association convention in San Diego in 2002 when one of the keynote speakers referred to Internet advertising as part of a "burger and fries combo." Yellow Pages advertising was the burger for local businesses, some of which might want a few Internet fries to go along with that burger. There's no doubt where the beef is now.

My point is that amazing secular growth opportunities are usually only amazing in hindsight. Which means that some of the skepticism facing current potential secular growth opportunities—virtual reality, cryptocurrency, autonomous vehicles, robotics, commercial space, life longevity, cannabis— may well prove to be misplaced. Just as that skepticism toward Internet opportunities was misplaced. With new amazing secular growth opportunities will come premium growth investment opportunities that need to be analyzed.

This Internet growth opportunity is far from over. The Covid-19 crisis likely permanently accelerated the adoption of Internet services and applications, allowing best-in-class management teams more opportunity to tap into high-growth revenue opportunities. The growth runway for the leading Internet companies is still long. There is still stock-picking to be done in net land!

In terms of the unusually low interest environment, there is no doubt that this has been a tailwind behind some of the most successful high-growth tech stocks of the past two decades. If most of the profits for a business are out in the distant future—which is the case for early-stage companies and/or ones in near-term aggressive investment mode—then low interest rates strongly boost the value of those long-term profits. High interest rates reduce them. That's why high-growth, high-multiple, limited profitability stocks trade off aggressively on rising interest rate fears.

I have no idea what will happen to interest rates in the future. I do know that interest rates have been relatively low for some time (10+ years) because inflation concerns have been tempered. But one major source of inflation tempering over the past 20+ years has been the increasing influence of technology on the global economy, especially Internet technology.

The Internet has had a fundamentally deflationary impact on large swaths of the economy—retail, communications, information, travel, advertising, entertainment, etc. It has done this by increasing price transparency, removing friction, and increasing selection and options. Amazon, Alibaba, eBay, Etsy, Shopify, Walmart.com, and many other companies have made it cheaper and more convenient to shop. Google and other companies have made it dramatically easier to access information. Facebook and other companies have made it much more practical for small businesses to market their wares locally, nationally, and globally. Airbnb, Booking, and Expedia have brought enormous efficiencies to the travel research and booking process. Video and audio subscription services like Netflix, Hulu, Disney+, YouTube, Spotify, and Apple Music have dramatically reduced the cost of entertainment for consumers.

There are other deflationary examples, but you get the point. And Internet technologies are here to stay. So their fundamentally deflationary impact should linger for some time. It may even become greater. Interest rates may rise dramatically in the next 5 to 10 years, valuationally challenging high-growth stocks, but this isn't a given. And at the end of the day, my strong sense is that fundamentals will still trump interest rate movements.

Finally, there's the issue of drawing stock-picking lessons from the most successful stocks. Guilty as charged. But this book also draws lessons from plenty of failures and also-rans—Blue Apron,

Zulily, Groupon, eBay, Pandora, Grubhub. I believe the whys and hows of the successes and failures apply broadly to all growth stocks . . . or to stocks that are presented as growth stocks.

QED.

HERE COME THE REGULATORS

Another thing happened while I was writing this book. Big Tech (principally Apple, Amazon, Facebook, and Google) came under intense criticism. Five bipartisan bills were introduced into the House with the goal of "reining in Big Tech." A new head of the Federal Trade Commission was appointed, in part based on her groundbreaking published article, "Amazon's Antitrust Paradox," which was highly critical of the company. And a federal judge threw out an antitrust case that was filed against Facebook by 48 state attorneys general. That's 96 percent of all the states! Clearly these companies have become highly controversial. At least with political representatives and regulators. Among consumers, surveys have consistently rated these companies as highly trustworthy, especially Amazon, but also to a large extent Apple and Google. But this is clearly a new dynamic that investors will have to deal with.

In fairness, this dynamic isn't that new. Regulatory scrutiny of these companies has been building for years. And mostly for the right reasons, in my humble opinion. These companies have clearly become very powerful platforms. And if you are looking for examples of very aggressive business practices, you can probably find them with these companies. Whether this means they broke laws, should be fined, or should be broken up, I don't know. I'm not a lawyer.

But I am a student of Internet history. Arguably among the most experienced students of Internet history. Certainly of Amazon, Facebook, and Google. And I do worry that the thrust of some of today's legislative and regulatory actions is based on a not completely full understanding of Internet history. When the House Judiciary Committee released a report in mid-2020 that asserted, "There is mounting evidence that the dominance of Online platforms has materially weakened innovation and entrepreneurship in the U.S. economy," and "Our economy and democracy are at stake," I thought the conclusions were a bit excessive and wrote a short report detailing what I thought were missing elements from the report. Also, as a small nit, I objected to my name being misspelled in the public record—my research was cited in the report, but the footnotes referred to Marc S. Mahaney. Mon dieu!

You didn't buy this book to read my political views, so I'll just make three quick points. First, the argument that Amazon, Facebook, and Google reached their dominant positions through anticompetitive practices just isn't true. As I detail in Lesson 7, Amazon upended the original king of online retail (eBay) and gained market share from Walmart and others primarily because it was better at product innovation, because it offered a superior consumer value proposition, and because it consistently maintained a long-term investment horizon. These attributes still hold, though this may well change. Also, there were social networks and search engines before Facebook and Google. Facebook and Google simply offered consumers and marketers a much better mousetrap. This point still holds, though it too may well change.

Second, these companies have generated a lot of benefits to the American economy, democracy, and society. No, these aren't altruistic nonprofits. They're competitively capitalistic corporations. But their impact has been fundamentally deflationary. And these companies have removed friction from day-to-day activities like shopping, entertainment, information gathering, and communication. And these companies have made it much easier to express, broadcast, and discover information and opinions. These are beneficial consequences.

And third, the broad sectors in which these companies compete remain highly competitive. A lot of small businesses were destroyed as a result of the Covid-19 pandemic. But it also led to the creation of a record number of new businesses, especially Internet companies, and especially online retail companies. How hard would it be to build a new Amazon that competed with it across all its business units? Very, very hard. And it would be hard to compete successfully in online retail in any one segment. But companies like Chewy, Etsy, and Wayfair have done it, by focusing on compelling consumer value propositions, relentless product innovation, and outstanding execution. And the dramatic rise of Shopify and TikTok shows that great innovation and customer focus can still power very large new entrants into online retail and online advertising.

And that's all I have to say about that.

WRAPPING IT UP

I have been lucky. Covering Internet stocks over the last 25 years has been exciting and stimulating. It has also been humbling. I have made many stock-picking mistakes, several of which I have detailed in this book. Two in particular clearly stand out in my mind.

In July 2006, Yahoo! reported disastrous June quarter EPS results. Revenue came in light versus Street estimates, the company's September quarter outlook was soft, and the company announced that its long anticipated search engine improvement program (nicknamed Project Panama) would be delayed. YHOO shares crashed 22% the next day and hit a 52-week low. And YHOO was my number one Buy recommendation. I was a young analyst at Citi trying to make a name for myself and had been aggressively pitching YHOO as a Long. Another three-egg omelet on my face. I got on the morning call with Citi's sales force and lamely tried to defend YHOO shares and my call. I then spent the next three hours on the phone talking with clients about what I thought was happening with Yahoo! and apologizing for my call. Sometime late that morning, my research director (Matt Carpenter) called me to ask how I was feeling. I told him the truth—I felt awful. He responded: "Good, it means you care. Now figure out how to pick stocks better." About a year later, Yahoo!'s then CEO Terry Semel resigned amid mounting criticism of the company's lack of success. And somewhere along that way, I downgraded YHOO to Hold, having learned the hard way to be more dispassionate with my stock calls and to focus more on fundamentals.

The second incident occurred more recently. In February 2020, I hosted a casual dinner with the fellow parents of my sons' high school basketball team. I normally don't talk stocks at social events, much preferring to talk about current events, good books, the latest fashion trends (kidding), high school basketball (not kidding). But someone asked me about UBER, so I explained why it was my top pick at the time. UBER was in the high $30s. A few weeks later the Covid-19 virus really started to hit the United States, and I watched UBER shares collapse briefly to $15. Knowing that close friends may have bought UBER shares on my recommendation and lost money in a short time put an extra sting into that collapse for me. Another lesson in humility. Another reminder that there will be blood, at times due to factors completely beyond the control of the company or the analyst. UBER bounced back strongly and outperformed nicely for the full year, but that feeling of having let down friends—of not warning them sufficiently of risks—stuck with me.

Humility is a great attitude to take toward investing. If you don't have that, you'll likely get blown up in the market.

A lot of respect and recognition will also help. As the Benjamin Graham saying goes, "In the short run, the market is a voting machine." And votes change all the time. Expect to see significant volatility around stock prices that is completely unassociated with the companies' fundamentals. Recognize that this will happen.

But also recognize the other part of the saying, that the market "is a weighing machine" in the long term. I have seen this play out time and time again with technology stocks. The highest-quality names—in terms of revenue growth, earnings quality, management teams, value propositions, product innovation, and TAMs—have been the best stock performers over the long term. They have been dislocated many times—for company-specific and for market-general reasons—but their stocks have followed their fundamentals. As the latter (the fundamentals) have become stronger, the former (the stocks) have risen. The market respects fundamentals over the long term. So work to identify high-quality names, check to make sure their valuations are ballpark reasonable, and/or look to swoop in on those dislocated (DHQ) opportunities that are sure to arise.

For much of my career, I have faced skepticism about tech stocks, and Internet stocks in particular. There has been an implicit bias in the market against high-growth tech companies. There is the belief that they aren't high quality. That they are just trendy. That those high multiples they often carry are just bull's-eyes for the next wave of innovators. Yet a small but notable percentage of these have emerged as very high-quality companies and very high-quality stocks. It turns out Amazon did become extraordinarily profitable. And became a ten-bagger many times over. There were other examples. And there will be other examples. High-growth tech stocks should probably always be a limited part of an individual investor's portfolio, but they should be there.

To wrap, my second-oldest son is in college and has become interested in the stock market. He mentioned to me recently that he and his friends were looking for books to read on how to invest. Carter, I truly hope this book helps.

As for the other readers of this book, I recall the saying of one of my mentors, Joel Levy. He helped run the research department at Citi when I was there. Joel worked at the firm for 30 years and passed away much too early from pancreatic cancer. One of my favorite of his sayings was, "Make 'em think, make 'em laugh, make 'em money."

Well, hopefully, this book has given you some new ideas and ways to think about investing in tech stocks and in high-growth stocks. Hopefully, you have enjoyed some of the stories I've laid out here. And hopefully, this book will help you invest successfully and make money. If all three of these hopes transpire, my lucky streak will have continued.

ACKNOWLEDGMENTS

I want to give big thanks to the many individuals who helped me with this book. Yes, all the mistakes and errors in it are 100 percent mine, but plenty of people generously provided me with feedback and ideas that were invaluable. At the top of that list are my colleagues Shweta Khajuria, Ben Wheeler, Jian Li, and Spencer Tan, whom I have been lucky enough to work with for the past several years as part of the Internet Research Crew, first at RBC and then at Evercore ISI. They read all the lessons and provided tons of feedback and suggestions. I am especially appreciative of the significant help Jian Li provided in thinking through and producing many of the book's exhibits. Marc Harris—my research director and friend for most of the past decade—also provided lots of constructive criticism—as well as one of the catchier lesson titles. Over the course of almost 25 years, I have benefited from debates and discussions with a very large number of institutional and retail investors and industry experts. Several of them read and commented on part or all of the book draft and provided highly useful commentary—Hero Choudhary, Jimmy Wu, Ashim Mehra, Heath Terry, Nick Lawler, Bob Lang, Glen Kacher, Spencer Rascoff, Rich Barton, Lise Buyer, Barry McCarthy, Russell Goldsmith, Lanny Baker, Chris Connor, Brooke De Boutray, and Glenn Fogel. Also, Jim Cramer provided inspiration, as well as some great ideas early on about how to structure the book. Scott Galloway provided a ton of encouragement early on in the process and helped me get the project off the ground, as did Brad Stone. And Adam Lashinsky pretty much kicked off this whole process by inviting me to give a talk on my top Tech stock picking lessons back in 2018 at the Fortune Tech Conference in Aspen, CO. Finally, I want to thank my literary agent James Levine and the thoroughly professional editors at McGraw Hill—Stephen Isaacs, Judith Newlin, and Patricia Wallenburg. Attitude of gratitude.

INDEX

Page numbers followed by *f* and *t* refer to figures and tables, respectively.

ABOUT THE AUTHOR

Legendary analyst **Mark Mahaney** has been covering Internet stocks on Wall Street since 1998, with Morgan Stanley, American Technology Research, Citibank, RBC Capital Markets, and now Evercore ISI. *Institutional Investor* magazine has ranked him as a top Internet analyst every year for the past 15 years, including 5 years as number one, and he has been ranked by the *Financial Times* and StarMine as the number one earnings estimator and stock-picker. In addition, TipRanks has placed Mahaney in the top 1 percent of all Wall Street analysts in terms of single-year stock-picking performance.

Mark lives in Lafayette, CA with his four sons.